GATHERING
LIGHT

GATHERING
LIGHT

Essays of People and Place
from the Leelanau Peninsula

By Kathleen Stocking

Rivertree Press

Many of these pieces appeared, in various forms and at various times, in the following publications, and I would like to thank the editors of each: *Leelanau Enterprise, Blue Magazine, Glen Arbor Sun, Leelanau Conservancy Newsletter.*

Illustrations:
by Kristin Hurlin

Cover illustration:
Morning by David P. Grath
(42" x 36" oil on canvas).
Originally shown at the Dennos Museum in 2017
and now in the private collection of Lisa Siddall.

This book is dedicated to

the people of Leelanau County.

An early morning walk is a blessing for the whole day

– Henry David Thoreau

Table of Contents

Preface and Acknowledgements i

Spring
Old Shores...1
Curtis Cluckey, Mushroom Hunter 17
Ruby John, Native Fiddler 23
The Johnson Family, Early Empire Pioneers 33
Alligator Hill...49

Summer
Houdek Dunes 85
Jonah Powell, Lake Leelanau Musician 91
Chippewa Run 99
Meadowlark Farm 107
North Manitou Island...................................117

Fall
Living on the Narrows 137
Kehl Lake...153
Pierce Stocking, Park Maker 159
Becky Thatcher, Artist 171
Native Wild Rice and the Fall Harvest 181

Winter
Orchards and Orphans...................................199
Hank Bailey, a Part of the Place.......................209
The Storm 225
Vineyards and Hopfields................................233
Where the Land Ends 239

Preface and Acknowledgements

This is my second book about the Leelanau Peninsula, a book I told everyone I knew, thirty years ago, I would never write. When my first book about the Leelanau Peninsula, *Letters from the Leelanau*, was published in 1990 by the University of Michigan Press and became popular over that summer and the next, I was caught completely by surprise, and I think the University of Michigan Press was, too, since initially they only printed about 500 copies. I know, because when I asked for more copies it took weeks to get them. The book sold over 10,000 copies back then and is still selling. Over the ensuing years people—both on and off the Peninsula—have written and called, and told me they wanted another book just like it.

At the time, I had nothing more to say about the Leelanau Peninsula. I'd written those early essays over the course of a decade, between 1979 and 1989. After a period of freelancing for downstate magazines and newspapers in the late 1970s, I was asked to be the "up north" writer for *Detroit Monthly* by the brilliant Kirk Cheyfitz. He somehow managed to convince me that, even though I'd never written an essay in my life, I could do it. "Just go toward what you're drawn to," he'd said, sage advice to any writer. But then, after a decade of serendipity, Kirk Cheyfitz, my visionary and intrepid and funny editor, was pushed out or, as he said, "Put on the window ledge at the tenth floor and given a shove."

The essays for *Detroit Monthly* had been written deliberately with a down-state, urban audience in mind. Over the course of a decade writing for a city magazine

I had almost unconsciously learned what people wanted
to hear about people in the country. I knew what to say
to connect them to where I was and, in the process, over
the course of many years, felt like I was losing the origins of my own authenticity. At the same time, magazines and newspapers were changing, closing, dropping
from sight, becoming more market-driven and more in-
sipid.

Computers, too, were changing everything, not just
technologically but psychologically. In 1990 there was
an Internet, I think, still in its infancy, but it wouldn't
be long before ordinary housewives and carpenters,
much less intellectuals and doctors, were Googling to
find out the symptoms of throat cancer, for example, or
the details of the Peloponnesian Wars as related by
Thucydides. We weren't there yet, but you could feel it
coming. The phenomenon of people watching baseball
on their I-phones or reading books on their Kindles was
a decade or two away, but you could sense something
like that on the horizon.

My country seemed to be changing in other ways as
well, and I wanted to understand those changes. I had
been reading and reading and reading in my little farmhouse, but knowing things from newspapers and books
is not the same as knowing things firsthand. Following
Kirk Cheyfitz's advice, I went toward what I was drawn
to. First, I went to teach in the prisons and homeless
shelters of California. I wanted to understand why
America had more people in prison than any country in
the world, including Russia. I wanted to understand
why we were abandoning our kids and our families in
unhealthy and unsafe homeless shelters. After California, I found a job online to teach at a school for the elite
in El Salvador. I wanted to understand that country's
relationship to my own; I wanted to understand the Revolution there; I wanted to understand why Archbishop

Romero had been murdered by a government of the wealthy backed by the United States, in a packed church while he was saying mass, speaking on behalf of the poor. What was America, my beloved *'tis of thee* country, doing out there—supposedly on my behalf? Then I did two tours as a teacher in the Peace Corps. I wanted to understand more about the Third World and more about my government's role in that world. Coming and going for 17 years, from my house near the big woods on the outskirts of the village of Lake Leelanau, living and teaching in several different cultures, as well as traveling whenever I could to other countries near where I was working overseas, plus the sheer passage of time, aging, gave me the perspective I was seeking.

Meanwhile, during the years that I was ranging far and wide and then returning, I would sometimes be home for a few months and write little pieces for the *Leelanau Enterprise*, the *Glen Arbor Sun*, *Blue Magazine*, *Traverse Magazine*, and, for a while, working through a special program to give paying work to seniors, I wrote for the newsletter of the Leelanau Conservancy. Some of those several pieces, most substantially changed, have been adapted for this book, always with the written permission of those publishers.

Almost 40 years have gone by since I first started writing about the Leelanau Peninsula. A lot has transpired. Brigadoon, a mythical land of happy people living behind a veil of mist, which is how I described Leelanau County in a piece for the *Detroit Free Press Magazine* in 1979, is not Brigadoon anymore. There have been a lot of changes, many of them for the better. If you live long enough in a small remote place, you can see a population grow and change over the successive generations. I think I can see the outlines of a distinct culture emerging on the Leelanau Peninsula. This is a culture arising out of a more rudimentary version of the same thing, a culture that expresses some of the best goals of democracy: inclusion, tolerance, fairness, openness, respect for the rule of law, public education, nurturance of children, protection of natural beauty, freedom of thought and speech, and taking responsibility for the future with the actions we take today.

Living in a village where one can see and experience democracy in microcosm, and alternatively, living and working in Third World countries—most of which range from straight-up fascism to corrupt oligarchies; places where almost all of the information is false or censored, or both; places where the poor live with routine violence, routine food insufficiency and have no access to education or a court of law; places which invariably call themselves democracies no matter how much oppression there is—is the best way to understand democracy in macrocosm.

Democracy is not some abstract notion that appears from time to time in textbooks, or that comes in a kit you can order online. Democracy is the slow messy process of everyone having their say and it originates in the human community naturally. I met a woman in Thailand, a fellow teacher, who had grown up in a small mountain community in the Philippines where everyone lived in grass huts. She said that when anything happened that people felt they needed to talk about, they met at the Firefly Tree, a tree at the edge of the village where the fireflies liked to hang out. People would just drift toward the tree until most of the people had come together, and there everyone would have their say about whatever was on their mind. Democracy is innate in the genome. It's the essence of being human.

Democracy is what undergirds strong, caring, creative people and their communities. Good things can happen when intelligent people are educated and feel totally free to talk to each and share ideas, anywhere and anytime.

There's something inspiring about being in a place like Leelanau County where people are doing a lot of good things and they aren't doing them just for the money. They have a purpose that's palpable. Yes, we all need to earn a living, but money alone can't be the sole goal or it gets old. As far as I can tell, Leelanau people are trying their hardest to pay attention to what matters most: *love*—family, friends, church; *beauty*—keeping the scenic beauty of the hills and orchards free from development and the towns free from urban sprawl and public beaches free of pollution; *knowledge*—schools, libraries, the Internet; *creativity*—art, music, crafts, theater; *healthy food*—organic farms and subscription agriculture; *nature*—taking care of birds and wildflowers, trees and fishes, and making sure the soil, air, and water are healthy; *due process*—respect for public dialogue in and out of the judicial system; *free speech and free thought*—every art fair, every newspaper, every line at the grocery store, every public meeting, and every school is a part of people's practice of free expression.

There are more high-minded endeavors on the Leelanau Peninsula than you might think possible in such a small place. Northport Energy, and a group of University of Michigan graduate students, decided in 2018 that they will try to create a Leelanau Peninsula with 100 percent renewable energy by 2030. The late Tom Kelly started Inland Seas in 1989, after he saw what Pete Seeger was doing on the Hudson River, in order to teach kids how to understand and protect the water in the Great Lakes, so they'll grow up to be scientists and engineers with the knowledge and passion needed to care for the largest body of fresh water in the United States. The Leelanau Conservancy, founded in 1988, has protected over 13,000 acres outright from development and has another approximately 21,000 protected with conservation easements (where the land stays in private ownership but the owners agree not to allow commercial or other development). The Glen Arbor Art Association has been supporting art and artists since 1983 and they currently give after-school art classes to kids, in addition to dozens of other programs. The private Leelanau School, begun in 1929 at the height of the Great Depression, has an environmental stewardship and outdoor learning program, unlike anything in the world because of the rare and beautiful natural surroundings. If "the perception of beauty is a moral test," as Henry Thoreau famously said, then the teachers at the Leelanau School, not to mention the moment-by-moment immersion in the beauty of nature, are teaching that to their students.

Part of this spontaneous do-gooding on the Leelanau Peninsula is that the beauty of the place draws people and inspires them, too. They start to like their neighbors. They want to give back and, no small thing, they need something to do, some kind of project that gets them up and out of the house in the morning. The sense of connection to the land and to each other is the glue that creates community, creates democracy, creates hope, creates love.

If you want to see democracy in action, go to America's Leelanau Peninsula. Out of the people's sense of connection to others—and their taking care of their children and their land—has been created, over time, a culture of people looking out for each other, working for the common good. This is the very definition of democracy: liberty, fraternity and equality.

There are more than 120 nonprofits and well over two hundred civic and social groups on the Leelanau Peninsula that one can be part of and for which one can volunteer. There are bike groups and rowing groups, church groups and theater groups, quilting groups and yoga groups. There's a wildflower rescue group.

And then there are the lone, spur of the moment individuals trying to make a difference for the better. When I came back from teaching in El Salvador, and learned there was a morning and a place set aside for recycling old paints and even bathtubs, I went to a road on the outskirts of Suttons Bay, dropped off my things, and when I was all done, driving out the long road, at the exit was a little old lady passing out free pine seedlings from the trunk of her station wagon. It was a bitterly cold but sunny spring day, and there she was, all perky and happy, sparkling just like the sunlight, with those fingerless gloves that street musicians use so they can play in the cold. When I accepted my tiny pine seedling, and asked her what group she was with, she said, "Not with a group. Just doing it." She smiled and added, "For the fun of it."

There are lots of places all across America, with wonderfully caring people and similarly wonderful and messy democracy, with good libraries and great music groups, volunteers turning out in droves to rescue wildflowers and raise money for someone who needs a bone marrow transplant, just like the Leelanau Peninsula. But this is the place in America I know. And so that's what this book is about, the place I know, and the people I love.

I have many people to thank for their kindness and support. It was Carolyn Faught at the Leelanau Conservancy, for whom I was writing at the time, who first recommended Leslee Spraggins as a proof reader and Leslee has been a godsend. A good proof reader is intelligent, wise, patient, kind, painstaking, eager to look up things they don't understand and verify things they do, willing to wait to see how the meaning unfolds, and then, if they still don't get it, make a gentle note in the margin, and of course can do all the other things, too, like grammar and spelling. Leslee is a rare find. In my last book, where I garbled the geography of El Salvador, Leslee got the mountains and oceans back in their right places and rescued me from publishing to the world my disastrous sense of spatial relations. All the expert help I have received with the essays in this book notwithstanding, all the errors are my own and no one else's.

David Grath, a painter who let me use the image of his painting, *Manitou Dreams*, for the cover of my first book about the Leelanau Peninsula, has now again, given permission for me to use the image of another painting, *Morning*, for this second book. David has a way of seeing into the inner soul of a place. His work is emotional, moody and peaceful all at the same time. He can express feelings with the subtle use of color. Kristin Hurlin is a Glen Arbor artist I've known and admired for many years. Her careful, botanical renditions of the natural world are marvels of keen perception. I was thrilled when she agreed to do four pen-and-ink trees, four seasons, to illustrate this book: spring, summer, fall, and winter. When I broached the idea with her, she understood instantly. She said, "It's about time." Yes, this book is about the passage of time. Scott Wilson at VADA color in Traverse City has earned his sterling reputation for quality work. Jen Isbell at the Copy Shop on Eighth Street helped me formulate the manuscript for Julie Taylor, who in turn helped get the book ready for Versa Press in Illinois where Carri Kober and Tom Frank, consummate professionals, were easy to work with.

The people who helped during the time of writing this book are myriad. First and last is Alan Campbell, the recently retired editor and owner, with his wife, Deb, of the *Leelanau Enterprise*. There's Carolyn Faught, Communications Director at the Leelanau Conservancy as well as others at the Conservancy I felt privileged to meet in my time there: Tom Nelson, Director; Matt

Heiman who handles conservation easements; Board Director, Ed Ketterer; and docents Lou Ricord and Marsha Buehler. Jacob Wheeler, editor and publisher of the *Glen Arbor Sun*, took many pieces from me. Dave Taghon, the Director of the Empire Museum, was always available to answer questions. Francie Gits, Director of the Leland Museum, and her longtime assistant, Kim Kelderhouse, were good about giving whatever information they could find. Will Thomas, Dick and Sue Hanson, and several volunteers at the Northport Area Historical Society provided invaluable help with research. The Traverse City Copy Shop's owner, Dan Ricard, and his staff, including Alisha Cochran, Jennifer Isbell, Bonnie Morton, Phil Rajala and others were unfailingly friendly, professional and competent. Librarians everywhere helped me, including several at the Traverse Area District Library (TADL): Amy Barritt, Archivist; Bryce Bush, Director of Adult Services; Katherine Carrier, Reference Librarian; Michelle Howard, formerly a Reference Librarian and now TADL's new Director of Adult Services (Bryce Bush went to a Lansing library); Betsy Meyers, Director of Programs; Matt Wiliford, Director of Marketing; Kim Wiggins, Adult Services; Ben, Brian, and Becca; all the Sound and Sight staffers; all the Computer Lab helpers; and the entire staff and all the volunteers at the TADL have always been fabulous. Dave Diller at the Glen Lake Community Library is a great librarian and has assiduously collected and preserved rare local books. Bradley Chaplin, newly the Director at the Suttons Bay Public Library, plus his assistant Jane Suppes, and longtime staffers Pat Wolters, and Suzanne Rogers, give their best to the community, especially in helping children learn to love books. Peg McCarty and Sarah Bearup-Neal at the Glen Arbor Art Association gave moral support to me, as they do to all artists and writers. Marsha Meyer, the programs manager at the Portage Public Library when my first book came out, became a friend, as did her husband, Michael Dunn. My new neighbors at Riverview Terrace in Traverse City and the wonderful management there have been a blessing, including but not limited to: Sue Albee, Tony Applegate, Bev Bechler, Dan Binder, Jane Bishoff, David Carr, Tom Carr, Ellen Corcoran, David DeMerchant, Doug Faust, Jim Friend, Dennis Hardy, Gene Hominga, Eric Hoover, Flint Horton, Carley Jankowski, Louis Kahan, Janine Khoury, Roxanne Johnson, Pam Kole, Alisa Korn, Tony Lentych, Elizabeth Loeher, Norma Loper, Lucy Lynn, Rose Miller, Samir Mubarek, Paul Olson, Michelle Reardon, Dale Roberts, Marie Schaffer, Jo Simmerson, Leslie Sladek, Angie Szabo, Patty Szabo, Jeff Turner, Marilyn Vogel, Betsy Zeeryp, Jane Zimmerman and many more whose names I'm still learning; Charlie Edwards, Dave Gourlay, and Ken Sands on the maintenance staff, are the best in the world. Friends and fellow artists whose kindness and moral support have meant so much include Susan Cordes of Northport; Tricia and Shawn Denton and their three children, Cecelia, Thomas, and Ursela in Maple City; Gracie Dickinson Johnson on Glen Lake; David and Pamela Grath in Northport; Marlene Hahnenberg in Lake Leelanau; Kristin Hurlin and her husband Paul May in Glen Arbor; Martha Meek and Catherine Southwick in Suttons Bay; Teddy Page in Cedar; Lynne and Bill Perkins in Suttons Bay; Nancy Priest in Lake Leelanau; Amy Russello and Hank Bailey of Cedar; Leslee and John Spraggins in Northport; Mary Sutherland and her twin sister, Patricia "Tish" Waddell, in Glen Arbor; and Linda Szarkowski of Northport. Bob and Darlene Revnell from Long Lake, provided expert and genteel help in getting me settled in my new apartment. Jim Brye, owner of Radio Shack in Suttons Bay, and all of his staff, including but not limited to Rink Smith and Roger Suppes, have been endlessly patient with my technology challenges. Gary Garanem, a good man, gave me a job when I needed one. Pamela Grath's Dog Ear Books in Northport, a salon more than a bookstore, is, like Sylvia Beach's Shakespeare and Company in Paris, an oasis. Vic Herman and Amy Reynolds, owners of Horizon Books in Traverse City, and their excellent staff, Lois, Margaret, Marta, Jinhee, and Jill, some of whom have been with them since the 1960s, and many others, are second-to-none in terms of their love of books and writers. At Marathon Automotive on South Airport in Traverse City, Antoine Gleason, Marty Goetz, Trevor Hinds, Frank Jodoin, Ron Martinek, Rob Michels, Edward "Eddie" Petty, Ross Schofield, Dave Sorowitz, Erin Winfrey and a dozen other service people, technicians, and mechanics have kept my Honda Civic on the road. At Inacomp, on Eighth Street in Traverse City, Tom, Jordan, and Guy helped with all kinds of computer issues. I admire people who can do things I can't, whether they're gifted artists or gifted auto mechanics, brilliant window washers or brilliant book sellers. All the good people I've known over the years who have been my neighbors, my safety net, my friends, have been vital to my survival. I am grateful for any and all who are still my friends, which can be hard sometimes, and still in this world, which can be harder.

Spring

Old Shores

Go stand on the beach at Good Harbor Bay some beautiful day. Contemplate the majesty of Whaleback in the distance to the north, jutting out into the waters of Lake Michigan, knowing as you do this that bald eagles are there. A bald eagle can see a fish from a mile away and swoop down and get it. You know you cannot do this, except in your dreams.

Turn and look at the sand cherry growing on the blonde beach. Think about falling in love, like the newlyweds in the newspaper in their 90s who have decided that life is not yet over, the wedding photo showing their ancient, age-spotted, infinitely wrinkled hands, touching. Think about the glaciers that receded and advanced, retreated and moved forward, countless times over two-plus-million years and created the very shore upon which you are standing.

We live on a peninsula that has experienced numerous lake stages of prehistoric Lake Michigan lapping at its perimeter. The three, major prehistoric "great" lakes were: Lake Algoma, Lake Nipissing, and Lake Algonquin and over the last 11,000 years, give or take a few hundred years, these lakes successively formed the border of the Leelanau Peninsula. Don't confuse the names of these prehistoric lakes with other lakes you might have heard of by the same or similar names, we're talking about ancient lakes here, not any modern ones.

Dick Cookman stands at the corner of St. Joseph Street (M-22) and Jefferson Street in Suttons Bay, in front of Enerdyne, his science-themed store full of telescopes, binoculars, microscopes, science kits, science toys, robotic kits, books,

rocks, minerals and much more. Cookman is a retired Northwestern Michigan College (NMC) geology and astronomy professor. He resembles Gandolph, the Druidic wizard in the
Hobbit stories and he talks like James Stewart in *It's a Wonderful Life*, the 1946 black-and-white, classic Frank Capra
film. He points across St. Joseph Street—M-22—eastward toward the bay and says, "From here to the shore of the bay,
that used to be part of Lake Algoma." He turns in the opposite
direction and points up Jefferson. "That alley up there, by the
water wheel, by the park, that's about where the shore of
Lake Nipissing would have been. And if you go farther up the
street, where the hill starts, that was the shore of Lake Algonquin."

To imagine the Leelanau Peninsula's shores in former
times, over the last 11,000 years or so, picture a three-tiered
wedding cake shaped like a wobbly isosceles triangle made
by kids. The triangle is pointing north, or northward, on an
eastward slant. The top layer is Algonquin. The middle layer
is Nipissing. The bottom layer is Algoma. Three layers, three
lakes. The waters of those former lakes are now part of the
present-day Lake Michigan.

Now that you've imagined the Leelanau Peninsula's three
prehistoric shores as the edges of a kid-made layer cake, consider that all along the edge of each layer, the kids took bites
out as they were assembling, and then they frosted it unevenly with big, goopy, lumpy frosting: that's the peninsula.
Each shore goes approximately along the edge of the current
peninsula, in these three tiers, but was eroded in several
places by wind and waves.

Whaleback, for example, as seen from Good Harbor Bay,
the nose pointing into the water, has been eroded right up to
the imaginary whale's imaginary mouth. Good Harbor Bay,
if you're still standing there, is the modern shore and if you
go back up the road, the way you came in, you will go up a
series of "risers" like the bleachers in a stadium, up and over

the swampy ripples of old Lake Algoma shores, until you get to M-22, and the rough stand-in for the old Lake Nipissing shore. Beyond that is the oldest shore, the shore of Lake Algonquin.

Geology is interesting psychologically because to approach it, at least for me, requires examination of the fabric of space-time and the physics of consciousness. I think this is because it's hard to take in any span of time greater than one's own. In one lifetime, we can see small changes—a shoreline shifts here, a hill erodes there, a field is planted with cherry trees, a forest is cleared and a subdivision goes in—but the main contours of the land that a person sees all around every day basically don't change. And so, unconsciously, we make an internalized, non-verbal, false assumption and believe that these things don't change, at least not in any way that's going to impact us in one lifetime. To imagine changes that would make a difference to us, we would have to imagine a self that is thousands of years old. That's really hard to do, at least for me. So, we need to intellectually embrace the idea of the changes, even when we can't see them; that's at the core of geological awareness.

Michigan's fragmented shorelines, according to James Walter Goldthwait, an early American geologist who received his PhD from Harvard in 1906, are hard to pin down with any precision. Goldthwait, always fascinated by glacial geology, wrote in 1908, "Around the borders of Lake Michigan are many fragments of abandoned shorelines, which start at different heights above the present lake. Where the cutting back of cliffs at the present level of Lake Michigan has been vigorous, the old shorelines have been partly or wholly destroyed for stretches of up to twenty-five miles. It follows that old shorelines preserved at one locality, do not necessarily correspond with those at a neighboring locality, either in number or in order."

Given that the shorelines of the Leelanau Peninsula are fragments, you can still see them, albeit fragmentally, and more importantly, feel them. When I was growing up above Sleeping Bear Bay, I would walk down a large hill, maybe 400 feet high, and then up and over eroded, two-or-three-foot high old shorelines for half a mile or more, all the way to Lake Michigan. These old shorelines—and there are many—are maybe similar to furrows in a field, but shallower and more widely spaced; and there are trees and bushes and ground pine and wintergreen growing in and on the furrows. Although I was a kid, I knew without being told, that these furrows had been made by something. Later, when I was older and my father put in a road to the lake, a straight road, I could still see and remember the furrows on either side of the road, and what it had felt like to go up and over them. Still later, I learned they were former shorelines and that the waters of Lake Algonquin had once lapped at the base of my mother's hill.

We had a driveway that sloped and, in the spring, when a lot of snow melted on hot days, we would reshape the slush and snow into rivers and streams. A leaf was a boat. A pile of mud and snow was a continent. We were masters of all we surveyed and could create the world in our own image, or if not that exactly, then into something we alone imagined, and when we tired of one configuration, we could do it all over again, something different. Jean Piaget, the Swiss clinical psychologist who studied how children learn, believed that one of the ways children learn math is by studying water displacement. But you don't need to be a clinical psychologist to know that children love to play with sand and water, or even that children learn by playing.

Glen Arbor was underwater 11,000 years ago. What is now Sleeping Bear Bay, in that earlier period, extended all the way to Glen Lake and indeed included it. Then, there was a river delta, with a marsh between Lake Michigan and Glen

Lake, the river winding through, the river bed changing over time, as rivers do. You can still see some of the old river beds in Glen Arbor, places in the wetlands where it looks like a very large fat-tired, unicycle drove through the marsh and left a meandering, single, faded track, a few of them in different places. From the present outlet of the Crystal River near the Leelanau School on M-22, to the western edge of the small town of Glen Arbor near the Christian Science Church on M-109, that whole area was long ago a mix of marsh and water all the way to Glen Lake. Eleven thousand years ago, Glen Lake was a bay of Lake Michigan, or technically, a bay of Lake Algonquin.

If you want to understand what an embayment is and how one is formed over time, drive the coast road, M-22, from Frankfort to Manistee, where bays of Lake Michigan are becoming inland lakes. The road goes through an area that is largely undeveloped. For part of the drive you have the 3,600 acres of the preserved Arcadia Dunes—on both sides of the road—and the wide expanse of Lake Michigan over in the west. (The Arcadia Dunes are funded by the Charles Stewart Mott Foundation in Flint, Michigan and managed by the Grand Traverse Regional Land Conservancy in Traverse City.) See, and marvel, at how the marsh and lake at Arcadia are being gradually closed off from Lake Michigan; or how, at Onekama, the outlet between Portage Lake and Lake Michigan is "in process" and is slowly being closed by a sandbar. The almost imperceptible transition, from embayment to inland lake, is still happening, and you can see it along this stretch of the Lake Michigan shore.

Traverse City, like Glen Arbor, was a river delta, too, in one of its past incarnations. Although you can't see all the old river beds, you can go back to South Airport Road and see the hill that rises on the south side of South Airport, the prehistoric shore of Lake Algonquin, marking the northern edge of the old river delta. A childhood friend and former student of

Dick Cookman's at NMC, Jeanne Foglesong, described a field trip in Professor Cookman's geology class that began, of all places, at the Cherryland Mall. Jeanne was puzzled by how a geology field trip could start there. Cookman pointed south, to the ridge behind all the stores along South Airport Road, and explained that the ridge, 11,000 years ago, was the shoreline of the ancient Lake Algonquin.

If you've lived on the Leelanau Peninsula for a while, you can kind of feel the layers laid down by the glaciers and the glacial lakes. You've walked up and down over those rises that were once the shorelines of ancient lakes so many times that it makes perfect sense to you that there was something here before, a different configuration. But try to explain this to someone new to the area now that all the cars and houses are here, covering everything up, and it's awfully hard to have it make any sense.

Tricia Denton, a friend with a degree in environmental science from Michigan State University, agrees to ride with me around the perimeter of the Leelanau Peninsula to see if there's a way to understand the old lakeshores using some big geological survey maps I'd found. I appreciate this because she has a demanding life, working for the Glen Lake Watershed, spokesperson for Michigan's Infant and Child Mental Health Association, head of the Leelanau County League of Women Voters and a hundred other similar endeavors, in addition to taking care of her three children. Her brilliant and intrepid husband of 20 years, Shawn Denton, travels for his work, so she keeps the hearth fires burning. Busy as she is, she always makes it seem like she has all the time in the world to do something.

I'm driving. Tricia is in the front with the table-top-sized, laminated, geological survey maps and her calculator, turning the maps this way and that, trying to read the tiny elevation numbers on the maps and estimate the elevations in relationship to the present-day shore. Her daughters—Cecelia, a lanky and taciturn teenager who likes botany and zoology; and Ursela, a talkative redhead who likes art, half the age of her older sister—are in the backseat of my Honda Civic, eating dried blueberries I'd brought for them. The big laminated maps are unwieldy. The map elevation numbers are in meters; these have to be converted to feet so we who didn't grow up with the metric system can get a better grasp of the different heights. Tricia reads out an elevation, and I try to look around and see what this means. It's early spring and so there's almost no traffic, a good time to drive and look around. At some point the dried blueberries spill as they're being passed from front to back and little, dried blueberries roll into every crevice of the car.

We drive out to Cathead Bay where her aunt is trying to sell a lake lot, driving along the shore-side dunes past big, new, ostentatious houses, built into the sand hills, houses like something on Cape Cod. What happens when the wind blows? Does the sand get into the houses?

There are still piles of old, decaying snow in the woods, in the shaded areas under the cedars. The red osier dogwood, called red twig dogwood by my father, is the bright red of late spring in the dark swamp areas. Soon marsh marigolds will be up in the watery ditches, blazing forth with their astonishing yellow, but for now the landscape is shades of black-green, black-gray, dark-gray, and black. The sky is gray, like mouse fur. Even the water in Lake Michigan is gray, steel-gray, like something in the military. We nearly get stuck in the muddy driveway of the lake lot. One of her daughters finds some weasel bones, at least we think they're weasel bones, and she wants very badly to keep them. We decide it's time to go home, wash weasel bones, and read.

We stop at Pamela Grath's bookstore, Dog Ears, in Northport. Pamela is, like the Leelanau Peninsula itself, an anomaly. She reads hundreds of books a year. She is deeply steeped in literature, speaks fluent French, has a Ph.D. in philosophy from the University of Illinois in Champaign-Urbana where she studied with James Wallace, father of David Foster Wallace, the award-winning author of *Infinite Jest*, and knows the title of almost any book, new or old, and the author. Her husband, painter David Grath is, Pamela says, "working himself like a rented mule," preparing for a one-man show at the Dennos Museum. His studio and gallery are adjacent to the bookstore. Tricia buys books for her kids, and Pamela tells us about a place north of Eastport, off U.S. 31, where there's a park with all the shorelines labeled.

Once back in my Traverse City apartment, eight floors above the Boardman River, I get out a geology textbook, *The Geology of Michigan*, by John A. Dorr, Jr., and Donald F. Eschman published in 1970 by University of Michigan Press. I open the textbook. I look at the river, flowing by so slowly. I see a duck swimming up-river, effortlessly.

Every time I look at the river, listed on early maps as the Ottaway River, I'm reminded of how Traverse City was a river delta and how the river's path shifted many times over the last several thousand years. Across the river from me is Hannah Park, an Ottawa burial ground, according to the *Hinsdale Archeological Atlas of Michigan*. Wilbert Hinsdale, born in Ohio in 1851, saw the Native heritage being erased and, as head of the Archeology Department at the University of Michigan, charted, with his students, all the Native villages, burial grounds, and trails all over Michigan. This prodigious effort is how I know where things used to be. A similarly inspired early observer of the area, Dr. M. L. Leach from New York State, walked all over northern Michigan and wrote about it in the *Grand Traverse Herald* in 1883. He recorded an Ottawa campground, at a place they could pull their canoes up onto a grassy bank, directly across from Hannah Park, right about where I now live. It makes sense that their burial ground would be on a steep bank across from their campground.

I'm skimming through the geology text. It's starting to snow lightly, snow that's gray in the gray afternoon light so it looks like soft gray feathers. The earth got warmer and then colder, many times over, and as glaciers melted and froze, the lake levels rose and fell back down through endless time. Pudding stones have different-colored pieces of red chert (jasper) in them, something to do with the glaciers, something that happened a long, long time ago. Perhaps I'm just tired, but there are so many different names for all the glacial lakes, and so many different maps on so many different pages, all with different water lines, that I finally give up. What I want is a visceral understanding, something I can carry around in my head and mull over as I go about my daily rounds; but even if I were to memorize all the different names for all the different lakes, all the different elevations, all the different water lines, and all the different dates, which it seems like I'd have to do to start making sense of it all, I'm not sure where it would get me. It will be months before I decide to give geology another whirl.

Pamela is right: the best place to see the gradual progression of shorelines, from the modern one today, up through all the others, is the Antrim Creek Natural Area in Atwood, almost exactly opposite Northport as the crow flies. Thirty miles north of Traverse City on U.S. 31, turn west (on a northward slant) at the hardware store in Atwood, go down Rex Beach Road, drive two miles to the Lake Michigan shore and the Antrim Creek Natural Area. It's labeled. The reason it's easy to see the ancient shorelines here is that there's no development. There's just the land and Lake Michigan. Also, no small thing, the Michigan Department of Natural Resources (DNR) has helpfully installed a canopied information kiosk. The lines on the DNR map show how the old shores correlate visibly with the surrounding topography.

This was a Native campground for thousands of years. When people still used birchbark canoes, it was the shortest

distance across Lake Michigan to the tip of the Leelanau
Peninsula. The shore where the waters of Lake Michigan are
lapping the sand, is the present one. The next shore is the
shore of Lake Algoma, up about 10 or 15 feet, and this is the
one from about 3,000 years ago. Nipissing is next, another 20
feet or so, and this is the shore from about 5,000 years ago.
Finally, quite a distance up the slope, maybe half a mile, is
the oldest shore, that of Lake Algonquin, from about 11,000
years ago. The old Lake Algonquin shore is contiguous with
the road at the top of the hill, the Old Dixie Highway. Abstract information and visible reality converge at last to create understanding.

This area, called Kitigaaning, or "garden area" by Anishnaabeg people, according to information on a Michigan Department of Natural Resources sign, was used right up until
the advent of the Europeans. There was a visible foot trail,
the Mikana, a north-south path that followed the upper ridge
of the Lake Michigan shoreline and went from Antrim Creek
to Traverse City. A few miles north up the Lake Michigan
shore, at Norwood, there's an outcropping of bedrock lime-
stone containing chert, or flint, used for spears and arrows.
Flint-knapping is hard to do. One of the young men who
helped me move from Lake Leelanau to my apartment above
the river, said he learned to do it in Boy Scouts but it was
years and years before he could do it successfully. Pieces of
chert found hundreds of miles away, indicate that it was a
trade item. Archaeological discoveries show continuous
human habitation at Antrim Creek for more than 4,500 years.

Native people may have been here long before 11,000
years ago, too—many thousands of years earlier, when the
lake levels were so low that they could have walked from
Antrim Creek to Northport in a direct line, east to west, on a
northern angle. The information on the sign at the Antrim
Creek Natural Area, the DNR notes, is provided in part by

Charles "Chuck" Cleland, retired curator of Great Lakes archeology and ethnology at Michigan State University.

An article in the *Chicago Tribune* in 2009 reports that divers in the Grand Traverse Bay found "a mysterious pattern of stones rising from an otherwise sandy half-mile of lake floor." A blogger called it "an underwater Stonehenge." One of the divers, Alisa Korn of Traverse City, told me in 2017 that there was a drawing of a mastodon on one of the rocks. This image can be found online. If the drawing wasn't a hoax, then the rock formation would have had to have been established at least 10,000 or 11,000 years ago because, according to all sources, mastodons disappeared from North America between 10,000 and 11,000 years ago. It's even more probable that such a rock paddock would have been made many thousands of years ago, two or three times the amount of time since the mastodons disappeared, when the lake levels were low enough for aboriginal hunters to make an enclosure into which they could chase a mastodon and take it down. Hank Bailey, a member of the Grand Traverse Band of Ottawa and Chippewa Indians is reported in the article as saying, "There's a lot that we still don't know."

Michigan is unusual. Look at the globe. Look at North America. Michigan is the only inland land mass, surrounded on three sides by not only water, but fresh water. And the Leelanau Peninsula is a peninsula on that peninsula, all of it carved by glaciers. This otherworldly liminal landscape is unique but, for me, it's home. Home is home. I'm part of this. Or, it's part of me. That's what home is, a place where you don't know where it ends and you start.

Alan Arbogast, professor and chair of the Department of Geography, Environment and Spatial Sciences at Michigan State University wrote to me in an email about the ancient lakes, "We don't really think of them as three lakes, which implies independent (from each other) water bodies, but rather stages. If you think of it that way, then the focus becomes an evolutionary tale that reflects the very dynamic nature of the lake through time, one that is related to the interactions of many complex factors. The shoreline of Lake Algonquin, for example, represents a time when the lake was certainly much higher due to massive amounts of glacial meltwater (the ice front was draped across the northern end of Lake Superior). But there was also another factor that contributed to this apparently higher lake stage. That factor was the depression of the landscape into the upper mantle because of the weight of the ice. The landscape has since bounced back (continues to, actually) such that it appears that the lake at that time was incredibly high."

About four hundred million years ago, Michigan as we know it didn't exist. It was a coral sea down near the equator, according to geologists, before the plates in the earth's crust shifted. Remnants of that time can be seen in the Petoskey stones, fossilized coral, that are found on the shore. Trying to calculate geologic time in relationship to one's own lifespan, can be relied on to bring on an uncomfortable moment of comeuppance, as one confronts not only one's own insignificance but, relatively speaking, that of all humanity. To get some idea of something that took place 400 million years ago, if 400 million years is reduced to a year, a human who is seventy years old has lived only a few seconds of that year, just barely long enough to bend down and pick up a Petoskey stone, if it's a small one.

The mysteries of the past stay with me all the way back from the Old Dixie Highway in Antrim County to Traverse City, and I muse over events in the last few years that were caused by global warming and the resultant melting ice. The ice shelf off Antarctica in 2017 lost a piece of itself the size of Delaware, an event documented by the National Aeronautics and Space Administration (NASA). It's floating out there ready to terrify the next Titanic. A 106-year-old fruitcake, it was reported in the *National Geographic* in 2017, was just found in Antarctica, and was "in excellent condition" according to the person who found it. Glacier melt in the Yukon in 2017, cut a channel from the Alsek River to the Slims River, according to an April 2017 article in the *New York Times,* so the water from the Slims River now goes into the Pacific instead of the Bering Sea. It happened almost as fast as the way we rerouted our "rivers" in the slush of the driveway in the spring. Because of climate change, according to scientists, what happened to the Slims River, a process that would ordinarily take thousands of years, happened in a few months.

Back in Traverse City, after stopping briefly at my apartment, I'm once again heading toward the Leelanau Peninsula. If you drive M-22 north out the east side of the Leelanau Peninsula, starting at Tom's Food Market, you will see the current shore of Lake Michigan in the east, where the sun comes up, adjacent to and overlapping, and sometimes contiguous with, the most recent prehistoric Lake Algoma shore. Your car is on M-22, the coast road, a rough approximation of the old Nipissing shore. But this is not absolute. Although M-22 (also called West Bayshore Drive North along this stretch) is a solid asphalt road, the exact synchronization with the old Nipissing shore is not. This is because wind and waves changed things over time. To your west, where the sun goes down, 600 feet up that bluff, the first hills will be the old Lake Algonquin shore.

I'm heading to the lighthouse at the tip of the peninsula, north of Northport, to meet Jeanne Foglesong. In Greilickville, just north of Traverse City on M-22, the traffic is backed-up and stalled, everyone waiting. A traffic accident? No, ducks crossing. When we finally start moving again, I see them truckling along through the park, a mother duck and her little ones.

I've known Jeanne Foglesong since grade school. Her father, John Eichstadt, who went to Princeton when Einstein was still there, and who graduated with a degree in math and came to the Leelanau Peninsula bringing a little of that eastern élan with him, was one of my teachers. He taught at the Leelanau School, where he was my sister Ann's teacher; then he came to the Glen Lake Community School, where he taught my other three sisters and me. The Eichstadts lived on Glen Lake and so we were neighbors, and Jeanne was my sister Barb's classmate and friend. Jeanne is a Realtor with Coldwell Banker, so she sees a lot of the peninsula. She's honest and patient, good qualities in a Realtor. Jeanne, like her father, is good at math. She was the one who helped me figure out the length of a human lifespan relative to the approximately 400 million years since Michigan was a coral sea down near where Florida is now, where if the approximately 400 million years is reduced to a year, humans have been on earth a few seconds of that time. I would never have been able to figure that out by myself, and even now that I know it, can't take it in. We are meeting at the Leelanau Conservancy's Lighthouse West Natural Area. I've asked her to walk with me out the trail toward Lake Michigan. I don't know what's there and I want to know.

We come to a 100-foot-high ledge, almost a sheer drop, that descends to a dark, rocky terrace that extends west, approximately another 500 feet, to the shore of Lake Michigan. That ledge, undisturbed by any bulldozers, is primal and strange. It would seem to be some vestige of the Lake Algonquin shore. Jeanne, Professor Cookman's one-time student, chooses this moment to confess that she's afraid of bears, although she's never seen one. I have seen bears a few times, always at a distance, in the Rocky Mountains and in the mountains of Appalachia, and on the shores of Lake Superior in Canada. I am not afraid of bears, but it's the kind of desolate place where one might have such thoughts. It's a dark and stony area. Native people would have never camped here. They wouldn't even have buried people here. Too many stones. The tree canopy is dense and so the light is dim. The stones themselves are almost black. Everything feels dark. The sense of a land uninhabited by people, of endless time, is inexplicably there like someone breathing you can't see.

"Do you know an owl can hear a mouse from 30 feet away?" I ask.

She laughs. "Did you say that to tease me about the bears?" I like to be with someone who knows my quirks.

Four billion years ago there was minimal life on earth. It was almost nothing. We were nothing. How did a world without so much as a mouse—or an owl to hunt it—become a place with two-legged people, old friends from school, kidding around about bears and owls? That's the kind of question that rises up in the human mind in such a place. But there are no bears. There are no owls. At least not any that we can see. Owls hunt at night. And bears don't like to be where people are.

Months later, on a day that the sun is dazzling and the whitecaps on Lake Michigan are like a million toy sailboats, a fantasy regatta, a day when the wind is from the west, I'm down at Good Harbor Bay again. I walk toward Shalda Creek where I used to bring my children when they were little. I would read and they would play. Here they could reroute the creek as I had once rerouted slush and meltwater in the driveway. They would rearrange the sand and water for hours at a time, day after day, as glaciers had once done on a much larger scale to the whole place. I'm not sure about Piaget, but it feels to me that the physics of consciousness is partly derived from the way we internalize geologic formations and geologic time. When we do it while surrounded by breath-taking beauty, which we don't think of as breath-taking beauty because we aren't thinking, because we're unconscious of the surrounding natural beauty even while immersed in it, it makes us who we are. It shapes how we experience our existence. This is only a hypothesis, but it's possible that when you live on the shores of a stunningly gorgeous glacier-made peninsula, your sense of impermanence is both unconscious and permanent and your expectation that there will always be amazing beauty all around you is, too.

Curtis Cluckey, Mushroom Hunter

His work is washing windows, but his passion is mushrooms. His dream is to grow them commercially.

Cluckey meets me in Art's Tavern on Lake Street in Glen Arbor, just before noon on a muggy May morning. We both order burgers which are excellent here. He's been washing the windows at the Bethlehem Lutheran Church across the street. By reputation and in person, he's the Glen Arbor version of legendary Johnny Appleseed, a quintessential backwoodsman with good skills, good stories, and good integrity, a great window washer and a gifted mushroom finder.

"There's a lot more to Curt than meets the eye," says Anneke Wegman of Lake Leelanau, wife of Guy Plamondon who owns Plamondon Shoes on Front Street in Traverse City. Cluckey's been a Plamondon family friend for two decades. "We love his stories. Once we held him hostage until he put in five pieces of a very hard 1,000-word puzzle just so we could hear his stories," she says. "The most important thing about Curt is that he's always been very good to our children." She's hoping to have Cluckey teach her youngest son, a budding naturalist, some of his mushroom lore. "I trust him. We could use more good guys like Curt." In a day and age when being trustworthy is coming back into vogue, Cluckey has that old-fashioned quality in abundance.

When Curtis "Curt" Cluckey was in his late teens, he tells of how he rode a bicycle north from Ludington, where he'd been staying with his grandparents, to the Leelanau Peninsula. "The bike was a one-speed Huffy. I think it probably had three speeds at one time, but it was broken." He laughs. "It took a week." Today with a good bike, he says, a person could do it in a day. I ask if he was wearing a helmet and spandex and he says he wasn't, but it probably wouldn't have helped with that particular bike. "I slept in pastures. You'd be amazed at how close you can be to the road and still be invisible. I had a pup tent and a sleeping bag. It was May. It was cold in the morning. I had to get up and get moving."

He found the Leelanau Peninsula to his liking, got a job washing windows with Bill Burmeister of Northport and, except for some time out in Montana and a few different excursions around the United States, has been here ever since. "I worked for Bill for 13 years," Cluckey says. "A few years ago, I bought the business from him." Leelanau Window Cleaning is listed in the Leelanau phone book.

When Cluckey travelled, he says he rode the freight trains and hitch-hiked. "I found I could take an empty can and put in paraffin and cardboard and make a little cooker. I ate beans. Potatoes. I never ate anything that cost anything. I shopped at the co-ops."

"I always worked. I was a dish washer at a Big Boy. Wherever I went, I'd go to the temp agencies. They'd put you to work right away. In Seattle I put in foundations. I went east, too. I shoveled snow in Boston. There was a lot of warehouse work. I took odd jobs. Anything to earn a few dollars. One place they paid to check the size of your aorta. My aorta was good-sized because of all that work." Like Woody Guthrie and Jack London before him, and of course, Johnny Appleseed, he loved his country and wanted to see it in its most unvarnished state.

"In all of my travels I always spent time in nature. I think the United States is so beautiful. In Washington State there were farms and forests," he says. "Now it's all developed. The forests are becoming farms and the farms are becoming cities." Once he bought a used bike from a yard sale and traveled along a western lake.

"I've had the same clients for years," Cluckey says about his window washing. "I do advertise, but mostly I get referrals. People don't hire someone to come in their house unless they know someone who had him do work for them."

He had said over the phone that he didn't usually eat in restaurants, not in the habit of it and also saving his money for his mushroom-growing business. Eating at Art's Tavern in Glen Arbor is a festive occasion. He's wearing what looks like a new Carhartt t-shirt and definitely new Dickies canvas pants because the tag is still on the back of his pant leg where he hadn't thought to look for it. He's dressed up for this. Cluckey is exactly the kind of guy you'd trust to teach your son how to find morels or come to your cottage and clean the windows. He's as genuine and gentle as a leaf or bird.

"He's a very honest person," says artist Beth Bricker. On a recent day, Beth says, "when it was cold and sunny, Curt was working with my sister and Bill [Cherry and Bill Stege], at my grandparents' old cottage. He does a great job. He entered into the conversation with us." Cluckey says he charges by the window, not by the hour, so that way if he and his customers get into a conversation nobody needs to worry about the time. It makes for a more congenial work atmosphere.

When morel mushrooms were more plentiful on the Leelanau Peninsula and Cluckey lived down in what's called "the hollows" on Plowman Road, he would find the morels and sell them at the nearby upscale Burdickville restaurants, LaBecasse and Funistrada. (The State of Michigan no longer allows morel hunters to sell to grocery stores and restaurants.) According to Josephine Arrowood who was his neighbor at the time, "Curt was a good neighbor. One spring he plowed for me."

Cluckey says in that earlier time in his life, about 20 years ago, the morel hunting was better. "The hills above Glen Lake were great for 'em because they haven't been logged [since the Sleeping Bear Dunes National Lakeshore was established in 1970]. The habitat is intact. Logging changes everything."

One of the reasons Cluckey says he wants to grow mush-rooms to sell is that they're disappearing from the woods. "The mushrooms that grow on trees, have been there thou-sands of years. They don't move around. They have a symbi-otic relationship to the trees. If the trees are gone, the mushrooms go dormant [in the soil]. They won't come back until the trees come back." Cluckey has a business partner and together they hope to go into the mushroom-growing business. "We're looking at a 20,000-square-foot building in Cheboygan. We've got a business plan."

Cluckey says he comes from a long line of American pio-neers. "I'm named for my great-grandmother. Her name was Violeta Curtis Pierce." I tell him that Pierce was my father's name, and that according to family lore it had been a sur-name of some family member in a previous generation. We might be related. Pierce was the last name of his great-great-grandfather on his mother's side, Cluckey says, and that man had been a frontiersman who was an aide for Kit Carson. "My grandfather Pierce helped Kit Carson map the Oregon Trail."

He thinks he likes to be out in the woods because that's his family's background. He learned the names of the trees from his grandfather. "They came, probably, from England, probably 400 years ago." Like many of the early English pio-neers, the people in the Pierce and Cluckey families kept moving west, into the wilderness, as the eastern United States became more developed.

Mushrooms, Cluckey says, are rich in Vitamin D. They're also a source of protein and boost the immune system in ways scientists are just beginning to define. Shiitake mushrooms have been proven to fight cancerous tumors in mice, accord-ing to a classic book on the subject, *The Mushroom Cultivator*, by Paul Stamets and J.S. Chilton, a well-worn copy of which Cluckey carries in his truck. The Chinese have been finding medicinal uses for shiitake mushrooms for centuries.

One of the ways he cooks morels, Cluckey says, is to dip them in batter—the same kind of batter one would use for onion rings—and then deep fat fry them. Morels are hollow inside. Gently slice the mushrooms in half and soak them in salt water and allow them to drain on paper towels before cooking. And, of course, one needs to know how to identify morels or to trust that the morel hunter knows. Morels are the northern Michigan version of French truffles, rich-tasting and uniquely satisfying. People who grew up in the wilds of northern Michigan learn their value as a cooking ingredient. They can make an ordinary meal exquisite.

Morels can be chopped up, browned in a little butter, and used as a steak sauce. A dish made with small green zucchini, a few chopped green onions, morels, heavy cream, ziti and a grating of Reggiano Parmigiano is delicious, with the cream making everything taste like the wild mushrooms; the black morels are best for this. Morels dry well and once they're dried can be kept for years. The dried morels are great crumbled and added to spaghetti sauce.

"I like to be outdoors," Cluckey says. "I like to be in the woods. It's cool under the trees. It's good exercise." He doesn't stick to the woodland trails in his mushroom hunting but goes up and down the hills, through brush and over treefalls. "I like to explore new places. Mushroom hunting has taken me all over Michigan, down to Cadillac and up to Munising. It's like a sport, except you don't need a license."

Other areas of the state, away from Lake Michigan, are often better habitat for mushrooms, according to Cluckey. "This area is arid, maybe because it's a peninsula sticking out into the water, but it's dry and breezy." More humid, inland woods are often better for mushrooms. Mesick, for example, is prime morel habitat.

"Morels grow under ash trees, mostly, and some under elm trees," Cluckey says. "But with the emerald ash borer coming in and killing all the ash trees, morels are harder to find. Last summer I was in the places where I used to find morels under the ash trees and they weren't there anymore. And every weed was covered with the ash borer." Ash borers are a small beetle and, true to their name, are a brilliant emerald green. It's a rare and scary shade of green with a flashy metallic sheen to it.

"I've studied mushrooms," Cluckey says. "Elm oysters, they grow on trees, and they're delicious. I've grown shiitake, brick-top mushrooms." He wants to grow mushrooms indoors and sell them to grocery stores around Michigan. "If we actually do it, we'll be selling at least 1,000 pounds of mushrooms a week."

He finishes his lunch and pushes back from the table. It's time to head back to the church job across the street. It's beautiful outside. "It's a dream," he says of the idea of growing mushrooms. "We all need to have a dream. It might happen. I'd be happy if it did."

Ruby John, Native Fiddler

Ruby John is a jewel of a girl. Her name fits her. She's also a gifted and versatile fiddler. One balmy Friday evening in mid-June she's entertaining families at the Little Traverse Inn, fiddling in the Ruby Sky Band with some of her friends: Dane Hyde, who sings and plays guitar; Katie O'Conner, a singer and Irish dancer; and John Driscoll, a flautist and singer. The next week she'll play for a staff dance at Interlochen Arts Academy's opening of summer camp. And after that, at Tucker's in Northport. She's known for playing a Métis-style of fiddle as well as Celtic, and standard country-and-mountain-style.

"Métis means half," Ruby says.

The Métis-style, as she explains it, is a style of fiddling based on an early mix of French and Native music—and, as the years went by, some bits of Scots-Irish and English, according to musicologists—that arose out of a combined culture that began in the late 1500s in northeastern Canada. "When the French fur traders came from France and had children with Native people," Ruby explains, "they developed their own style of fiddle-playing. I don't consider myself a traditional Métis fiddler because I didn't grow up with it, but I love the sound and love to play it. I like all different kinds of fiddle-playing, all the different regions and the different styles, it's like all different kinds of dialects." She likes bluegrass music, too, which can sometimes show Native influence.

Métis fiddle-playing is related to, but not the same as, the Cajun music popularized by the band, BeauSoleil. In the case of Cajun music, the French influence occurred when the rebellious and unruly French Acadians, some of whom were Métis, were sent to French Louisiana in the mid-1700s after the British seized power from the French in Canada. The Louisiana south, sold by Napoleon so he could pay to put down a slave revolt in Haiti, wouldn't become part of the United States until 1803. Cajun music, which sometimes partakes of elements of Creole music—a mix of black, white, and Native influences, a music popularized by the Neville Brothers, among others—is French-influenced-Native-born music in the southern bayous and backwaters of the Mississippi delta.

Graeme Leask, the Scot proprietor of the Little Traverse Inn says he's glad to have Ruby there. "I like to support the local music scene, the local musicians, but Ruby's traveling so much now, with her music, we hardly ever see her." Graeme bought the historic Inn in 2010. The Inn itself dates to the late 1800s. "I love the people. I've made great friendships." He gestures around. "This is the community living room." His menu, kind of a London pub menu, offers fish and chips, shepherd's pie, and several Indian dishes. "It's comfort food from all parts of the world," he says. Haggis is prepared well here, but the best, so the customers say, are the French fries and mashed potatoes. "Scots know how to cook potatoes," Kaz McCue, an art teacher from the Leelanau School, says as he tucks into his mashed potatoes, with some of the skins on, on an evening a group from the Leelanau School is celebrating Robert Burns's birthday. In the summers Kaz bartends at the Inn.

A lot of American music, including that of Johnny Cash and Elvis Presley, both of whom believed they were part-Native, shows indigenous influence. When DNA tests came in, it turns out Presley was indeed part-Native, but Cash, to his chagrin, was not. Joan Baez is part-Mexican which means she was part-Native from south of the border. Buffy Sainte-Marie is Cree from Saskatchewan. The blues song, *Black*

Girl, as sung by Lead Belly and others, with notes in a minor key, can easily be imagined as a Native song with just vocals, and those strange catching noises in the throat, and may have been such a song in its origins.

Dane Hyde says he's known Ruby for about 10 years and played with her for about five. "I think she's awesome. She's respectful of her elders. She's respectful of the music and the work. I've watched her grow from a student to a huge resource for this area. She travels all over and comes back with new music for our community."

Ruby also plays, every chance she gets, at the Medi Lodge (formerly Tendercare) in Suttons Bay, an assisted living place. It's her community service, her way to thank all the people who have helped her in her career, and pass it on. Often her mother, Cindi John, is with her. Ruby and her mother have been doing this for years. The residents adore Ruby, according to Marilyn Vogel, a former care-giver there.

In 2008 Ruby was invited by Anne Lederman, a fiddler from Manitoba, to attend the Elder Youth Legacy Workshop in Toronto, the only Native young person in the group from the United States. She says she studied the Métis-style for four weeks with several elders, including James Cheechoo, Lawrence "Teddy Boy" Houle, Colin Adjun, and John Arcand. Ruby is scrupulous in naming and crediting all the musicians who have mentored her. She began studying the fiddle when she was about 10 years old. "A fiddle is basically a violin with a flatter bridge," she says, "the difference [between the two] is the music you play on them."

I first met Ruby one winter when she and her two older brothers, Cameron and Alex, were being home-schooled at the tribal library where their mother worked as the librarian; I'd been brought in to help with literature and history. When Ruby and I met again recently to talk about her becoming a professional fiddler, neither of us could remember what I'd taught her. She remembered that one day I'd brought in what she called a French Silk Pie, Quiche Lorraine, something I'd forgotten. Her parents, Ed and Cindi John were there in the library, on a seasonal break from fishing. Her parents own the Treaty Fishing Company and from early spring to late fall run the Linda Sue, an excellent fishing boat named in memory of Cindi's sister, out of the tribal marina on Grand Traverse Bay. Winter is their downtime.

Ruby was quiet and shy when I knew her as a preteen, but at 26 she's outgoing, poised, seeking ways to connect and put me at ease, remembering the pie, talking about going to Kentucky to a fiddling event with her mom. Clearly the years of performing in public have honed these social skills. She has long, black hair and looks distinctly Ottawa, but seems to blend in naturally wherever she is, whether it's a Celtic band at the Little Traverse Inn or a Native event in Canada, swimming through it all as unselfconsciously as a fish, no matter how uncharted the waters.

For me, Ruby isn't separate from her family. Yes, she's a fiddler in her own right, and years and years of studying with different fiddlers have made her a good one, but I always remember the presence of her mother and her father. When I go online to see videos of her playing, I come upon one that takes place in what I instantly recognize as the old Kitchi Minogining (Garden of Learning) youth center and library. There she is, being videotaped, playing her fiddle, while George Trudeau, an Ottawa language teacher and musician from Manitoulin Island in Canada, stands, elegant and lively, at the piano. Ruby is obscured by the large bookcases, until her father, almost imperceptibly, comes behind her and gently ushers her from the shoals of the bookcases into the open near the piano where the camera can see her. Ruby, as all children are, if they're lucky, was a group effort.

Ed and Cindi John had to find a way to navigate the minefield of the 400 years of unceasing—at times inadvertent and at times deliberate—destruction of Native peoples by the invaders; and—in the resultant chaos—keep their marriage and family together, and do it in a way that affirmed their cultural heritage. Having the treaty rights restored in 1980, after endless court battles, helped. Treaty rights gave the people in Peshawbestown federal recognition, as well as treaty fishing rights, and ushered in a period of renewal. Bible-study groups helped, too, according to Cindi. Ed and Cindi's success with fishing and keeping their family together is a testament to what tribal elders mean when they talk about the current Native Renaissance.

Initially Ruby's mom, Cindi, took fiddle lessons with Ruby and Ruby's two older brothers, Cameron and Alex. "When I was fourteen," Ruby says, "I told my mom this was what I wanted to do." Her brothers liked the fiddle, but not enough to pursue it full-time. Neither of her parents play music, but she says she has a great-grandfather on her mother's side and a grandfather on her father's side, both of whom were musicians, one a fiddle player and one a pianist. Ruby's mom, Cindi, is part-Ottawa from the Grand Traverse Band and part-Irish by way of Appalachia. Ruby's father, Ed John, is Ottawa through-and-through, with family roots in the Great Lakes area that go back uncounted millennia.

Ruby, after deciding she wanted to study the fiddle, took lessons from Traverse City music teachers Chris Williams, Jan Ostroski, and others. "Lee Sloan was in his nineties when I started studying with him. I studied with Bob Saddler in Cadillac. I worked with George Trudeau. He lives in Traverse City and we still play together. We played for the Fall Festival two years ago in Canada, in Wikwemikong [on Manitoulin Island in Lake Huron where Trudeau grew up]," Ruby says. "I played old-time Canadian fiddle and George played keyboard."

Trudeau remembers the first time he heard Ruby play, some 13 years earlier, "I said, 'Ruby I can chord for you [on the piano]. And she said, 'A lot of people say they can, but they

can't.' Then I did. Oh my gosh, we hit it off, right from there."
Trudeau comes from a musical family. His mother, he says,
was "a church organist and a fantastic honky-tonk piano
player" and music came naturally to him; by his teens he was
playing in bands. "Another thing about Ruby," he says, "Any
chord, she can name it, just like that." Not all fiddle players
can do that, he says.

Chris Williams remembers Ruby as a young student. "I
started teaching Ruby when she was maybe nine. It's been a
joy to see her develop as a musician and as a person. She's
one of the few Native fiddlers. If we include Canada, there's
more." Williams first encountered the Native style of fiddling
when she met Nick Bailey (now deceased) in Manistee. "The
sound, to my European-trained ears, just had a different
twist to it. Then I watched *Medicine Fiddle* [a 1991 film by
Michael Loukinen about Native-style fiddling, now on-line]
and saw that he was part of that tradition." Williams talks
about certain tunes, such as "Red River Jig," "Little Johnny
with His Bandy Legs," "Big Bear," "Maple Sugar," and others
that can be played both in a traditional European way and in
a Native way.

Ruby plays all over Michigan and across the border into
Ontario: Garden River, Sagamok, Manitoulin. "Last summer
was the busiest I've ever been. What took a toll on me was
the traveling and being away from home." Home is the rural
Leelanau Peninsula. "I love coming back. The peace and quiet
all around me. My family." She helps her parents, as does her
brother Cameron, with packing fish for the Farmer's Market.
Recently Michigan State University awarded Cindi John a
grant to teach Ruby how to smoke fish the traditional way of
their culture.

Ruby and I are having lunch at Fischer's Happy Hour
near her home. Paul Fischer is here, down from the Upper
Peninsula where he likes to go to hunt and fish and has a second home. His parents came from the east side of Detroit in

1947 and bought the tavern when it was just the front room, with the family living in the back and upstairs. His father and grandfather, Paul says, were always in the beer and delicatessen business. Paul says he could remember his father talking about Detroit during the Depression, bootlegging, the Purple Gang. He looks around. "Everyone comes in here. The farmers would come in here in the summer," Paul says. "They'd spray at night. They'd leave their sprayers out back. I always worried about them driving home at two in the morning." He glances over at his daughter, Kristi, a tiny, energetic young woman. "She's the third generation," he says. "She owns it now."

At the Traverse City Farmer's Market on a Saturday morning, Ed John is selling fish, greeting customers, while Cindi hands a gift to her son's girlfriend's toddler. "I love you," she says to Cameron. "We're a pack," Cindy says, turning to me, "We work together." Cameron works on the boat with his father and Ruby helps with the fish, too, when she's not fiddling.

Ruby's parents, Cindi and Ed John, learned how to fish from Native fisherman, the late Art Duhamel, who taught himself. Duhamel was a handsome and charismatic man who, following a hellish childhood in foster homes, orphanages, and juvenile detention centers, became a master welder and worked on the Alaska Pipeline and the Mackinac Bridge; he also spent some time in prison. Duhamel—articulate, rough-hewn, athletic, intelligent, determined, and famously imperfect in his personal life—fought for federal recognition of Native treaty rights all through the 1970s and was ultimately successful. In honor of that fight, the tribal marina is named for him. "Art did a lot of things that were dangerous [like fishing in subzero temperatures in snow storms from a small, open boat]," Cindi says. "Ed and I try not to do some of those things." They did not know how to fish when they started, but after 30 years, they're experts.

"It was a lifestyle choice for my parents," Ruby says. "My dad loved being out on the lake, loved fishing, and my mom loved my dad. I've helped with the fish my whole life. I clean fish boxes. When I was little, I helped my mom thread needles to mend the nets." When Ruby was first born, she slept in a handmade, white pine fish box, crafted for her by their non-Native landlord, Earl Chervenka, who rented them space to mend their nets in his warehouse on Lakeview Road.

Now, with her mother's tutelage, Ruby is looking forward to learning how to smoke fish. "The secret to good smoked fish," Cindi says, "the secret to good fish, is to have it very fresh. We pull our nets every day. We set them at night and pull them in the morning."

Ruby says her favorite fish is the whitefish. She has two recipes she recommends that are quick and easy. She sprinkles a little Old Bay (paprika, dry mustard, salt and pepper) spice on a fillet and wraps it in tinfoil and bakes it for 30 minutes. "Easy cleanup," she says. Another way she likes to eat whitefish is dipped in ranch dressing, rolled in Panko crumbs, and baked. These recipes work well for lake trout, too. Pierre Charlevoix, the French nobleman and Jesuit priest who first came to North America in 1705, described the Great Lakes, the largest body of fresh water on earth, as having water so pure a traveler could drink from it anywhere, and the waters were teeming with all kinds of fish. He wrote, "of these, the whitefish is the most esteemed for the richness and delicacy of its flavor and there is universal acquiescence that no other of the fish kind can excel it."

We're down by the tribal marina, bathed in humid, sugar-maple smoke from the smoker, while Ruby plays her fiddle, cross-tuned. There's a big, blue tarp over us to keep off the rain. The gulls are swooping and calling out along the breakwater. The sounds of the gulls rise and fall, countering the sounds of the fiddle. Clouds come close to the water. It's overcast, intermittently raining. The rain silently accumulates in little pockets of the tarp and then, suddenly, when we're least expecting it, cascades off with a big splash. The water out in the bay is blackish-gray-green where it's deep and grayish-green where it's shallower. "You can see the wind pushing the lake down," Cindi John says. "It's moving through. I hope it moves through before we go out to set our nets." The smell of the smoked fish is familiar, comforting. For how many eons have humans been gathering at the end of the day to smoke fish?

"Traveling and going places," Cindi John says, "that was Ruby's college." She opens the smoker and checks the fire below the fish. "Patricia," Cindi says, "the woman at Inter-lochen [Patricia Hoekje Reeser, who recently had Ruby play there], we met her in Bayside Travellers. These people, lawyers and doctors some of them, but we just knew them as musicians. They supported Ruby."

"When I was young and travelling to all these places," Ruby says, "what kept me from getting into trouble was all these wonderful musicians who live here. Their support kept me from doing anything foolish." She starts laughing, "When I was about 18 and had my first boyfriend, constantly on the phone with him, Charlie [at a bluegrass festival in Kentucky] grabbed my phone. He hung up on my boyfriend. He pulled me aside where my mother couldn't hear and he said, 'You tell me you want to be professional. You're young. You're a woman. You'll get pregnant. It'll be over for you. Do what you say you want to do, or don't say it.'"

"We have all these families," Cindi says, "Bayside Trav-ellers, our immediate family, the tribe, *Bible* study groups, music teachers, bluegrass festivals, people in Canada."

Ruby wants to move into a more innovative kind of fid-dle-playing called "open-tuning" which basically means changing the key the different strings are in, which will bring her closer to the strains of Native sounds found in some styles of fiddling. It reaches deeper into the heart and the unexpected shifts are stirring. Dane Hyde describes the sound that Ruby gets on her fiddle with her cross-tuning as, "like the half-tones in the bagpipes." The twelve-tone scale, which is traditional for European music, leaves out some possibilities and, Ruby says, "Cross-tuning opens things up more."

Ruby picks up her fiddle. "Those gulls," Ruby says. "They walk around with a big bunch of grass in their mouths." She imitates the sound. "Prupp, prupp. They *talk* to each other." She tucks the bow under her chin and begins to play "Red Prairie Dawn." The smoke and the music drift out over the water.

The Johnson Family, Early Empire Pioneers

In 1880 Levi Johnson and his wife, Anna, were deeded 120 hilly acres looking east over Glen Lake. The grantor on the deed was Ulysses S. Grant, the President of the United States. There is, from that spot, a panoramic view of Little Glen Lake, Alligator Hill, the Narrows, and some of Big Glen Lake. Prime view property in Leelanau County is currently selling for about $100,000 an acre, but of course in 1880 no one would have thought to pay for the view: the fertility of the soil would have determined the value of the land. Virgin soil that had never hosted crops was said to have produced wonderful-tasting food.

Assuming the Johnson's 120 acres had already been timbered-off, probably by the Northern Transit Company (NTC), the company that, with a 24-vessel fleet took out most of the virgin pine on the Leelanau Peninsula, the Johnsons showed good timing. Thirty years earlier and they would have had to cut the timber themselves with an ax and carry in their supplies, probably on their backs as horses were hard to buy in the early days on the frontier.

In those days, the hills there had a few natural springs, according to several old-timers, and so the Johnsons probably had a freshwater spring on the property. If they did, this saved them the trouble of digging a sand-point well. They would have needed money for tools, building supplies, and animals. That they were industrious we can surmise, since they survived. They were wise, too, or fortunate, or both wise and fortunate, not only about the time they chose to come to

Northern Michigan, but in their choice of a home site. They had cleared land, virgin topsoil, and were a 15-minute walk from Glen Lake where they could have watered their animals, carried on year-round fishing, and enjoyed summer bathing. Ice that they took out of the lake in the winter would have kept their milk and meat cool in the summer.

This is not to imply that the Johnson family had an easy time of it. Pioneering required the skills of timber cutting, carpentry, tool making and, of course, farming, gardening, animal husbandry, hunting, fishing, cooking, soap making, and knowledge of home health remedies, not to mention physical strength and stamina, and character qualities such as flexibility, optimism and determination.

Frontier living involved ceaseless toil. Bringing water from the well in a bucket, many buckets, and splitting firewood, lots of firewood, had to be done constantly. Yes, on a nice summer day, you could do your laundry and listen to the songbirds and watch the clouds in the sky while you did it, but not in the rain and snow; and there was often rain and snow. Laundry was the chore women hated most, not only because of all the hauling of the water, and the heating of the water, but because it had to be done in a big tub in the yard, the clothes scrubbed on a washboard, backbreaking work, and the soap, made from lye, ruined one's skin. The clothes had to be wrung out, something requiring the out-sized hands and out-sized strength of a shot-putter or a champion arm wrestler. As Ray Welch, an Empire man from a long line of pioneers, said, "It was all work." Maybe you could go a month without washing clothes but stop hauling water and chopping wood for a week, for instance, and your whole, carefully constructed existence was up for grabs.

Public television did a reality TV program in 2000, *Frontier House*, to see which of three couples could master the arts of homesteading during a few months in the wilderness. The sheer drudgery of it, much less the isolation, took its toll on the contestants, even with "experts" to help with things like tree cutting so no one would get hurt. By contrast, in the real world of homesteading, random accidents were a given. Just like in *Little House on the Prairie* there was always the risk of Pa getting lost in a snowstorm or a bear stealing all the food.

According to Ray Welch, from the family for whom Welch Road is named and the closest neighbor of the Johnsons, a man who grew up in a time before people in Leelanau County had electricity or running water, the Johnson family was hard working and respectable, a welcome addition to the community. Ray Welch was employed as a gardener for my father, Pierce Stocking, when he told me this in 1974. He had been born in the early 1900s and would have been a child when the Johnsons were his neighbors. Dorothy Fradd, the daughter-in-law of Frank Fradd, from a family of the earliest English immigrants in Empire, said her father-in-law told her that the Shaugers, Welches, and Johnsons, who all lived near each other, socialized and celebrated holidays together.

The Johnson home, as Dave Taghon, Director of the Empire Museum, explains it, would have been at the top of Welch Road off M-109, in what is now the Sleeping Bear Dunes National Lakeshore. The home had been built by Frank Fradd Jr., born in Empire, and his father, Francis Fradd Sr., born in England, both excellent carpenters. Frank Fradd's mother was Ida Shauger, daughter of Daniel Shauger who homesteaded near the Johnsons on what was known as Shauger Hill. Daniel Shauger, Frank Fradd's maternal grandfather, a large man, six feet tall, was said to be able to carry 125 pounds on his back from Glen Haven to his home, without bothering to put his burden down even when he stopped to talk to someone. I've heard a few stories of such exceptionally strong pioneers. People were probably stronger then; they had to be.

Frank Fradd, according to Bill Bolton, the now-retired su-
pervisor for the village of Empire and for whom the Empire
Airport is named, "was a slender fellow." Bolton, too, had been
a builder and thought Fradd's good reputation as a builder
was well earned.

The Johnson house was moved in the 1920s, after the
Johnsons were no longer there, to the Breithaupt Farm down
the slope, closer to Glen Lake. The fact that the home, after
50 years, could be moved, indicates that it was well constructed. The Johnson's sturdy home was conveniently located, an hour's walk to Empire in the south and an hour's
walk, in the opposite direction, to the sawmill and tram line
at the mill pond, at the end of Little Glen Lake. The tram carried lumber two miles north to Glen Haven. People could and
did ride the flat cars back and forth from Glen Lake to Glen
Haven.

The Johnson family lived about an hour's walk from the
Brotherton School near North Bar Lake, according to Taghon.
This was where the Johnson children attended before the
Springdale School was built near their home on Welch Road.
At that time, there were approximately 7,200 rural, one-room
schoolhouses scattered over the state, the idea being that
every child should be within an hour's walk of education.
Michigan's virgin timber made it one of the wealthiest states
in the union—from about 1860 to 1920—and the state department of education had enough money to send a photographer
around to take group pictures of the students with their
teachers, photos usually taken outside, with the building in
the background, because the out-of-doors provided sufficient
light for the early-day cameras.

One of the Johnson's neighboring homesteaders was John
Dorsey. Dorsey was about five-feet tall, according to his great-
grandson, Jim Dorsey, and according to many other accounts,
very strong and an amazing fighter. No one wanted to fight
with John Dorsey; he could knock a person out in a flash. He

was also intrepid. At the age of 19 Dorsey had sailed the Great Lakes in his own sailboat. His family had left Ireland to escape one of the many famines. His father died when they arrived in America. His mother remarried, was widowed again, and she herself died when Dorsey was a teen. He had been considering the priesthood but when the church would not allow him to attend church without paying for the pew, he struck out for parts unknown. He sailed into Glen Haven on his one-man sloop in 1851 and taught the Ottawa fishermen there how to make barrels to ship their fish to Chicago. He became fluent in Ottawa and through his fair-dealing earned the respect of the Natives. He went to fight in the Civil War even though he had a young family. John Dorsey, by all accounts, was a man of sterling integrity. When Dorsey died in 1903, some of the Ottawa fishermen he'd worked with in Glen Haven back in the 1850s, came to his funeral, some traveling quite a distance, some on foot.

Anna Johnson, according to Dave Taghon at the museum, was a midwife. The neighbors called her, "Auntie," an old-fashioned term of respect for a woman who was not literally a family member but was a person trusted and accepted by the family. Anna Johnson's work as a midwife would have required a person of congenial temperament and reliable competence. "A good midwife," according to Soranus of Ephesus in the second century AD, has good hands and "has her wits about her, is possessed of a good memory . . . [and is] robust, loving work." Elizabeth Dorsey, wife of John Dorsey and a close neighbor of Anna Johnson, was also a midwife. It might be expected that the two women shared their knowledge with each other and took turns doing the work, so that if one couldn't go, the other could.

Customarily midwives were not paid with money, but with food, labor, or goods. Mrs. Johnson's work as a midwife might thus have improved the standard of living for her family, but probably not by much; like most midwives, she surely often worked for free. Mainly this important service to the community would have engendered the good will and loyalty of the neighboring settlers. Historian Bruce Catton said, "On the frontier, if you helped others, they helped you, and took you at your own valuation."

Anna Johnson was a good cook, according to the oral histories archived at the Empire Museum. She reportedly cooked at D. H. Day's Inn in Glen Haven and, in the early 1900s, when Day shifted from lumbering because the trees were mostly cut, she worked at Day's cannery across the road. The museum has a photo of her standing outside the cannery.

The Empire Museum has a photo of Levi and Anna Johnson and two of their children in an 1800s-style, horse-drawn, doctor's buggy. The photo shows a young, good-looking family. They are apparently prosperous, judging by their clothing and the above standard quality of the buggy and the horse. Levi Johnson looks manly and stylish in his traditional man's flat cap, or golfing cap, noble and diffident at the same time, probably feeling protective of his beautiful, young wife holding their newborn infant daughter, Faith; and proud of his son, Levi Jr., who is looking away from the camera, dressed in a fine suit of clothes and sporting a soft flat cap like his father's. The Johnsons would have two more daughters, Hope and Charity.

We cannot totally read Levi Johnson's expression, but we are drawn to the photo, coming back to it again and again, trying to conjure his thoughts, his life, compelled by the way he is holding the reins of his handsome white horse so confidently.

Anna and Levi Johnson were just like any other enterprising pioneer family, with one difference: they were black. How did they happen to come to Empire? What was the racial climate in the area at the time? If Ray Welch is any indication, the fact that the Johnson family was hardworking was enough to make them good neighbors. That Mrs. Johnson was a midwife would have made her family vital to the community. Her husband would have been part of this, because he would have had to drive her to the neighbors to deliver a baby and return home to take care of his own children, while his wife waited for the neighbor's baby to come into the world. The midwifery would have made the Johnsons highly valued by their fellow pioneers.

The Civil War, which had ended in 1864, was described by Pulitzer prizewinning Civil War historian, Bruce Catton, as that "immense convulsion which changed so many things so greatly." Levi and Anna Johnson may have made their way north after being catapulted to freedom by that nation-wrenching experience. It's also possible, given how prepared the Johnsons seemed to have been for frontier living, that they were the descendants of some of the 600,000 freemen, many of whom were multiracial, according to William Katz in *Black Indians, a Hidden Heritage*, people who'd been living all over the continent for centuries. "Except for the first settlers at Jamestown," writes author Benjamin Quarles in *The Negro and the Making of America*, "the Negro's roots . . . sink deeper than any other group from across the Atlantic and [they] helped make America what it was and what it is."

We don't know what brought the Johnsons to Empire. There are no diaries or letters, as far as anyone knows, from the Johnson family. We know there were lots of jobs in the timber industry on the coast of Northwest Michigan in the late 1800s. If the Empire Lumber Company was putting ads in the newspapers in Belgium, which according to Empire immigrants from Belgium, they were, then they were desperate for workers. The work required people of good strength and stamina, and a steady temperament. Women, too, could work in the lumber industry, usually as cooks, sometimes as laundresses. Good cooks, especially, were highly valued. It's not something everyone can do; probably one person in a thousand is a really good cook.

We know there were steamers coming up the lake from Chicago and that passage on the steamers took about three days and cost about seven dollars a person. Often travel was on the open deck. Passengers had to bring their own bedding and food. This would have been a risky trip for anyone but would have been especially so for someone black. They would have had to have been careful, as anyone would, not to be vulnerable to ordinary thieves as well as to avoid more sophisticated schemers who looked honest but weren't.

If they had come up following the Civil War, did they come knowing someone? Had they met a Union soldier from the Civil War, perhaps someone like Dorsey? Had they nursed him when he was injured? Did they come randomly, just taking their chances, perhaps heading to Canada where they knew they'd be safe, but maybe stopping in Glen Haven and discovering the work was good and the people were, too? Maybe Mrs. Johnson had delivered the baby of someone on the boat coming home to Empire, earned their respect and gratitude, and was encouraged to stay once the boat stopped in Glen Haven. We simply don't know.

African Americans who were enslaved were, according to law, not allowed to read and write since, so the thinking went at the time, if they were literate, they might write their own freedom papers. That notwithstanding, people who worked on the plantations were often well-trained in all kinds of crafts: management, carpentry, toolmaking, farming, the care of horses, or, for women, in cooking and other household endeavors.

The Johnsons appear to have been highly skilled in a variety of ways and, given that, they may have also been educated. Maybe the Johnsons came from a background where their families had been free for many generations, living in New York City or Boston or anywhere, and thus knew how to read and write. That they were good survivors, had many skills, and knew how to find a builder of good character, and get along with their neighbors, like the Dorseys, the Shaugers, and the Welches, seems apparent from their homesteading success.

Northwestern Michigan would have been, relatively speaking, a safe haven for an African American pioneer family. A group of abolitionists, including writer Bruce Catton's parents, had established a racially integrated academy in Benzonia, 25 miles south of Empire. These people were from Oberlin, Ohio. Oberlin was known as "the town that started the Civil War" because of the abolitionists' willingness to risk their lives to help runaway slaves. Several African American families settled in what is now Benzie County when Benzie was part of Grand Traverse County in the early days.

There were also several abolitionists in prominent positions in the area, including Morgan Bates, the founder of the Traverse City weekly newspaper. There were two missionaries, the Reverend George Smith, a minister to the Ottawa in Northport, and Reverend Peter Dougherty, a minister to the Native people on Old Mission, both abolitionists.

Besides the Johnsons, there were at least two other known African American families in the area that is now part of the Sleeping Bear Dunes National Lakeshore, according to Taghon: the Hall family and the Skinner family. Some of these children, judging from the school photographs, may have also attended the Brotherton School on Voice Road, the Drake School on Fowler Road, and the Aral School [part of the late 1800s and early 1900s logging community named after the Aral Mountains in Europe, at Otter Creek, at the end of Esch Road in the Sleeping Bear Dunes National Lakeshore; no longer there]. Several children from the Hall family are shown in the state-archived photo of the Aral School. According to Calvin Murphy, a member of the pioneering, mixed-race (Native, black, and white) Joe Davis family from Benzie County, and a Vietnam veteran who now lives in Bear Lake, some of the Hall children, perhaps all of them, according to one of his grandmothers, died in a house fire in the early 1900s.

Families often moved to be near the most recent timber-cutting operations because that's where they could find work, so possibly the same children, at varying ages, might appear in photos in different schools. Census records show that the Boston family near School Lake in the northern part of the Sleeping Bear Dunes National Lakeshore was a black family. We know from the oral histories recorded in *Some Other Day (Remembering Empire)*, that there are nine black people buried in Maple Grove cemetery on M-109.

The presence of African American pioneers and African American workers in the lumbering industry within the area of the Sleeping Bear Dunes National Lakeshore is an important part of both the history of Michigan and the history of the United States. However, the management of the Sleeping Bear Dunes National Lakeshore, despite their many events and displays featuring white pioneers in the area, has not seen fit to include informational programs about the several African American people who worked in the timber industry, nor have they chosen to include the history of those African American families like the Johnsons, the Davis's and others who homesteaded; this leaves the distinct impression that the bureaucracy of the local national park service, and perhaps those at the top of this federal bureaucracy as well, are only interested in history if it is white. However, for those who might be interested in something more complete, historic photos of African American pioneers in Leelanau and Benzie counties can be seen at the Empire Museum, the Benzie Area Historical Society, and in the history room at the Traverse Area District Library.

Dorothy Fradd, in charge of the Maple Grove Cemetery for the town of Empire, met me there one May afternoon in 2018 and showed me where the Johnson family was buried. The people buried there would have included Levi and Anna

Johnson and their son, Levi Jr., who died of typhoid fever in the early1900s. Perhaps other family members were there, too. None of the names are listed on the small gravestone. This marker is what Mrs. Fradd calls a "foot stone" with the single name, Johnson, on it. This is a small, plain piece of cement about eighteen inches long, a foot wide, and four inches thick. The graves had been moved from the Johnson homestead to the cemetery sometime in the early 1900s. This kind of reinterment was a common practice, according to Mrs. Fradd.

An indication of the racial mores of the day in the Empire area where the Johnsons lived, is that the African Americans were buried within the Maple Grove Cemetery proper, on M-109, and the Native Americans out behind it. One explanation of the cemetery slight to Native people might be that the Native tribes had been displaced from their land only recently in Michigan and were still, in the minds of some people, the enemy. Pioneers on the Leelanau Peninsula were just beginning to settle in, in the 1860s, after the last treaty with Native people was signed in 1855; meanwhile Native people out west were still fighting pitched battles with immigrants, and some of those immigrants might have been relatives of people in Empire. The last of the Indian Wars took place in Arizona in 1918.

Regarding the apparently benign attitudes toward black people in the 1860s in Northern Michigan, some of the settlers there had fought on the side of the Union in the Civil War. Michigan had been an anti-slavery state from the beginning, and the homesteaders who were veterans, or knew veterans, would have been predisposed to support what they regarded as the pro-Union, anti-slavery purpose of the Civil War. In his book, *Michigan*, Bruce Catton has written about the African American Morgan family in East Jordan. The Morgans were pillars of their community. They owned the brickyard. Mrs. Morgan gave piano lessons. When Mrs. Morgan died at the remarkable age of 107 in 1951, the entire town shut down for her funeral. In Empire, based on views expressed by Ray Welch, racial discrimination against his neighbors, the Johnson family, was out of the question.

The Brotherton School and the town of Empire sprang up almost overnight in the 1860s, in what had previously been a virgin forest peopled solely by Native tribes. Unbelievable change occurred over a mere 20-year span of time. For example, the man for whom Voice Road was named, the road on which the Brotherton School was located, was Ernest Voice, from a family of wilderness missionaries and abolitionists. He was an accountant and manager for the Empire Lumber Company and would have been in a position to hire Levi Johnson or any other African American.

The Empire Museum has a photo of Empire Junction, a railroad-stop and timber operation, on the Platte River during the late 1800s, and several of the workers in the photo are visibly African American. Voice's grandfather, George Smith, was the abolitionist who had established the Indian Mission at Northport in 1855. One of Voice's aunts, Mary Smith, had married Payson Wolfe, an Ottawa sharpshooter from Northport, who served in the American Civil War. Edward Voice's mother, Arvilla Smith, wanting to finish her education at Oberlin College in Ohio, was accompanied by an Ottawa guide, perhaps even her brother-in-law, Payson Wolfe. Her family knew she'd arrived safely when her guide returned to Northport, according to the Empire Museum's oral histories.

By the early 1860s supplies were available in both Empire and Glen Haven—lumber, tools, cloth, needles, candles, beans, rice, flour, sugar, lard, kerosene, livestock—but, more importantly, there were jobs. It took 20 to 30 men an hour to unload or load a steamship, according to the book, *Sleeping Bear, Yesterday and Today*, by Glen Haven writer, George Weeks. Any strong, healthy laborer could find work in the lumber mills or on the docks for the standard dollar a day. Trained sawyers, teamsters and foremen, being harder to find, would naturally earn more.

The wilderness was disappearing fast, but in Michigan in the late 1800s, when the Levi Johnson family arrived, nature was still bountiful. Wild berries were everywhere: grapes, elderberries, mulberries, cranberries, strawberries, raspberries, blueberries, and blackberries, all of which could be preserved by drying or canning. Quail eggs, a delicacy, could be found in the spring and so could the Michigan version of truffles, morel mushrooms; both could be preserved for winter, the first by pickling and the second by drying. There were countless varieties of fish in all the lakes and streams. Rabbits could be snared and larger game could be taken with bow or gun. Passenger pigeons, flightless when nesting, could be caught with one's bare hands. Maple syrup and ginseng were cash crops.

The Erie and Welland Canals were finished in 1825, bypassing Niagara Falls, so there was a way to ship goods on the Hudson River to Manhattan. The Illinois and Michigan Canal in 1848 connected the Illinois River to the Mississippi and the Gulf of Mexico. The Soo Locks were finished in 1855. The Baltimore and Ohio rail lines connected the eastern seaboard to the Midwest by 1860. The railroad to the west coast was finished in 1869. The Chicago Sanitary and Ship Canal, connecting the Chicago River to the Des Plaines River, opened in 1900. The Great Lakes shipping company, the Northern Transit Company (NTC), could take lumber out of Glen Haven all the way to Ogdensburg, New York, gateway to the St. Lawrence. Everywhere the Native people had once gone by canoe and on foot, the big transport companies could go, too, by rail and schooner.

A little girl in Leland in 1857, Theresa Manseau, arriving with her father Antoine, writes of how wild roses and balsam scented the air after the rain. We know from her diary that it took four men a day to put up a shelter. We don't know if the Johnsons had help from their neighbors in putting up a temporary shelter, while waiting for the Fradds to build their house, but it's likely. We do know from the Empire Museum's collection of oral histories that the home of another African American pioneer family, located near the Maple Grove Cemetery on M-109, burned to the ground and their neighbors, both white and black, came and helped them rebuild. The strong abolitionist sentiments held by some prominent members of the community, combined with the early settlers' need for mutual support in order to survive, seem to have to outweighed, at least at that time, any other concerns.

After Abraham Lincoln signed the Homestead Act of 1862, the trickle of immigrants soon became a flood. Mary-Elisa (Stayaert)Van Slambrouch (also spelled Van Slambroch), Dave Taghon's grandmother, a Belgian immigrant to Empire who just narrowly missed crossing the ocean on the Titanic, wanted to follow her sister, Louise, to Empire. She also wanted to come to Empire because her new husband, Leon Van Slambrouch wanted to avoid conscription. One in three of all the young men in their Belgian village of Maria-Aalter were required to serve in the military and often never came home. Maria-Elisa's man, Leon, in addition, wanted to work outdoors, according to the Empire Museum's oral histories. He probably also wanted to hunt and fish, something not generally allowed in Europe unless one lived in a castle.

These excellent oral histories were recorded in 1974 by the Empire Area Heritage Group; with few exceptions, the members of the Empire heritage group were relatives of the first settlers. The Van Slambrouchs felt assured of employment because relatives said there were good jobs. In fact, when they arrived, they discovered the lumber company was running two shifts, that's how busy the mill was. People were pouring out of Europe to come to America. Mrs. (Stayaert)

Van Slambrouch said that the train to Michigan in 1912, "was so crowded, we had to stand from Buffalo to Grand Rapids." They travelled by train, presumably seated by this time, on the last leg of their journey, all the way to Empire. There were trains—and train tracks—criss-crossing Northern Michigan then, and little depots, something now hard to imagine as the passenger trains are gone and even the cargo trains have been phased out and almost all of the tracks have been removed, everywhere. Some of the former railroad tracks in Leelanau County have been converted to bike trails.

Alexis de Toqueville, the French aristocrat who visited the Great Lakes in 1831, saw a magnificent wilderness and foresaw all of the development that was coming. He knew the Europeans were on their way. "This lake, without sails, this shore, which does not yet show any trace of the passage of man, this eternal forest which borders it; all that, I assure you, is not grand poetry only; it's the most extraordinary spectacle that I have ever seen in my life. These regions, which yet form only an immense wilderness, will become one of the richest and most powerful countries in the world. Nature has done everything here," de Tocqueville wrote, "a fertile soil, and outlets like to which there are no others in the world."

Like other early settlers on the northwest coast of Michigan, many of the African American pioneers on the Leelanau Peninsula left their farms in the 1920s and presumably the Johnson children were among them. Some in the Skinner family may have stayed in the Benzie area and several members of the large, mixed-race Davis family stayed (one member served in the First World War by passing as white), and some relatives are still in Benzonia and in Thompsonville, but others have left. By this time the soil had worn out, the jobs in the timber industry were gone, and there were other and better opportunities elsewhere. Many of the children of the early settlers, both black and white, left for good jobs in the Detroit auto factories, more marriage possibilities for their adult children, a choice of churches, better schools, more stores, electricity, and just generally all the comforts of urban living.

Alligator Hill

This is a story about a mill, a marriage and a hill near the small crossroads town of Glen Arbor. This is a story about America. It's a story that covers roughly a 110-year period, from when my parents were born in 1908 to the present. This covers a span of time when horses have been replaced by cars, when the last of the Ottawa women selling baskets from their canoes around Glen Lake have been replaced by people on jet skis, when letters and books have been replaced by telephones, television and the Internet, and hundreds of species of fish, plants, birds, butterflies, frogs, and animals have become extinct due to deforestation and pollution. This is the story of Alligator Hill where I grew up, a 500-foot-high deposit of glacial till stretching unevenly, green and vaguely amoeba-shaped, for two miles or more in every direction between Sleeping Bear Bay and Little Glen Lake, between Glen Haven and Glen Arbor, between the Sleeping Bear Dunes and Big Glen Lake.

Growing up, I saw Alligator Hill up close, either from the back of my horse or on foot, and from that vantage point it did not look like an alligator. Although people say it kind of looks like an alligator on Google maps, presumably based on aerial photos, when I was a child, I would have never seen it as an alligator except for the rare times I was at the top of the dunes looking east, or on the south side of Little Glen Lake, when the leaves were off, looking north. The alligator name always seemed a little inappropriate to me, like an anachronism. It references a tropical creature in a non-tropical place, and at the same time, surely unintentionally, seems to hint at the Devonian past, the so-called "Age of

Fishes" 450 million years ago, when amphibious alligator-like creatures called Tiktaalik, according to a February 2014 entry on the *Live Science* website, crawled in shallow water and when, to make things even more confusing, the continents were in different places.

In February 2018, I started making day trips from my apartment in Traverse City back to Alligator Hill, just to see it. From Inspiration Point, on the high, south side of Big Glen Lake, looking northwest, Alligator Hill looks like a sleeping cat with its chin on one arm and a furry tail stretching lazily east and north toward Glen Arbor. This is a large cat, perhaps the cartoon cat, Garfield, disguised as a dark green forest, taking a nap. From this vantage point you can easily see how Glen Lake was once part of Lake Michigan, an embayment, with only that very low, mile-long sandbar which constitutes Glen Arbor, separating the two bodies of water.

When you can see with your own eyes how, as recently as 11,000 years ago, glacial Lake Algonquin was here, and there was no land where Glen Arbor is now, it'll make your mind reel. When you've regained your balance, you can deliberately try again to collapse time and imagine how slowly, ever so slowly, over many centuries, Lake Michigan and Glen Lake became separate entities.

Glaciers are not only unnerving emblems of vast unimaginable changes in the earth we live on, in the past, before we got here, but imply the possibility of vast unimaginable changes in the earth we live on, in the future, holding within that prospect, the extremely unwelcome possibility that, just as we were not around in the past, we might also not be here in the future. Ice came. Ice left. Continents shifted. We are continually finding out new things about this planet. The March 2018 *National Geographic* revealed a just-discovered, previously unknown event, a time "when life got big" about 570 million years ago, and there was a sudden "profusion of complex creatures" which resembled plants but were tiny organisms, and their fossils became imbedded in a random piece of the Canadian Shield, the earth's oldest layer of rock, on the shore of the northern Atlantic, where we can go and see them and try to understand this better. I'll bet you can't think about this for very long without feeling peculiar about the passage of time and everything that goes along with that.

Jane Goodall, the scientist famous for her love of the great apes and her decision to go live with them and study them up close, in the winter 2018 issue of *Parabola*, talks about the "explosion of intellect" in the human, somewhere along in the last 100,000 years or so, something that allowed us to communicate—a brain that "sets us apart from other animals," even the apes she adores. This is a mysterious planet and our place on it is a mystery, too, and nowhere are you more likely to feel that than from the high lookouts on the Leelanau Peninsula, a glacier-sculpted land that, relative to most places, hasn't been here all that long.

Early Native people—the people who have primacy of place because they were on the Leelanau Peninsula long before anyone else—according to Thomas Vennum's book, *Wild Rice and the Ojibway People*, had a campground on the east side of Big Glen Lake for thousands of years: grains of charred wild rice have been found there, and arrowheads. They would have arrived in those ingeniously constructed birch bark cargo canoes, big enough to hold everything, light enough to be carried, and seaworthy enough to withstand the most fearsome waves. Some of the first maps of the peninsula, on file at the county planning department, show a Native sugarbush, a seasonal camp for making maple syrup—at the far west end of Alligator Hill, on the north shore of Little Glen Lake—still extant at the close of the 19th century.

Looking west from Inspiration Point, one sees the Sleeping Bear Dunes. The dunes were created over an 11,000-year time span by the prevailing westerly winds and stretch north and south for a dozen miles or more, about 400 or 500 feet above Lake Michigan. The name of the dunes originated with indigenous people who navigated in canoes, using such landmarks as they could find to make their way along the Lake Michigan shore. This particular landmark was a small knoll at the top of the western edge of the dunes, only visible from the west, out on the water. Native guides said the knoll resembled a "couchant bear," *l'ours qui dort*, or *l'ours couchant* in French, and reclining bear, *mokwa ganweshin* in Ottawa. (Many Native guides in the area of the Great Lakes were from the Ottawa tribe, a group known for travelling wide as traders, and thus having knowledge of regions beyond their Ottawa villages.) The name of this knoll, over time, would be misconstrued to mean the entire dune. The knoll, photographed when it was still intact in 1938 by Fred Dickinson, is now disintegrating.

The name for this landmark knoll was recorded in the journals of two of the first handful of white men to visit the Great Lakes several centuries ago: Francois-Xavier de Charlevoix, a French Jesuit explorer who came from France between 1705 and 1709, and again between 1720 and 1721; and Henry Rowe Schoolcraft, a surveyor for the United States Department of War, who traveled up the Lake Michigan shore in 1822. The appellation of the landmark knoll was relayed to these two explorers by their Native tour guides, pilots of those 35-foot long, birchbark cargo canoes. These canoes, tied with spruce root and sealed with pine or spruce resin, were surprisingly seaworthy and light enough to be carried. This would have been during a time that all the land of Michigan still belonged to the Anishnaabeg. The Anishnaabeg—literally "the original people"—were expert navigators. They knew the stars. They knew the weather. They knew the vagaries of the Great Lakes. They knew how to stay safe. They knew how to build and repair their canoes. They knew how to make quick shelters and how to keep themselves supplied with food while they traveled. Without the Native guides the exploration of the Great Lakes would have been nigh unto impossible. It still astonishes one to contemplate how recently the Great Lakes were unknown to all people other than those of Native ancestry.

Alligator Hill is now part of the Sleeping Bear Dunes National Lakeshore. They've turned the area around the old charcoal kilns into a parking lot. One Sunday morning I'm there quite early, in a milky fog. I park next to a big white Tahoe with Ohio plates, empty, someone already hiking. The trail's now in a different place. Parts of the charcoal kilns are still here. For a while my father, Pierce Stocking, had made charcoal with the scraps from the mill. You would load the kiln, like you would a wood stove, only instead of burning the wood, you would kind of cook it at a low temperature, slowly, like you would a pot roast in the oven, only of course much longer, for days, finally breaking it out and dousing it with water and letting it dry, packing it up to sell.

I began coming when I was a toddler, with my father, an early 20th century lumberman for whom the Pierce Stocking Scenic drive in the Sleeping Bear Dunes National Lakeshore is named, to his lumber mill. We lived in Cadillac and would get up at 4 a.m. to eat something and then be on our way. We had an old black Ford with runners on the sides. I seem to remember that M-115 wasn't paved all the way and that parts of the road were still under construction.

We would arrive at the mill at 7 a.m., when the men were given breakfast: buckwheat pancakes, sausage, fried fish, fruit pies, applesauce, bacon, biscuits with gravy, eggs. Oleomargarine, whipped white grease, came in big tubs and if I was there when it was being prepared for the table, I got to put in the yellow food coloring and watch it be stirred. I had my books to keep me busy, because each day my mother would send me off with a different selection, but when I wasn't reading, I watched the food being made. The yeasted oatmeal bread was made with honey, salt, brown flour, water, powdered milk, cooked oatmeal, eggs, lard, bacon drippings, and it was the best bread ever. Bean soup with a meaty ham bone, a goodly amount of onions, celery, celery leaves, carrots and a little garlic, was good, served with cornbread. Johnny, the cook, liked to get vegetables past the lumberjacks. A man who wouldn't dream of putting a spoonful of carrots on his plate, didn't even notice if there were vegetables in the soup or meatloaf. Johnny's meatloaf had grated carrots, small pieces of red bell pepper, parsley, and mushrooms, if he had them. The top of the meatloaf was covered with tomatoes, home-canned with celery, onion and green bell peppers, and baked at a low temperature for two or three hours; the tomatoes made the meatloaf more tender and also became a thick, meaty, tomato gravy for the scalloped potatoes. The scalloped potatoes would have some of the skin left on (more vitamins and minerals), a little grated onion, salt and pepper, and baked in a thick milk gravy made with reconstituted powdered milk, with a little paprika and dry mustard.

Nothing was wasted. The bean soup, three days later, would be added to more freshly cooked great northern beans and baked with blackstrap molasses, tomato paste, dry mustard, a little brown sugar, ham scraps, ketchup, bacon pieces, coarse salt, and a little vinegar. And those beans, mashed, and then served on oatmeal bread with sweet pickle relish and the smallest amount of finely sliced raw onion, were excellent.

Johnny Buckwheat, the cook, was my friend. A tall, skinny, good-natured man, too old to be a lumberjack, he taught me how to tie scraps of paper to long pieces of twine and get the kittens to chase these paper "mice." There was always a cat in the cookhouse and often kittens. Those shanties were porous. Mice could, and did, get in anywhere. It was hard to keep all the food—50-pound bags of flour, oatmeal, rice, sugar; crates of onions, apples, cabbage, carrots, potatoes; tubs of sauerkraut; hanging dried spices—always secured in metal bins. Cats were the sensible solution. Johnny Buckwheat knew how to delight and amuse a child. He would serve me cold water in a warm glass that had just been pulled from a pan of hot water and grin as he watched my surprise. He treated me with kindness and respect, pretty much the same way he treated the kittens and the cat, come to think of it; just another kitten in the cookhouse. He didn't hover or talk baby-talk to me, but he was aware and knew when I was bored, or sleepy, or hungry. Children aren't always hungry at mealtime and sometimes they're hungry when it's not mealtime. A grilled peanut-butter-and-jelly sandwich—with thinly sliced, stale, homemade, whole-wheat bread and a generous amount of grape jelly—could be perfect with a glass of cold well water. Lunch was at noon: meat and potatoes, lots of homemade bread, many vegetables, and pies and cookies. My father used to marvel that the men wanted the sweets the most and that sugar was the cheapest of all the foods he had to buy.

Johnny could make a pea soup with canned peas that was wonderful. It was thick, and could double as a gravy. I think he made it with some kind of stock, maybe beef bones or pork or chicken, thickened with milk gravy, some chopped onions that disappeared in the soup, and maybe some canned spinach. The only time I've ever had soup like that was in a tiny French restaurant in Manhattan. I could never duplicate it, although I tried many times. Now that I think of it, Johnny may have been French.

A good cook knows what fits with the mood of the weather and the mood of the people. A good cook knows what tastes delicious and what is healthy for the human body. Well-fed men, and horses, are good workers. My father said Johnny could make shoe leather taste like filet mignon. I never thought about it at the time, since I was little and preferred a peanut-butter-and-jelly sandwich, most days, to meat. But I think now, remembering back, I think Johnny not only pounded the meat, ground it, and slow-cooked it, but also brined it, putting it in a salt solution to tenderize it. He also made something that I think now was like the German sauerbraten, slow-cooked beef that's been marinated in vinegar and spices for a few days and turned.

The men didn't talk when they ate. "Please pass the potatoes," and "Thank you," was about the extent of it. They were polite. They never overate. They took what they could eat and cleaned their plates. They thanked the cook when they left the table. Contrary to what most people think about lumberjacks, these men were not brawlers. My father hired athletes. They moved in a gentle and fluid way, like dancers. Some were, of course, giants, but most were not. The hard work was more about pacing and stamina than brute strength. Not all of the men who worked at the mill lived there, but most ate there. The work was physically demanding and dangerous; the men needed to eat right so they would have their wits about them.

My father worked both at the mill and in the woods, mainly trouble-shooting, but also doing the heavy labor. Hard work was the founding principle of his morality. He had enormous energy and drive and part of the respect he had from his men was that he could outwork them. When the men came to work at 8 a.m., my father had already been up since 4 a.m., and when they went home at 4 p.m., he would still be driving back to Cadillac. Once home, if it was summer, he'd work until dark in his garden; and if it was winter, he'd be shoveling snow and cutting wood. He found rhythmic work, like hoeing weeds and stacking wood and shoveling show, relaxing. It was his time to think.

There was a mechanic at the mill, Irving Blough, a rough-hewn genius whose fedora, rimless from wear, looked like a fez. That hat was part of him. He lived under it. His hands, like any good mechanic's, were black from machine grease. My father treated Mr. Blough with deep deference and paid him extremely well. Mr. Blough was never told what to do, he was asked, politely. Mr. Blough could fix anything. He was a rare find, a treasure, not the kind of person you run across every day or even every lifetime, and my father knew it. The lumber mill, built in 1948, a mile from Glen Arbor, was one of the last traditional lumber camps, with slab-board housing for the workers and a slab-board cook shanty, little different from the lumber camps of previous centuries. This would end in the late 1950s when the camp was demolished, and Irv Blough built a portable mill for my father, one of the first.

The work in the woods, how to cut a tree so it fell right, was part geometry, part instinct, part long experience, and for some of the more problematic trees, the men waited for my father's judgement. Many decades later I learned from an old farmer in Buckley, Elmer Pavlis, that my father was one of the only people in Northern Michigan who knew how to "tune" a saw blade, one of those big, round blades used in the mill to make lumber. He did it by tapping gently with a fleece-covered wooden mallet all around the blade until it was back in "true"—the word Pavlis used to describe tuning a mill saw-blade. Anyone could go through the motions of tuning a saw, Pavlis said, but only one in a million could get it exactly right. Saw blades were expensive. Pavlis said my father never charged for this.

In the spring the leeks and wildflowers would bloom all around the mill and up the surrounding hills, the woods full of trilliums, both red and white, Dutchman's breeches, pink and yellow lady slippers, gay wings and trailing arbutus under the pines, mayflowers, jack-in-the-pulpits, spring beauties, yellow trout lilies, and tons of morels. The leeks are still plentiful; the deer don't eat them. Most people don't eat them, but they can be delicious, as I discovered when John and Leslee Spraggins invited me one Sunday morning for brunch at their home near Northport. The Spraggins live on a hill that might be the highest in Leelanau Township, at the north end of the peninsula, where you can see everything for miles. If the peninsula is like an old-fashioned clipper ship heading north, their home would be the crow's nest. John cooked leeks, which he called ramps, in a wok with a little oil. They puffed up wonderfully, like little elliptical balloons, and then settled down again. The ramps tasted a bit like spinach with a little onion underlayment, and had the texture of spinach. John served them on an omelette and I loved the taste, rare and new and familiar at the same time.

The red trilliums, the lady slippers, the morels, the polygala or gay wings, and the trailing arbutus are something I haven't seen on Alligator Hill in years. In some places, in the swamps, where no one ever goes, they can still be seen. Anyone born in the last 50 years would never notice the loss of these flowers from the everyday places, that's how long they've been gone. According to Edward O. Wilson, professor emeritus and honorary curator of entomology at Harvard, writing in the *New York Times* March 4, 2018, a process of species extinction that used to take a million years, is now so accelerated that we will have destroyed half of all species by the end of the century. I have an intimate relationship with Alligator Hill. This is my true home, where I live even when I'm not there. I can feel what's missing and it's as if part of me is gone. The changes in the woods and the cultural changes between the middle of the last century and the beginnings of this one, are huge.

The full-time residents on the Leelanau Peninsula in the 1940s and 50s were referred to by tourists as "locals," a pejorative term, which now, ironically, in 2018, is an appellation of esteem. When I went to the University of Michigan in 1963, my fellow students in Ann Arbor, many from large cities like Manhattan, Chicago, and Detroit, learning that I hadn't grown up in a city, would ask me if I was from a farm. When I tried to explain that I was from "the woods and lakes" it was hopeless and so I gave up and accepted that the closest I could come to anything they had a reference for was a farm. 'Yes,' I said, 'I'm from a farm.' They knew what farms were. They had seen pictures.

I saw the transition from the last vestiges of the timber industry to the rising tourist industry, from a time when nature was associated with barnyard manure, biting insects, and manual labor (under the hot sun or during a snow storm), to a time nature, often now with a capital 'N', was esteemed as vital and vanishing and called ecology, from nobody having wine with dinner to everyone doing it, from everyone smoking cigarettes to almost no one smoking cigarettes, from the disparagement of homosexuals to the legalization of same-sex marriage, from girls who got pregnant out of wedlock being forced to give away their children to women deciding to have and raise babies on their own, from teachers ridiculing disturbed children with learning disabilities to special education, from subsistence farms with windmills to organic farms with solar panels, from burying toxic waste in the backyard to recycling, from suspicion and prejudice toward people of color to acceptance and tolerance, from relegating women to lower paying menial jobs as office help to bringing them into the business mainstream, from parents routinely beating children with a belt to it becoming a crime, from sexual abuse being a dark secret to it being openly discussed, from eating white, Styrofoam-like bread laced with chemicals to a demand for organic, brown, whole-grain bread, from telephones with a party line to I-phones, from women wearing hats and gloves to women wearing Levi's and mini-skirts, from commercial and residential development being considered wonderful advancements to the preservation of natural beauty being esteemed as the way of the future.

Everything's changed, especially in the woods. Environmental groups proliferate, but developers and their advocates sit on zoning boards and so they get their way. And America is not alone in its destruction of nature and its denial of it. The Japanese are into "forest bathing," where they go and marinate in nature in a sentimental way, but they still club to death the almost-extinct dolphins. The French have loved gardens and parks ever since Monet's *In the Garden* painting in 1895, and before, with the Tuileries in 1564 and the Bois

de Boulogne in 1853. Parc Monceau, installed in 1778 by the
Duke of Chartres, cousin to King Louis XVI, near the fabulous Avenue des Champs-Élysées, is where Marcel Proust
played as a child. There are over a thousand public gardens
and parks in tiny France, but France, a country slightly
smaller than Texas, has more nuclear power plants—the kind
that could poison everything for a hundred miles in every direction if there was ever a Chernobyl-like accident—than just
about any place on earth. People in the aggregate, in terms
of their understanding of the destruction of nature all around
them and how nature is needed to sustain their lives, have
not yet caught up to the reality. We're just slow that way.

The shacks of the mill-hands were rough wood and tar
paper, like fish shanties, but bigger. There was often no glass
in the windows, but a blue-green, heavy-gauge plastic with
tiny squares, like graph paper. At night, light came from
kerosene lamps with wicks that had to be trimmed. Water
was hauled in buckets from the well—the well with the long-
handled pump, over near the mill in the center of a clump of
cedar trees. Everyone had guns.

Each house had a wood cookstove in the shedlike kitchen
off the back, and a regular woodstove in the living room. The
kitchens were an almost-detached part of the house because
that way, in the case of a kitchen fire, the whole house would-
n't go up in flames; kitchen fires were fairly common. Hanging blankets served as doors between rooms. The houses were
permeated with the smell of wood smoke: stale wood smoke,
fresh wood smoke, and the present moment's wood smoke.
Dirt was swept down the open cracks between the splintery
floor boards. This was a way of life that had existed in backwoods America for something like the last 400 years. Women
with a knack for making a place comfortable could make
these humble homes inviting and beautiful: geraniums in
flower boxes, a piece of pretty oil cloth on the kitchen table, a
blue-green-and-pink-and-gold picture of Jesus in a gilt frame,

wildflowers in a glass jar on the unused woodstove in the summer, embroidered pillow covers, a colorful scarf draped just so from railroad spikes on either side at the top of a window, and the good-cooking smells of an apple pie, redolent with cinnamon, or ginger cookies—heavy on the ginger.

There were outhouses behind each house; toilet paper was a page from a Sears and Roebuck or Montgomery Ward catalogue. Garbage was buried or scattered in the woods. Clothes were washed with Fels-Naptha, a big bar of rough yellow soap. This was done by hand in a washtub with a scrub board. Each house had a shed entranceway where there were onions, cabbage, carrots, potatoes, and apples. Once I took the black leaves off a cabbage and the woman of the house chastised me, saying those leaves were keeping the cabbage fresh. I learned something.

There was one Ottawa family at the mill. The woman in the family made birch bark and porcupine quill baskets. I would watch her soften the quills in water, so they could be pushed through the holes she had punched in the birchbark. Sometimes she dyed the quills, using Rit dye. The father in this family, an excellent worker, a quiet man who didn't drink, would later go to prison for molesting children. This man had been separated from his family at a young age and put in a government orphanage where he was unloved and abused. The current separation of children from their mothers at America's southern border will "create monsters" as Pulitzer Prize winning reporter Seymour Hersch said in a 2018 CBS interview; psychologists quoted in a June 2018 *Washington Post* article said the same thing in more academic language. But you don't need to be a prize-winning reporter or a psychologist to know that it's wrong to separate children from their mothers; it creates wounds that never heal. Things people repress in order to survive live on in the subconscious and are expressed only by repeating them in similar acts against others; in a way, it was amazing that this Native man survived at all, and not surprising that he was psychologically damaged.

My father moved his entire family to Alligator Hill in 1952. My father came from a long line of pioneers and felt more at home with broad horizons and no neighbors in sight. My mother came from a background of town living; she was accustomed to libraries and parks. She'd had 12 years of piano lessons. She could sing. She was well versed in literature, art, music, flower arranging. She had the social skills required for club memberships. This is the rule, as I learned it: nice women do not notice when bad things are happening to other people, unless it's a funeral in which case you say, "Sorry for your loss."

My mother knew what to say and when to say it. She had that indefinable something that set her apart from other people. Partly it was her looks. She had the most amazing, curly red hair, lots of it. She was tall. She had blue eyes that pierced. She was physically "ablaze". She had presence. She walked into a room and everyone turned to look. She had, as people said, "a lot of class." In contrast to what we usually think of when we think of someone upper-class, my mother swore like the boss of a bawdyhouse, at least when among adults, and her speech was an astonishing and unlikely mix of quotations from Shakespeare and profanity. Perhaps she thought it would throw people off balance, and challenge their unthinking assumptions about women, and give her an edge; perhaps it did. In a time, in the not so distant past, when all money and power rested with men and women's voices were not heard, she made sure that hers was. My father did not swear and he seldom raised his voice. My mother was always late to everything and my father was always not only on time but a few minutes early. He drove carefully, always following the speed limit and stopped at stop signs even if there was no one coming. My mother drove fast, well over the speed limit, often did not stop at stop signs and passed, even when she could not see if something was coming—either on the left or right; she wasn't choosy—around curves and up hills. She had accidents. Once she sheared off all her top front teeth and from then on wore what was called a "bridge". Her car insurance was the highest possible; she was in something called "a risk pool". It was terrifying to be her passenger. She drove, long after she had been declared legally blind and had her license revoked. I never understood these things, except to understand that my mother and my father were different kinds of people, as we all are. My four sisters and I were different from each other as well. They did what people expected them to do and said what people wanted them to say; I was the opposite.

When we first moved, my mother hated the house on the hill above Lake Michigan. She would learn to love it later, but at the time she hated it. It was wild, uncivilized, inhospitable. She watched the storms in November and thought about the ships that would sink and the men who would drown. She complained about the sound of the mill. She probably also hated the shacks of the mill-hands around the mill. Visibly, and in every other way, it was like the shacks of slaves around a mansion on a southern plantation. There was incest and alcoholism, malnutrition and disease, ignorance and wife beating; not in every home or even in most of them but in enough that you couldn't pretend it wasn't there. If she'd married a man with copper mines in South Africa, for example, some faraway place where poverty and hopelessness and dislocation and mental derangement and lack of learning caused terrible things to happen to the minds and bodies of the men who did the work, and to their families, she wouldn't have had to see it. She wouldn't have had to think about how the money was made that paid for her shoes, but now she did. She had always lived in a world with churches, educated friends, social clubs, streetlights, sidewalks, grocery stores, and a daily newspaper, delivered. Alligator Hill was not that world.

One of the mill workers had a child with his retarded daughter. His wife, a sweet and competent woman, became our babysitter. She would bring her husband's child by her daughter with her to work. The child, called "Dolly Cry" by my baby sister, seemed indeed to always be crying. These people are all dead now and I can tell the terrible secrets of that terrible time. I knew we were not supposed to know and were not supposed to speak of these things.

But what I learned then, and what has been corroborated over a lifetime, is that what people know and what they don't, is what they choose to know or not know. My sisters developed an uncanny ability to not see, and then to not think about what they had deliberately not seen; the only outward indication they had ever been witness to the suffering of the families at the mill was a deep and probably unconscious dislike, not to mention fear and disrespect, of poor people. We had things and the mill kids didn't; they did not want to think about it beyond that. The way I saw it, we had things *because* the mill kids didn't; that changes the equation.

My sisters and I all went to college. None of the children of the mill-hands did. Some of the male children of the mill-hands went to jail. Some of the female children of the mill-hands ended up in terrible marriages, or worse, prostitution. Several of the children of the mill-hands became alcoholics. These people were not like that because they were stupid and lazy but because they didn't have any books in their houses or enough to eat. Surely, they were also demoralized, unable to see how to change their circumstances or to believe that they could do so. The thing about the exploitation of people or the exploitation of nature—isn't that it's bad for the people or bad for the land, although it certainly is that—it's that it's bad for those of us who do it or ignore it. You cannot make your mind unaware of some things, by deliberately restricting your thoughts and feelings, and still become aware enough to develop your mind to its fullest potential. The unawareness affects the wiring in your brain. It impacts the way you love. It stunts you.

I think people support the exploitation of other people and natural resources because they have benefited from this in the past, are benefiting from it in the present, or think they will benefit from it in the future. I mentioned to one of my sisters, some years back, that I had always felt badly about my father's workers: they couldn't earn enough from their work to live decently or provide for the needs of their children. She said, "They were lucky to have those jobs." That was her way of seeing things. And the look on her face, a look I knew well, was: *Can't we talk about something more pleasant?* She knew, in a visceral way, that if one didn't have money, one could be Dolly Cry, and she didn't want to think about it. On some level I think she felt that if you didn't pick up the gun and pull the trigger, you weren't responsible if someone ended up dead or damaged. My perspective was different. I thought then, and think now, that if a person, by their actions, causes something bad to happen, or by their inactions, allows it, then they are responsible. But I grew up in two worlds, in the shacks of the mill-hands and in the house on the hill, and so I was less able to pretend that I could not see.

The move would break my parents' marriage, and for a time it would break each of them, and me, too. They had loved each other, wildly passionately, but that came to an end. My father had courted my mother by building the fire in the one-room school house where she taught, going over every morning at 5 a.m. so she could come in two hours later to a warm classroom. He brought her speckled trout and cooked them for her. He continued to bring her speckled brook trout, for a few years after we moved, and to keep a large vegetable garden for her, and to split wood for the fireplace. She preferred sugar maple; my mother's house smelled wonderfully fragrant, like maple syrup and ham, for years. But those things faded. My father had an affair. They drifted apart. They di-

vorced in the 1960s and, in the days before communal property, and because all the land was in my father's name, my
mother got only our house above Sleeping Bear Bay. My father eventually remarried, a tall redhead like my mother, but
unlike my mother in that she liked guns, hunting, and training dogs; my mother never so much as looked at another man
after my father. When my mother was in the hospital, years
later, with cancer, my father, now married to someone else,
showed up with two-dozen, long-stemmed yellow roses, crying. My father died in 1976, my mother 20 years later. Before
she died, my mother wrote a letter to her five daughters, saying she forgave my father everything and would see him in
heaven, and we would know this when we saw a rainbow. My
sisters referred to this, with a roll of the eyes, as "the letter"
and my niece, Kyla, dubbed it, "Grandma's myth." I did see a
rainbow, a double one. Make of that what you will. You cannot
say what another person's love is. Only the person knows.

My mother would find herself again in teaching, something she had always been good at but had discontinued when
she got married because, in the 1930s, they didn't let married
women teach. My father would find himself, after some years
would go by, in designing gardens and parks, something he
hadn't known he loved, but discovered that he did. I would
find myself in books, starting with the ones my mother left
around the house when she went back to get her Masters:
Ezra Pound, Wallace Stevens, e. e. cummings, T. S. Eliot,
James Joyce, Thomas Hardy, Walt Whitman, Gerard Manley
Hopkins, William Butler Yeats. We had a library full of books,
but I had read them; these were new books from my mother's
classes.

I would take them to read, hiding them up under my
blouse and heading out, saying I was "going to the mill" but
stopping three-quarters of the way down the south slope at
the barn where I took care of the horses. We usually had two
or three horses for the mill and two or three for riding. The
barn loft had a high window for loading in the hay and I could

read there, no matter the weather, bracing a bale—crossways in the open window—covering it with a tarp to ward against the needle-sharp straws, and then covering myself with horse blankets, my back against the bale with the natural light behind my head. If it was cold, I broke a bale, and covered the horse blankets with sweet-smelling hay. Hay is surprisingly warm. I loved the smell of the horse blankets and hay. I loved the smell of my horses. I loved their big eyes, like mirrors, like mystery. Sometimes I would take my book and leave on one of the horses, either Pal, a gentle palomino mare, or later, Highclops, a big chestnut gelding, heading up the old golf course roads that traversed the high hills, sometimes going down the road on the east side towards Glen Arbor, coming out by the Forest Haven Cemetery where someone told me Civil War veterans were buried.

Now, on yet another visit, I'm at the base of Alligator Hill again. Gray and black squirrels, thrilled with the sunlight, are scampering over the few patches of snow and the newly bare ground. This is the quiet beauty time for those of us who have always lived here, a time when the essence of the land seems to enter the people. For visitors lucky enough to be here now, with no one, they can find this, too. It's February, but the snow cover is like the end of March. The silhouettes of the bare-branched trees on the horizon are the kind the French like in their paintings and photographs. I'm thinking of Henri Rousseau's *A Carnival Evening* and Henri Cartier-Bresson's photos of Paris boulevards in March. A small, gray Subaru from Illinois with a "Wildlife" sticker is the only other car in the parking area, besides my own Honda Civic. When we were children, we used to calculate our worldliness, and the desirability of the place we inhabited, by toting up the number of out-of-state license plates we espied.

If the day was warm, when I was on my horse, I would head up to the top of Alligator Hill on the north side, above Lake Michigan, to what we called the [Lake Michigan] Look Out. There was an old, white, clapboard-sided building there that had been the club house for the fancy golf course during the 1920s. It was empty. I could read in there if it was raining, both my horse and myself inside.

There was a road at the top of Alligator Hill then, perhaps it's still there, that went north-south along the eastern edge of Alligator Hill, a spur that ended at a lookout where one could see both Big Glen Lake and Little Glen Lake. Once I walked my horse down this hill, thinking it would be a short-cut to the lake. I never did that again. It was too steep, for both me and the horse.

If I turned around at the Glen Lake Look Out and went back the way I'd come, I could turn west down the south side of Alligator Hill and arrive at the carriage house. This was a building that had housed both horses and cars, at the same time, a remnant of the Gilded Age. When we moved to Alligator Hill this combined garage and carriage house still had bales of hay and stalls for the horses, and a grease pit for the cars, a marvel to us as children because it was so clearly an exhibit of the transition between one mode of transportation and the next, like something in a museum.

The idea of the brevity of any existence is expressed perfectly by Vladimir Nabokov, the Russian writer who was brought up in fabulous wealth and escaped the Russian Revolution (and the peasants who wanted to exterminate his royal fabulous-ness), with nothing but his fabulous education. In the opening of his autobiography he writes, "The cradle rocks above an abyss, and common sense tells us that our existence is but a brief crack of light between two eternities of darkness." Even as a child, when I stood in the carriage house that was set up for both horses and cars, I was chastened by the awareness of the lightning speed of cultural change and the shortness of any life in the grand scheme of things.

It's believed that human beings domesticated horses about 5,500 years ago on the Steppes of Mongolia. Like computers in my lifetime, awareness of the usefulness of horses quickly spread. They made life easier. For thousands of years horses were a part of everyday life all over the world and then, within an incredibly short span of time, five decades or less, that changed. These magnificent creatures carried us into battle, worked our farms and timber, and took us shopping. Where would we be today if we hadn't had horses? People on their own can't haul logs out of the woods, not easily, or pull a plow for days, or cover hundreds of miles on foot in a few weeks or stand patiently while a girl lies in the grass, propped against a saddle, and reads a book.

Once I went looking for a natural spring which I'd heard was down the hill from the old Water Tower and somehow, on a sunless day, got turned around, becoming hopelessly lost. I climbed into the saddle, leaned forward over the saddle horn, moved my legs, shook the reins and my horse got me out of the woods and back to the trail. From there, we both knew how to get back to the barn.

If I kept going along the southerly road, along the border of the old golf course, I'd end up back at the mill. However, more often I went north across the fallow fields that had been golf fairways, where we still, even up into the 1960s, could find old golf balls, and from there south again to the barn. In those days, in season, there were wild strawberries, wild raspberries, wild blackberries, and wild plums. The wild plums had spikes on their stems.

Alligator Hill was seen by the early developers as possessing a rare and wondrous beauty, unlike anything in the world, and they were not wrong. Opulent exclusivity, both natural and manmade, was what they were selling. The hills, garlanded by blue lakes, stretched in several directions. The wildflowers in the spring, set in among the green trees and the sudden glimpses of the bejeweled waters, were so beautiful and smelled so good, you felt transformed. The light around the peninsula is often vaguely pink, something about the evaporation off the water someone said. The only landscape I've ever seen with that kind of light, so many high hills, and so much water, is Istanbul. In ancient times, when Istanbul was still Troy, and even later when it was Byzantium and Constantinople, it must have been like this. Alligator Hill, Yeats's "Byzantium."

The grand vision the developers had for the Day Forest Estates was bold. They imagined, "A permanent Summer White House for residents of the Gold Coast of Chicago or Millionaire's Row of New York." An ad in the *Traverse City Record-Eagle* from June 27, 1927 reads: "Each estate will command an individual setting with a marvelous vista. A Magnificent Golf Club House will be located on the bluff. [There will be] an eighteen-hole golf course, beach and tennis club fronting Lake Michigan, a provision for a polo field, an aviation field, winter sports facilities [and places] for bathing, swimming, and boating. The Day Forest Estates will be *so restricted* [my italics] as to ultimately become America's premier summer community." The real estate developers, the high rollers of a previous century, were drunk on their own dreams. With each honeyed phrase, the exhilarating language rose giddily, daringly, precariously, higher and higher. But it all came crashing down.

America was strewn, after the Gilded Age, with people who'd dreamed too big, or simply had an accident: lost an arm, a leg, a hand, a spouse, their mind. "Poor Mrs. M," my mother would say about a frail, once-beautiful woman we sometimes picked up hitchhiking, she and her three children: two, skinny, bluish-skinned, dark-haired boys, and a little blonde girl who looked like a baby Marilyn Monroe, all strung along behind her as if held together with an invisible rope. Did they always hitchhike in the rain? They always looked cold, wet, and hungry. I wanted to take them to my father's cook shanty, dry them out by the woodstove, and sit them down at the long plank table and say, "Eat." It looked like they could eat for years and not have enough.

The inside of my car, at the base of Alligator Hill near the charcoal kilns where I've parked while I look around where the mill used to be, trying to see what I can remember, is warm from sitting in the sun when I get back into it. It's a day of classic coastal clouds, white puffs with gray-blue undersides, in a friendly white sky washed with blue. The squirrels are still scampering around over the hard-crust snow, trying to find the goods they'd buried in the fall. "Now, where *did* I put those beechnuts?" But squirrels can't remember. They find their stash again by smelling.

When I leave the trailhead at the base of Alligator Hill, I drive due north, along the road where my Realtor sister in Seattle now owns and rents out my mother's house, then down the long hill where we used to walk to the school bus, and finally into Glen Arbor by the Christian Science Church. I pass the big restaurant on the corner where they have live music in the summer. I pass the Totem Shop where I worked as a teenager. I pass the Cottonseed which used to be the Dinette. My father and I would sometimes eat at the Dinette. One day the waitress asked me, as my father excused himself to go wash his hands, "How much does your father weigh?" I had no idea. Many years later I would recall this odd question, especially odd when posed to a child, and realize that for one out-of-her-mind moment the waitress had a schoolgirl crush on my father. All the stores are closed. Only Art's Tavern is open. It's been there forever. The solar panels on the roof are the only thing new.

I drive on toward the Leelanau School where I know there are recycling bins. I need to throw out the junk that's accumulated in my car. In 2011, the CBS show, *Good Morning America*—spurred by the cheerful and ceaseless lobbying of people all over the peninsula and, through Facebook and Twitter, all of the people they knew everywhere—announced that the area of the Sleeping Bear Dunes was the most beautiful place in America (for that year). Egypt has the Nile,

Tibet has the Himalayas, and the Leelanau Peninsula has the Sleeping Bear Dunes. The "Most Beautiful Place in America" title was bestowed partly on the basis of the number of votes and it's a testament to the energetic endeavors of well-connected and enterprising Leelanau people like Bobby Sutherland, Glen Arbor founder of the Cherry Republic. Bobby's family came to Glen Arbor on vacations in the 1950s and by the 1970s had moved to Glen Arbor. His father became the principal of the Glen Lake Community Schools. His father died young, in the early 1980s. Bobby, not wanting to leave Leelanau County when he came of age, created a business selling things with a cherry theme to tourists, first only t-shirts and cookies out of the trunk of his car, and eventually just about anything cherry-related, packed at his warehouse, shipped all over the world and also sold at his six stores throughout Michigan.

Typically, people who came to the Leelanau Peninsula over the last 70-plus years have brought skills and education with them, skills and education that allowed them to choose where they wanted to live. Some of the earliest of these so-called modern cultural pioneers, choosing to live where it was beautiful and arriving in the 1950s, became teachers at the private Leelanau School, located where the Crystal River flows into Lake Michigan. This school had emerged at the height of the Great Depression when a summer camp, Camp Leelanau, was carried over into the fall, winter and spring. John Eichstadt came from Princeton and taught math. Mrs. Dorothy (Knight) Lane came from Wellesley and taught Latin. Peppi Teichner came from Germany and taught chemistry and skiing. I knew of these teachers because my sister Ann was their student at the Leelanau School and because Mr. Eichstadt and Mrs. Lane taught for a while—full-time in the case of Mr. Eichstadt and part-time for Mrs. Lane—at the Glen Lake Community Schools where I attended.

Hans "Peppi" Teichner was an early member of the second wave of pioneers. (The first wave, from the 1840s through the

1940s, was largely European immigrants seeking land and an escape from feudalism, as well as a scattering of second sons, New England brahmins in the days of primogenitor, forced to seek their fortunes in the wilderness, usually in the dangerous and risky business of taking out the trees.) Teichner was a living legend. He had been teaching skiing in Spain when the Spanish Civil War broke out. The Jewish Teichner helped people escape Franco's fascist regime, out-skiing his would-be captors in the Pyrenees Mountains. He later served in the First Mountain Division in the United States Army, had an army buddy who enticed him to the Leelanau Peninsula, where Teichner came and carved out a livelihood for himself teaching skiing. He taught everyone from the beautiful Helen Milliken, the late wife of the longtime Michigan governor, William Milliken, to my sister, Ann, how to ski. Before Peppi, hardly anyone on the Leelanau Peninsula knew how to ski. By reputation and in person, Teichner was smart, funny, and brave, in addition to being an amazing athlete. His daughter, Martha Teichner, an award-winning New York City journalist, has given some of her family's land south of Leland to the Leelanau Conservancy in memory of her father, Hans, and her mother, Miriam.

Being who you are, where you are, changes the culture. One person can make a difference. Some people are one-of-a-kind amazing and they, and their legend, "seed" the culture in the way that "cloud-seeding" makes rain. On the Leelanau Peninsula there was the intrepid Irishman, John Dorsey, who sailed into Sleeping Bear Bay on his one-man sloop in 1851, and taught the local Ottawa how to make barrels so they could ship their fish to Chicago; a testament to the respect the Ottawa fishermen had for Dorsey is that, many years later, they found a way to attend his funeral. His high moral character impressed people and was something to aspire to. More recently, the late Bob Houdek, from a shy but illustrious family of Bohemian immigrants who came in the 1850s to

Gills Pier, helped as many people in need as he humanly could, right up until he died in 2010, just because he liked doing it. His level of compassion was an example to the community; we should all be more like Bob Houdek. Teichner had a palpable courage, even when he was no longer rescuing people in the mountains, and had a joyousness about life, too; another person who set a standard. People like Teichner, Dorsey, and Houdek make a lasting impact on a culture.

In the present time, Rebecca Lessard's non-profit Wings of Wonder rescues and rehabilitates raptors, releasing eagles and owls back to the wild. Kay Charters' non-profit Saving the Birds through Habitat encourages people to plant native species to keep the birds and butterflies alive; all those milkweed plants along the highways to feed the monarch butterflies are partly due to Charters' influence. Ottawa naturalist, Hank Bailey, part of the cultural renaissance in the Native community, talks to youth groups about Ottawa heritage. Jesus said, "Love thy neighbor as thyself," and on the Leelanau Peninsula, for the most part, we try to. As Will Bunek said once, before performing the chicken dance at the annual St. Mary School fund-raiser, "The Bible says 'Love your neighbor and your enemy'. That's easy for me because it's the same person." The culture, seeded by strong and decent individuals, grows over time in the directions they started for us. The presence of enlightened and educated people on the peninsula, and their children and grandchildren, and the continued migration of new people drawn to this culture, continues the pattern.

I drive back through Glen Arbor and decide to stop at Art's for a late lunch. I see Pam Warnes, a waitress here and an old schoolmate. She's limping. I ask her how she is. "Four grandchildren," she says, "they keep me going." Boys or girls, I ask. "Boys," she says. She has her mother's smile, the God's love smile, good for grandsons, good for anyone. When we grew up in Glen Arbor the town smelled of smoked fish. The

Sheridans and the Richardsons and the Killenbechs, I think, were still fishing, their nets drying under the trees in the pine-needle lane that ran behind the townhall.

D. H. Day's great-granddaughter, Vicki Finstad, works at Art's. Her mother, Patricia, is the daughter of D. H. Day's son, Robert Day. Vicki says, "Growing up I thought it was fun to see D. H. Day's name on things and know we were related. He's remembered [by us] as a man who cared about his family."

Much of the land that my father owned had originally been owned by D. H. Day, an earlier lumber baron; Day had sold it in the 1920s to the men who built the failed golf course. The prescient Day had bought up thousands of acres after the virgin pine had been harvested because he could envision a time in the future when there would be a market for the remaining hardwoods. In the early days of timber cutting, when they used crosscut saws, the softwood pines were easier to harvest than the hardwoods, and so pine was taken first. The taking of the timber, not just in Michigan, but all across America, was nothing new. According to James Defebaugh in *History of the Lumber Industry of America,* by the 1790s, New England was exporting 36 million board feet of pine annually.

There's a novel about life in the logging camps on the northwest coast, Ken Kesey's book, *Sometimes a Great Notion,* in which one of the sons of the mill owner writes the family motto, "Never Give a Inch." He writes it with a red pencil for marking the footage at the end of a log and puts the motto over his bed. Of course, it was ungrammatical. Taking advantage of natural resources and the human beings who do the hard work of harvesting them doesn't require good grammar. Violence isn't required either, at least not routinely, but looking away when someone was about to lose everything was expected, especially when your activities, either directly or indirectly, had caused the other person's losses and those losses were terrifyingly life threatening for them and their

children and the damage, even if they survived, would persist
through the next several generations.

Day had first come from New York State in 1878 and
would eventually establish a large timber operation in Glen
Haven, shipping the lumber out first by schooner, and later
by steamer, and still later by rail. Neither Day nor my father
clear-cut. That would have been stupid. It would have taken
more man hours, cost more money, wasted trees, ruined the
soil, and prevented future trees from growing. They did se-
lective cutting, waiting for the remaining trees to mature,
sometimes replanting.

Both Day and my father, as was the custom at the time,
allowed their workers' families to endure poverty, poor housing, and all the physical and emotional ailments attendant
on low wages and poor living conditions; they profited by this
and had more money to invest in timber, land, and things for
their own families because of it. There were no laws against
this, nor did they risk the disapproval of their peers. Neither
Day nor my father were doing anything out of step with the
values of their time. For my part, in relationship to my father,
I was deeply dismayed by the suffering of the children of the
mill workers, even as a child, on probably a subconscious
level, because the children of the millhands were my play-
mates. They were like brothers and sisters. My sisters and I
had easy lives, by most measures, with books and bikes and
nice clothes and plenty to eat. Brain damage from malnutrition is not reversible and the damage is carried over into the
next generation and the next. The children of the millhands
had hard lives, relative not only to my sisters and me, but to
children anywhere; they had no books or bikes, often didn't
have warm clothing or enough to eat. I was a kid but I knew
this was wrong. Children know. I couldn't have articulated it
then, I didn't have the words, but it stayed with me, is still
with me, which is why I'm writing about it, so people won't
look away. The exploitation of workers is still going on, in factories and farms and restaurants, all over America and all

over the world, and it is still wrong because it still damages
people and their children. Now that we have a universal civilization, thanks to the Internet, anything that impacts people anywhere impacts us all.

When someone you know does something wrong, it
haunts you. And when that person is your father, someone
you love, someone who loved you, too, unconditionally, someone who never complained or even commented when you got
carsick day after day, as I did on our trips to the mill, that
wrongdoing must be addressed and understood, so one can go
on living in a good way. Even when there's no love, but the
reverse—hate and enmity—and the person or people doing
something wrong are your captors in a war, it is deeply dis-
turbing. Once I read about an American soldier, a prisoner of
war during the Vietnam War, who found a hand in his soup.
It turned out to be the hand of a monkey, not a child's hand,
as he had at first thought, but he couldn't eat that day, or for
several days after, even though he was starving, as was
everyone in the camp: it took his appetite away. And that was
the way it was for me as a kid, and now, too, seeing what I
saw and feeling what I felt. My father understood perfectly,
far ahead of his time, what to do with land. He was called "a
visionary businessman" by writer Jim Harrison, one day
when Jim and I were talking about my father, because of my
father's understanding and appreciation of natural beauty.
My father was in the woods all the time, always had been,
and understood that doing right by it was a necessity for our
future. He did not have the same understanding about people, beyond those in his immediate family. It was exactly the
same thing, but he just never saw it.

Day had lofty ideas about how his own family should live.
He established a village with a school, a post office, a black-
smith shop, a granary, an icehouse, a slaughterhouse, a store,
a telegraph line, and eventually, in the 1920s, a cannery for
preserving cherries, according to George Weeks in his book,

Sleeping Bear—Yesterday and Today. Like a feudal lord, Day retained the deeds to the 100 plotted lots in the village. Day owned all the land, goods, and services; people could only buy things from him. He built ice-skating rinks and tennis courts for his children. Every Christmas, he took his family to Traverse City, in what his daughter Margaret described, in a wonderful letter reprinted in several places and on-line, as "a two-day orgy of hotel luxury and glorious prodigal shopping." They would travel by sleigh to Empire, and from there by train to Traverse City, embark at the Depot, and take a carriage to the elegant Park Place Hotel which at that time was a white, three-storeyed, wooden structure with a wrap-around porch; it looked like a big wedding cake.

Those were the days when, with a little luck, hard work, and ingenuity, a man could make a lot of money. Fever dreams of fortune fueled the pioneers who headed into the woods, but few ended up as rich as D. H. Day or my father. Like novice gamblers, most erstwhile entrepreneurs and adventurous pioneers, more typically took a loss. Forty-five miles south of Glen Haven, lots in the town of Kaleva, brilliantly and deviously named by developers for the Finnish mythical heaven, were sold to people in Finland in 1900 on the basis of beautiful pictures. People arrived to find nothing but timbered-off scrub pine and sand. They couldn't go back to Finland. They had sold everything to come.

Lumbering was dangerous, but for those who knew how to do it and were lucky enough to escape injury, it could be lucrative. In 1889, according to the Michigan Bureau of History, Michigan lumber outvalued all the gold in California by a billion dollars. From roughly 1850 to 1900 Michigan was the national leader in lumber.

Elizabeth Westman, an Ottawa woman born in Glen Haven sometime in the late 1800s, was one of seven children. In Glen Arbor, in a passage quoted in Robert Rader's book, *Beautiful Glen Arbor Township*, and published in 1977 by the Glen Arbor History Group, an ancient Mrs. Westman is recorded as saying, "We lived in a long building built by Mr. Day. The building was a short way from Sleeping Bear Inn. We were sharecroppers, too [they could have a portion of the food from the vegetable gardens they worked on Day's land], so we had enough food. We were given brown stamps for shoes and green stamps for vegetables." She is also reported as saying that there were large cranberry bogs around Glen Arbor and that her family harvested those cranberries. I never saw the cranberry bogs, but Kristin Hurlin, an artist in Glen Arbor, the woman who illustrated this book, told me over Thanksgiving in 2018 that she has picked cranberries in a swamp just north and west of the Glen Lake Yacht Club, so the cranberries are still there, at least at this time.

Two families of Ottawa fisher people were still living in Glen Haven when Day arrived, one of them the Westman family and the other the Jackson family, all thought to be related. Day employed them to cook, clean, and work odd jobs. These resident families caught fish, as they had for years, and shipped the fish to Chicago. Day charged them for the ice, the crates, the use of his dock, and the shipping, everything but the fish.

Day worked every angle to make money. He promoted tourism, becoming a leader in the state, heading up the Michigan Pike Association which staged auto rallies in Glen Haven. He was a founder of the Western Michigan Development Bureau. In 1922, with the lumbering business played out and thus no longer having a need for on-site workers, Day turned the old Ottawa fish camp into the D. H. Day State Park, donating the land to the State of Michigan, thus finessing the exodus of the last remnants of the Native families living there. The D. H. Day State Park is now part of the Sleeping Bear Dunes National Lakeshore. Day helped establish the Michigan State Park Commission and was its first chairman.

The developers who dreamed of getting rich with the nation's most exclusive and restricted golf paradise, put up imposing stone gates at the entrances all around Alligator Hill, announcing the Day Forest Estates. The stone gates were still there when I was a child and remained until the 1970s when the National Park Service (NPS), in an early phase of wanting things to return to a wilderness state, destroyed them. Later, in the 1990s, in another phase, this time of wanting to restore some local history, the NPS rebuilt some of the stone gates, but not all of them.

I get in my car and mentally prepare to go back to my apartment in Traverse City. For the past two or three weeks there have been signs on the bulletin boards, first only on the main floor, then on every floor—on the tack strip by the elevators—then finally *in* the elevators, "Please return the grocery carts to the lobby. They are for the use of everyone." The notes have become more adamant and frenzied with each passing day. People really do need to use the grocery carts. They use them to unload their groceries from the curb, and then take things up to their apartments; but the carts in the past were always returned to the lobby stairwell. This morning, when I left, the note said that if the grocery carts were not returned by the end of today, all apartments would be inspected, starting on the 10th floor, which seemed to imply that the office thought the suspect was on the 10th floor. What in the world could someone be doing with the grocery carts? I picture a tiny apartment—they are all tiny, 480-square-feet— with several grocery carts. Perhaps they are using them as cages for rabbits. They could cover the carts with plastic, poking holes for air. They could feed the rabbits with lettuce. But that's a lot of rabbits. And rabbits breed. That's a lot of lettuce.

Things like the mystery of the grocery carts is why I like living where I live. It isn't just the view of the Boardman River, but being around other people. People are always interesting. I love the intelligent, kind, legally blind man who goes out and cleans the snow off the cars of people who are in wheel chairs or hooked to oxygen tanks. I love the young man who's often in the lobby in his wheelchair, always with something positive to say to each passerby. During the solar eclipse of August 2017, I came home to find my fellow apartment dwellers, most of whom I'd never seen before, including several in wheelchairs, sharing the white square glasses, to view the solar eclipse, as excited as little kids. I love the sweet young woman who, during a picnic on the lawn, went and made conversation with everyone who was in a wheelchair, going from person to person, visiting with those who were unable to easily move around to socialize. These are the real beautiful people—not the ones with designer dresses, fancy sports cars, or mansions on hills—but the ones who reaffirm, every day, my faith in humanity.

The old Alligator Hill of the mill and the charcoal kilns, not the new Alligator Hill of the big, gravel parking lot and the labelled and marked National Park trails, is in my mind as I drive away from the area one last time, along Day Forest Road where I used to ride my horse when the road was little more than a two-track. I cross the bridge at the Glen Lake Narrows and watch a gull lift off the last of the lake's blue-green ice and fly toward the dunes. The lake is mostly open water now. I head up the steep Benzonia Trail. There's a lookout on the west side of the road, a short way before M-72, and I pull into it, rolling down my window, gazing south, out across the miles of forested hills rippling away toward the Platte River Watershed. I think I can pick out the low area of Crystal Lake and the harbor at Frankfort because of the mist rising from where they are. On this warm day I can smell balsam popple, also called Balm of Gilead, with its slight hint of bergamot, like Guerlain's Shalimar perfume. The Leelanau Peninsula must have been like a cathedral when the towering pines were here, this place of high hills and deep lakes, this headland surrounded by water and ice, this place of pink light, this promontory of blazing, wake-up dawns in the east and soft, lingering twilights in the west.

I turn on the radio. Then I turn it off. It's all school shoot-ings. I do my time-collapse trick. This time I start way before alligators, with the formation of the earth 4.5 billion years ago, racing through bacteria, worms, people, drawings on cave walls, right up to the present moment. I'm beginning to back the car around, as I'd once backed a horse around, to turn and go down the lookout drive to the Benzonia Trail when I realize, as I always do when I perform my time-col-lapse trick on myself, that reality is bigger than my moment in it. Reality has layers. The realization settles me down. I head south.

It's a soft, filmy, pale-blue, late February afternoon. Too warm for this time of year. The air smells like spring. I'm sleepy. The day is fading. Soon the songbirds and all the other birds will be migrating up the coast of Michigan. I glance into the woods at the side of the road. Here again the black and gray squirrels are running around. There are dark circles around the bottoms of trees. The blackness of the trees draws down the heat of the sun, so the white snow is effectively polka-dotted. The bare ground around the base of the tree trunks is where the squirrels are finding their food. I turn to go east, back to Traverse City. I pass the RV park, Indigo Bluffs, on the north side of M-72, closed for the winter.

But this is what I really want you to see with me: as I begin the hilly drive back to Traverse City, I see above the low eastern hills, slightly above the bare-branched trees, a floating, gigantic, opalescent, diaphanous, full moon, very close to the earth and enormous, wonderfully large and un-expected, a moon the shape of a balloon, as big as a house and with the pearly look of a crystal ball, in the blurry, bluish-lavender, hazy late-afternoon sky.

Summer

Houdek Dunes

Think of waves of sand, like a bolt of pale, champagne-colored, water-marked, Chinese silk, unravelling in front of you, going on and on, for a quarter mile or more, until the waves of sand reach the shore of Lake Michigan. Those waves of sand are succession dunes, somewhat covered with marram grass and spreading juniper and milkweed and birch and oak, but soft, tame, gentle, walkable, a place to take your children or your elderly relatives, a place to play, as the Houdek children did, a place to be easy and at peace.

"My grandfather used to take us here," Brad Houdek, a grandson of Julius Houdek, says. "That was Grandpa's thing. When my parents would go away for the weekend, and my brother and I would stay with my grandparents, he'd take us out hiking for hours." This land of dunes is the transition from the water to the hills, the land between shore and trees. The marram grass and the creeping juniper are transition plants, the pioneer stage in the foredunes, pioneers like Brad's grandparents and great-grandparents who came from Bohemia.

"We'd come home," Brad says, "Grandma would feed us. We'd fall asleep, completely exhausted." That was where Brad says he learned to love the out-of-doors. His grandfather didn't talk much. The sky and dunes and birds, the tiny creek, that was all there was and that was, in retrospect, powerful. The cosmos was vast. Humans were miniscule. That was enough to make one straight and keep one humble.

Delores Houdek, grandmother to Brad Houdek, says that she didn't learn English until she went to school. "They spoke

Bohemian at home," she says. Both her parents had been born in America but they spoke Bohemian: everyone they knew spoke Bohemian, too. Delores Houdek, born a Korson, was also a Houdek on her mother's mother's side. Helen Korson, the register of deeds in Leelanau County for more than four decades, said of her close-knit Gills Pier community, somewhat jokingly but not entirely, "The first generation we married each other. The next generation we had to go ten miles to Lake Leelanau to find partners."

The name Houdek means musician in the Czech, Bohemian and Slavic languages. (These languages came from a beautiful and hilly part of Europe that changed its name and its boundaries many times, a land largely now called Czechoslovakia, a region that was always changing hands because it was in between the ever-changing borders of Poland, Bavaria, Germany and Austria.) Joe Houdek, Brad's older brother, when an elementary school student at St. Mary in Lake Leelanau in the early 1990s, had his gift for music discovered by accident by Brant Leonard, a locally famous piano tuner. Leonard noticed, when he came to tune the pianos at the church and school, that young Joe was intensely interested in the piano he was tuning, and had perfect pitch, not something everyone has. Leonard told the parents, Bob and Vicki Houdek, and the parents got Joe a piano and piano lessons. The ancient Slovakian name "musician" was uncannily exact in this instance. Joe Houdek is now the Director of Music Ministries at the Parish of the Holy Spirit in Grand Rapids, Michigan.

The St. Wenceslaus Church was built in 1890, named for a 10th century feudal lord who, most unusually in the 10th century, helped the poor and thus was made a saint. The church can still be seen on a high glacial moraine in the north central part of the Leelanau Peninsula. From its belfry one can see the sweep of Lake Michigan on both the east and the west sides of the peninsula. The church was and is central to the surrounding Bohemian community, a close community that includes families such as Korson, Kalchik, Kolarik, Kovarik, Kirt, Jelinek, Novotny, Sedlacek, and of course, Houdek, many of whom have their names on the roads that wend between the drumlins falling away from the high spine of the peninsula. The Czech community is composed mainly of families with orchards. They deliberately chose this land, land that no one else wanted, because they knew the breezes (air drainage) would be good for their fruit trees. Their fair and kind treatment of their migrant workers is legendary and the same migrant families return to the same Czech farmers summer after summer.

There are lots of Houdeks, and, like the succession dunes, they came in waves from Bohemia, along with many of their fellow countrymen. John Houdek, born in Prague in 1835, came from Bohemia sometime in the late 1850s or early 1860s. He homesteaded the land that is now the Houdek Dunes. The original log home is still there, restored by builder Marty Easling who uses that and several other buildings as the base for his construction business. You can see the buildings there along M-22 about five miles north of Leland.

John Houdek's granddaughters, daughters of the Charles Houdek who inherited the land, and of Charles's wife, Anna, say their parents had a store there and two gas pumps. Leelanau artist David Grath who lives nearby says he remembers the store being there when he first visited the peninsula in the 1960s; it was the only store between Leland and Northport on the west side of the peninsula. There was also a flowing well. The grandchildren of that branch of the Houdek family recently built a deck in the Houdek Dunes Natural Area overlooking Houdek Creek. The deck, built in the summer of 2010 by the youngest generation, about 25 people in all, including spouses, especially those with building experience, was a family project, a surprise for the parents and grandparents. All the lumber had to be precut and hauled in manually by many people; there's no road to the creek, just a trail.

Karen Kirt, great-granddaughter of the first home-steading John Houdek, is proud of being a Houdek on her mother's side, proud of the deck. "Traversing the trails of Houdek Dunes gives me a chance to envision my grandfather, grandmother and the siblings, including my mother, working the land. Whether they called in the cows or farmed for sustenance, the Houdeks dedicated their lives to this property," she writes in an email. "I hope trail users will appreciate the past and create their own visions of the Houdeks in their minds as they use and hopefully embrace this land."

The Houdek Dunes Natural Area is as pleasant as a park and as accessible. Several generations of Houdeks recreated there. It was the ideal place for Grandpa Julius to take his grandsons. They fished for small speckled trout in Houdek Creek and walked through to Lake Michigan to go swimming.

Michigan is a land of sand and water and never more so than at the Houdek Dunes. The dunes, 11,000 years ago, were, like Chicago, under water. What was there was Lake Algonquin, now Lake Michigan, which included all of Lake Leelanau, connected to Cedar Lake and went almost to Traverse City. Most of the Leelanau Peninsula was under water. Two-thousand years ago Caesar was conquering Gaul and re-doing London, marching his troops around and teaching peasants how to build the Roman baths his men liked, but on the Leelanau Peninsula there was mostly only eagles and white-fish and marram grass.

Marram grass is still there. Marram grass grows well in sand and can go from one small tuft to a three-foot-diameter clump over a summer. The roots of the marram grass, where the sand has eroded from the wind, are a woody tangle, like someone's first attempt at a macramé wreath. The roots of the sand-reed grass, on the other hand, look like hair hanging from a shrunken head. The land and the little plants invite one to tarry, to dilly-dally, to lag, to look, to let the mind loose from its lists and requirements, the things that need to be done. For an hour or two or three, nothing needs to be done. Everything can wait.

A person cannot be immune to beauty, whether it's a sky-full of towering clouds or the discovery of a monarch butterfly's cocoon with its inimitable shade of celadon, dappled with shiny spots of gold, like gold leaf, containing the miracle of new life. (The cocoon is also called a chrysalis; chrysalis in Greek means gold sheath.) Monarch butterflies are in the milkweeds at Houdek Dunes. Monarchs like to eat milkweeds because it makes the birds not like to eat *them*. The "milk" of a milkweed, the white sap that oozes out of stems and leaves, if you've ever tasted it, putting a touch of it on the tip of your tongue, is horribly bitter—because it's toxic; but, in the way nature has, just to keep things interesting, the blossom smells softly sweet and good. If you find a monarch about to come out of the chrysalis, you can see the orange wings through the cocoon which turns black just before the butterfly emerges.

Monarchs migrate upwards of 3,000 miles, going from Michigan to Mexico at about five miles an hour, about the rate of a jogger. Where does such a tiny body find the energy for such a long trip? We don't know. It's a mystery. It's who they are. It's what they do, just like humans try to figure out patterns in the stars and write poetry and wear funny hats. These are the thoughts you can have in a pretty place.

Sit down somewhere, on the sand if you're young, or on one of the benches if you're not, and you'll see things you haven't really noticed since you were a kid and closer to the ground—the small, intricate patterns and processes of nature that one can only see when one is still and watching. All around you are the waves of succession dunes. As on the ocean, the rhythmic patterns are soothing. Look at the perfectly round hole of the wolf spider, for example, or the tiny cuneiform tracks of a bird, maybe a wren or a sandpiper. What have they written there with their cute little marks?

If you're near the creek, you might see the water striders, the small insects that use their middle legs like paddles to cross the water. Also, in the creek, if you happen along when they hatch, you might see horsehair worms, thin as a horsehair and maybe a half-foot long, and swimming, that date back 15-45 million years, before you were here, before anything was here, time so vast that the mind cannot take it in and must accept it, just like everything in Genesis, on faith. Luna moths sometimes hatch in the woods and if you see them, drying their wings, taxiing along on the leaves like little planes, you will never forget the pale green color of their wings, like moonlight, which is how they got their name.

Sit on the ground and feel yourself part of it. Look above at the leaves of the maple tree and see, in a way that you haven't for years, the faces in the shapes of the leaves. Look at the horizon and see the circus animals in the cumulus clouds. Pick up a small Petoskey stone and marvel at how it is part of the coral reef that was in Michigan 400,000,000 years ago when the land was under a saltwater sea. This is all yours, this *un*real estate, this beauty of the intangible. The air, which smells faintly of juniper, and tastes of gin, is the color of rosé wine, white wine that is pink because it is made from red grapes. In the distance we hear the gulls. Sometimes the simplest and most benign things are the most sublime.

Jonah Powell,
Lake Leelanau Musician

His hair. Even as a child, Jonah Powell, who was in my youngest daughter's class at the Leland Public School, had this nimbus of curls that one could see from a long way away and, of course, admire.

We would all see him from time to time, when he was a kid, in the halls at school or in the grocery store or in the library. He was instantly recognizable as: *Jonah*. As the years went by, sometimes we would see him playing his fiddle at various community events, up on the bandstand, a little tyke, but transcending age with his music. We all loved Jonah, even those of us who didn't know him but only knew of him. Then Jonah, like my daughter, his classmate, grew up and went away to college.

Time passed and then one day I saw Jonah and now he was an adult. He was helping to host a community potluck and benefit for John Rutherford, another musician, much older, a man who'd had a stroke. Jonah, a neighbor to Rutherford, was waiting to go on and play, along with some of his friends. It was a benefit put on by all the area musicians. Jonah's wife, the beautiful Carrie Hanson, was there, helping with getting the food out and making people feel welcome. Jonah's parents, Kathy and Clayton Powell—an elegant couple, as elegant in late middle age as they had been as young parents—strolled onto the gleaming hardwood floors of the old V.F.W. Hall and—gliding and graceful, seemingly effortlessly so, like Fred Astaire and Ginger Rogers in an old-time movie—danced the evening's first dance together.

Jonah, one day a while ago, now a young man in his mid-thirties, sits across from me in a restaurant in Lake Lee-lanau—the one that used to be Kejara's Bridge, run for decades by the Landry sisters, "the three red-heads," two of whom eventually became full-time hummus makers; one became a yoga teacher. The restaurant is now Fig's, named for Bryon "Fig" Figueroa who with his wife, three daughters and one on the way, hopes to buy it. "Usually they'd be here working with me," Fig says, "but today is a family day and they're going to the ultra sound [for the new baby]."

Jonah's eating an omelette and I'm chatting with him—and with Fig, the cook. I tell Jonah that I'm planning to ask him questions about his music and his life, but that I'll talk to the cook for a minute to let him eat.

Exactly as it was when it was Kejara's Bridge, the food is fresh, purchased from the local farms. The eggs are organic. The orange juice is squeezed fresh daily. You can get a burger or a burrito, either of which will be served with the most delicious tomatoes and greens.

"I love to cook," Fig says as he steps away for a minute from the hot stove. "I trained in nursing and did that for a while, but this is nursing, too. This is preventative medicine. If people eat healthy, they'll be healthy. I make the best food I can, and I love doing it." This little building has been owned, in addition to the Redheads and Fig, by Linda Ihme who sold ice cream and hot dogs and the place was called The Cool Spot; Linda moved on to establish the lucrative and thriving Vacation Rentals in Glen Arbor. It was also The Hot Spot, owned by Tim Nichols who sold pizza; Tim now has the popular Riverfront Pizza in Glen Arbor. The still-modest restaurant in the center of the Village of Lake Leelanau is now entering its fifth decade as one of the peninsula's starter businesses; it has provided the solid beginning for a succession of hard-working entrepreneurs who parlayed their success into something bigger.

Jonah talks about how he became a full-fledged musician. It started early. He says he was very young, maybe two years old, when he told his father that he wanted to play guitar. "My dad said, 'You don't want to do that. Everyone does that.'" Shortly after that, Jonah says he saw Itzhak Perlman playing the violin on *Sesame Street* and told his mom, "I want to do *that!*"

Jonah comes from a family of musicians. His father plays the guitar. His uncle, George Powell, a boat builder, plays the mandolin. Victor McManemy, a cousin, plays the guitar. Both his parents sing. Family friends, the Evans, are musicians. Jo Ellen Evans directed the choir at the Methodist Church where Jonah sang when he was growing up; and Jeremy Evans, who is the music and theater director at the Leland Public School, used to be the director of the Leelanau Community Choir that Jonah now directs.

Before Jonah had arrived, I'd spent some time walking around Lake Leelanau, where I'd lived for 36 years, revisiting some of the places. Lake Leelanau, which advertises itself as "the heart of the county," is a musical place. This is the culture out of which Jonah and a few other musicians—people like Joe Houdek who now heads the music department at a church in Grand Rapids; or Jonah's uncle, George Powell, who plays regularly at Martha's Leelanau Table in Suttons Bay, along with Sandy (Taghon) Dhuyvetter—arose. Every Wednesday afternoon there's a jam session at Dick's Pour House across the street from Fig's. Dick's Pour House has been there since the 1950s and is a place where you can play pool, buy a fishing license, watch sports on TV, and "find common ground," as longtime bartender Adam Sleder says. "People come to mourn. They come in here after funerals. They come to celebrate. They come in here after weddings, after high school graduations. They come to do business. They come to find information. And not just local people," Sleder says. "Travelers. Tourists [come in to Dick's]. They're trying to get a new perspective. They help me get a new perspective." Sleder is in a band, too: Soul Patch.

Jeanpaul Burnell, the kitchen manager at Dick's, doubles as the master of ceremonies for the Saturday night karaoke. People come. They sing. Poets, also, are not strangers to Dick's Pour House. Writer Jim Harrison, who died in 2016, lived in Lake Leelanau for several decades and used to drink at Dick's when Richard Plamondon was still the proprietor and bartender. Jim's poet friend, Dan Gerber, used to drink there, too, in his younger days. Dan grew up in Fremont, Michigan where his father founded the popular Gerber Baby Food line, now part of Nestlé, the world's largest food and beverage company. Dan Gerber and Jim Harrison both attended Michigan State University (MSU), where together they created the poetry magazine, *Sumac*. Tom McQuane, who writes frequently for *The New Yorker*, also met Jim Harrison at MSU, and also became a lifelong friend, also came to Dick's Pour House with Harrison. Dick's Pour House in Lake Leelanau has always been a favorite watering hole, not just for poets and musicians, but for everyone in the county. In an early poem Harrison wrote about "walking home from a tavern on a May night," a tavern very much like Dick's in a village very much like Lake Leelanau, "through a village with only three street lights, a slip of moon and still air moist with scent of first grass."

Local musicians gather at Dick's every Wednesday afternoon at 2 to practice. Today they're playing Ry Cooder's song, "Across the Borderline," with the sad refrain about "the broken promised land." Leelanau County has migrants, needed by farmers and respected by local people. Eight hundred Leelanau people recently signed a letter protesting the arrest of a beloved Hispanic man, a window cleaner who lives with his family across the bridge in Lake Leelanau. These longtime peninsula residents are the people Leelanau writer, Stephanie Mills, refers to as "the salt of the earth." The people at Dick's Pour House are the people poet Carl Sandburg was talking about, when he wrote about Americans in the heartland. Sandburg called them simply, "The people," as in, "The people, yes, the people. The people will live on."

The musicians are singing, "The Ash Grove" in the key of G, suggested by female accordion player Sandy Dhuyvetter, a Taghon on her mother's side (one of the many Taghons from Empire), who came back to live in Leelanau County after spending most of her life in California. The practice session for musicians, started by John Rutherford and Jim Neisinz, back in the day, became a tradition, and now includes Tom Allard, Barbara Abbott, Becky Abbott (Barbara's sister), David Borton, Sandy Dhuyvetter, Larry Hauzer, and Jonah's uncle, George Powell. One of the musicians is wearing a Leelanau Uncaged T-shirt. This refers to an annual music event in Northport, at the end of the peninsula at the end of the summer, with all kinds of bands, where the whole town comes out for one last hoedown in September. If you've never attended, you should. The incredible variety of everything— people of all ages, all races, all walks of life; street food such as fry bread and tacos; craft booths; art displays; face-painting for children; the music; the dancing; not to mention the sheer amount of buoyancy in the air—is well worth it.

Now again sitting across from Jonah at Fig's, I learn that Jonah's parents, who met while in the choir together at Grand Valley State College, love music themselves, and when Jonah was about four-years-old, they went out and bought him his first of many violins. Initially Jonah studied violin with Ellen Boyer, using the Suzuki method, and when she got a regular teaching job, he began to study fiddle with Fred Johnson in Kingsley, a renowned fiddler who played by ear. After that he studied for several years with Judy Gienow, the principal violinist at the Traverse Symphony Orchestra.

"The difference between a fiddle and a violin," Jonah explains, "is how it's played." The fiddle came with the first settlers from Ireland and Scotland and the music and the playing became part of America's backwoods heritage. There's a self-deprecating sense of humor in many of the American folk tunes. The song, "Bought Me a Cat," which goes through many animal sounds is a classic example. I once heard Jonah sing it all the way through in his excellent baritone, a capella and alone, at a concert.

Jonah left Lake Leelanau to study voice at Alma College and went from there to Ohio University in Athens where he received a Master's in Vocal Performance. While in Athens he also studied instrument repair with Dan Erlewin.

He says he supported himself during those college years with some music work, some family help, and also by painting houses. "I was lucky in my parents," he says. "They weren't concerned with practicalities. There was a lot of positive reinforcement." Now Jonah supports himself with a combination of music-related activities, including directing two choirs, repairing instruments, and giving music lessons. He's in four bands: K. Jones and the Benzie Playboyz, Cabin Fever, Hot Biscuits, and Runaway Mules.

"The two choirs fill in during the off-season," Jonah says. "People say, 'You guys look like you're having a great time' and that's because we are."

Teddy (Schlueter) Page, one of the women in Jonah's choir says, "I can't say enough good things about Jonah. He always has a smile. He's easy to work with. He's uplifting. Even if he wasn't the choir director, I see him in the community, and he's just a wonderful person."

Tricia Denton joined the Leelanau Community Choir a few years ago and says, "As a very shy, first-time-ever member of a choir at the age of 45, with no previous singing experience save around the campfire, Jonah was incredibly encouraging and supportive in an absolutely genuine way. Jonah loves what he's doing, loves being part of making us all feel successful, even a rookie like me. He's playful, hardworking, dedicated, supportive, and caring."

Denton goes on to say that she has been friends with Jonah's longtime companion and now wife, Carrie, for a number of years but never really knew Jonah. "Probably the thing that impresses me most about Jonah is the way he is with my friend. To see them dance together at their wedding reception, really, they *danced together*. This partnership is something they have both worked toward . . . like a lovely piece of music all on its own. And to hear him perform music in her honor, something truly intimate and passionate, it was beautiful to behold."

Jonah says his relationship with Carrie is important. "We have breakfast together. If I work late, I still get up to eat with her. Then maybe take a nap later." He's not one of those musicians who gets home in the wee hours, gets up in the afternoon, eats everything in the house, and then goes out to play music all night. He says, "Nothing good happens after midnight." His life is calm and orderly. He and Carrie have a vegetable garden they work in together. They have pets. They live next to his parents.

"Playing in four bands [in the summer] gives me enough variety to keep me interested, yet I don't have to learn all new tunes." Two or three years ago K. Jones and the Benzie Playboyz played with the Cajun band, BeauSoleil, from Louisiana. "It was a double bill," Jonah says. "We weren't covering for them. They weren't covering for us. It was a moment of achievement."

Sometimes the various bands play for family gatherings, weddings, social events. "We played a wedding rehearsal dinner," Jonah says. "It started raining as soon as we set up. We played during the cocktail hour—really high energy—then for the second set we had to tone it down, and we did it all really well, and it was a blast."

What motivates him?

He doesn't hesitate. "The joy of music," he says. "I'm happy when I'm playing."

The night I hear Jonah playing it's when he's performing with the Cabin Fever Band at Boonedocks in Glen Arbor with fellow musicians Tom Fordyce, Jim Curtis, Mark McManus and Joe Wilson. Words of an Eric Clapton song float out across the deck, "I've been tryin' all night long, just to talk to you . . . don't you need . . . someone . . . to talk to . . . "

The audience is families, people celebrating a birthday, people on vacation, or simply out for the evening with friends. There are children down front by the band, moving to the music. A grandmother gets up and dances with her grandson.

Someone says, "Music, the universal language."

The musicians are all wearing sunglasses, like those raffia replicas you see being sold on the streets in the Caribbean. Musician Tom Fordyce, an older, stocky man with a huge, almost comical moustache, smiles at a toddler and pantomimes a few moves in time to the music, dancing along with the child.

It's June 21, the day after the summer solstice. The sun doesn't officially go down until about 9:30 and, since this is northern Michigan, it will be twilight for quite a long time after that.

It's summer, and the music is playing.

Chippewa Run

There's a large field, remnants of an old orchard, a 65-year-old planting of pines, a marshy area, and a little creek on the outskirts of the village of Empire that you might miss if you didn't know it was there. There's a small parking area and a sign that announces that it's the Chippewa Run Natural Area. It was established by the Leelanau Conservancy in 2000 with the help of donations from Conservancy patrons and local people. It was one of the woodsy playing areas for Empire children and their friends in the Aylsworth, Davis, Deegan, Deering, Harriger, Lambkin, Norconk, Nowicki, Payment, Salisbury, Schmidt, and Taghon families, and a few other local families of long-standing, and they felt it was important to have it be there for their children, too.

Empire, a former lumber boom town, is a village of about 400 people on the shores of Lake Michigan. It's a crosshatch of little streets and alleys, half a dozen angling north and south, and maybe two or more going east and west. Community gatherings have always been a staple of the village. People are close. There's a place for ice-skating and a ball field. The town's only about a mile wide in any direction.

Micah Deegan lives about half a mile from Chippewa Run and he can watch bobcats out his picture window, feasting on the roadkill he brings home for them. One of the interesting things about bobcats, Deegan says, is they are neat eaters. They delicately tear off one small strip at a time, and do not gorge themselves. Coyotes are different, Deegan says. They put as much as they can into their stomachs because they will disgorge it back at their dens. But not bobcats. "They could be using a knife and fork," he says. "They clean their hands, they clean their face." Coyotes, Deegan says, approach any new area with caution, but a bobcat enters any arena "with grace and an air of regal confidence."

Deegan is the grandson of Versel Harriger, patriarch of one of the original Empire families, and he credits his grandfather with instilling in him a love and respect for nature. They spent countless hours together, hunting and fishing. Deegan says his grandfather was a member of "the greatest generation," a World War II veteran, a hard worker, a survivor of the Great Depression. "My grandfather taught me how to shake someone's hand, a firm grip, looking the other person in the eye. He always wore a hat," Deegan says, the old-fashioned fedora that's now come back into style, "but he never wore it straight. It was always cocked at a slight angle. We spent many hours conversating, talking about the things that needed to be said. I miss him." His grandfather taught him to observe closely, be ethical, not give spongy handshakes and appreciate natural beauty. "Once we were hunting and a wood duck landed. I was a kid so naturally I wanted to shoot everything I could. He wouldn't let me shoot it. He said, 'It's just too pretty.'"

The village of Empire is a good place for children since the parents usually know the kids haven't gone too far. They can't, really. Lake Michigan hems them in on the west side of the village and M-22 on the east side; the Empire Bluffs and the Sleeping Bear Dunes provide somewhat of a barrier south and north. The children are usually within hailing distance of their own or someone else's parents. It's a good place to grow up, the kind of village many older Americans knew as children: a center of civilization, surrounded by nature.

Chippewa Run is a lovable piece of land at the edge of Empire, one of nature's gifts, and people appreciate it. The creek is cold, spring-fed, a good and easy place for children to fish for brook trout; it goes underground occasionally but eventually wends its way to South Bar Lake, a mile or two down through the fields and swamps toward Lake Michigan. The cherry trees have been cut down, but there are still some people in their 70s and 80s, like me, who remember picking cherries there as children, the orchard filled with local families and the families of Hispanic migrants. For children, too small to last long at the picking, this was a paradise of painted turtles, some so tiny they must have just hatched, and the tin buckets for the cherries, it was quickly discovered, were perfect for baby turtles.

"Chippewa Run received its name after a local naming contest," says Dave Taghon at the Empire Museum down the road. People wanted to honor the Chippewa family, known as the Indian Jackson family, who had a seasonal camp there. Frank Fradd, born in Empire in 1892, visited the camp as a boy and wrote about this in a book of oral histories, *Some Other Day (Remembering Empire),* collected and published by the Empire Heritage Group. The camp was in a clearing, as Fradd described it. There was good drinking water from the spring and a cool creek in which to store perishables. Fish and game were smoked and dried. The housing was made of lightweight poles covered with animal hides and bark.

Fradd also reports that he could remember the virgin hardwoods all around the town of Empire, the oak trees three feet in diameter, with some maples four feet in diameter, and the gray elms six feet in diameter, a time when a clearing was less common than a forest. Frank Fradd roamed the entire peninsula during the Great Depression, looking for ginseng, which could be sold in Ohio for $25 a pound, good money in those days. Fradd describes trying to visit a bald eagle's nest when there were hatchlings in it and how the male and female eagles could see him, no matter how well he thought he was hidden, and would dive at him and hiss.

The land at Chippewa Run is slowly going back to the original forest, in a process of reverse aging called succession:

first the old orchard will decay; then the fields will fill with grass; then with sumac, juniper and wild strawberry; then with cedar, aspen, birch and pine; and gradually over time, it will become a beech and maple forest with more cover for birds and animals.

The village of Empire is itself an example of succession, albeit of human communities, and going forward in time, not back: from Native people; to early pioneers; to European immigrants; to the lumber boom town; to the classic village with a church and a bank; to the urban and educated retirees coming to live where there's still natural beauty; to the current influx of more than a million tourists a year from all over the world, just passing through, coming to visit the Sleeping Bear Dunes National Lakeshore. As in the case of ecological succession, all the stages overlap a little.

Lou Ricord, a docent for the Leelanau Conservancy, a scientist by vocation and avocation, a retired professor from Ohio University, often takes people on nature hikes through Chippewa Run. He meets me at the Glen Lake Community Library which is literally and figuratively in the center of town. Community events are often hosted at the library or at the townhall across the street. The librarian, Dave Diller, has brought in writers from all over Michigan and musicians from all over the world. Finnish-Laplander throat singers, Pia Leinonen and Joni Tiala, have been hosted by the library. Sean Gaskell, a man from North Carolina who went to Africa to learn how to play a 21-string African harp called a Kora made from a large gourd, has been hosted by Diller. One day in July 2018 there was a program for kids featuring Caribbean soul/hip-hop singers from Toronto. The library is a familiar setting for me. My friend, Carol Fittell from grade school, used to live in the house next door. Her father was in the United States Air Force and worked at the air base at the top of the hill, when Empire used to have an air base. I would sometimes ride my horse to Empire and tie it up across the street at what is now an antique store but used to be Mr. Lambkin's barber shop. There was a hitching rail there.

Ricord, a tall, handsome man with an easy smile, has re-searched the pocket gopher at Chippewa Run. One can see the little trails of the pocket gopher, under the soil, he says, but these gophers are nocturnal and one would be hard-pressed to see them in the daylight.

The pocket gopher has fur-lined cheeks, Ricord divulges with obvious delight. These cheeks, or pockets, have external openings and are used for storing the dirt the gopher pulls from the tunnels. The pocket gopher, probably finicky about dirt, can put its front lips behind its teeth so it doesn't get dirt in its mouth. To picture this, imagine big buck teeth, top and bottom, with expandable lips that can go behind the gopher's front teeth. The pocket gopher didn't just think of this one night after dinner—while drinking beer and watching TV, the Knicks and the Red Wings in a final playoff, his wife in the kitchen making mincemeat with brandy and listening to *La Traviata*—but evolved this, over thousands of years.

Wild irises, an electric shade of royal purple, dot the wet-lands along the sluggish, spring-fed creek that meanders through the old meadow. Sir John Lubbock, an English baron and friend and neighbor of Charles Darwin, felt that the wild iris is especially attractive to bees. To watch, as Lubbock did as a kid, a little bee alight on the lip of the sepal, the outer part of the flower, scrape his back against the down-hanging stigma, the bright yellow part of the flower, then crouch along the faintly striped tunnel to where the nectar is, inspired Lubbock to conclude that the complicated pollination of the blue flag iris led to a flower with a brilliant and beautiful color.

Traditionally in England, for at least the last five hundred years, and increasingly this is the case in America, too, since we mostly now all inhabit cities and suburbs at a great re-move from the countryside, there have been only two kinds of children able to explore nature: children from families rich enough to own a lot of undeveloped land around their houses; and children from farm families who worked the land. Urban dwellers are largely cut off from nature, except for excursions. A century ago in America, almost everyone lived with access to the natural world. The writings of Willa Cather and Mark Twain—Cather from the plains of Kansas and Twain from the backwoods of Mississippi—are replete with the sounds, sights and smells of nature because nature was all around them.

You'll discover, if you ask, that most people who love nature were immersed in it as children, not as a managed experience, but as a random one, where they had constant access without thinking too much about it, access that would allow them to catch a baby turtle in a bucket or watch a bee pollinate an iris. The meadows, cedar swamps, pine woods, and meandering creek at Chippewa Run are the kinds of things that used to be at the edge of every small village.

People who are aware of this loss of access to nature, and the loss of the understanding and joy that goes with it, are trying to bring back these things in whatever way they can. The Glen Lake School science classes, under the tutelage of teacher, Karen Richard, have made butterfly gardens in the schoolyard. My father introduced wild turkeys into the area back in the 1950s and big flocks can now be seen along the roads. The Leelanau Conservancy has an annual event where volunteers rescue and sell wildflowers from areas where development would otherwise destroy them. These efforts have been initiated by people who can remember when nature was beautiful, wild and abundant, and are carried on by people who want to see that kind of nature restored and sustained for their children.

Ed Ketterer, longtime chair of the Board of Directors for the Leelanau Conservancy, wrote in the *Leelanau Enterprise* in May 2018 that he grew up in a small Ohio town near Lake Erie. "It was easy to get to a wooded area . . . where my friends and I spent a lot of our free time . . . trying to dam the small creek, tracking animals, and watching birds." He attributes that childhood experience, plus summer vacations in the Canadian woods where he "first encountered the wonderful scent of pine straw in the woods on a warm, sunny day" to his debt of gratitude to nature and his work "to preserve it for future generations."

Fradd, writing in *Some Other Day (Remembering Empire)* that wonderfully gathered collection of oral histories, describes a migration of hawks in 1912, where they began migrating in September and continued through November. There were thousands of hawks in the sky, daily. No one knew why. Perhaps they had been displaced by timber cutting. This unusual three-month-long hawk migration was reported all over the west coast of Michigan. Fradd wrote that he never saw those particular hawks again.

Lou Ricord, like Frank Fradd from a hundred years earlier, both close observers of nature, says he saw a similarly strange phenomenon, when he saw blue jays flocking. "There must have been two hundred of them, maybe more," he says. "They were flocking in a field. People say blue jays don't flock. But I saw them."

There are green herons here, too, at Chippewa Run. These green herons are about a third the size of their blue heron cousins, and also chunkier and much shyer. Green herons are maybe about the size of a pigeon, but shaped differently, and with necks that can extend in an astonishing way and they have a very long beak, like a railroad spike. Green herons will fish the same way blue herons do, by wading in the water, and they walk like a water-wader, flipping their feet out in front of them and looking around. Both kinds of herons, blue and green, will drop things into the water, leaves or twigs, and when the fish come up to see what it is, they strike. They nest in the tops of trees near swampy areas. And when one takes off from the top of a tree, it sounds like what one imagines would be the sound of a horse in flight, if horses could fly.

There are lots of dragonflies here. The metallic blue-green sheen of the dragonflies' wings, like little mirrors, catches the sunlight as they flit over the stream. The wings seem to reflect the deep green of the cedars and the electric purple of the blue flag irises. The way the light bounces off the waters of the creek, bounces again off the cedars and the irises, makes the air seem to be the same color as the dragonfly wings, with glints of water-color, cedar-color, and iris-color, light that reverberates with these colors, light that seems iridescent. Dragonfly light.

On a soft spring morning, so soft and so quiet, with hardly any traffic yet on the roads, lying down in the blooming wild strawberries and daisies at Chippewa Run, like a deer, one can hear the bees and, farther away, the waters of the creek, rippling over the land, trickling this way and that, a riverine tenor counterpoint to the soft, alto hum of the bees.

Another student of nature, Henry Thoreau, writing in 1843, understood the thrill of wilderness. "Not yet subdued by man," he writes, "its presence refreshes him." Frank Fradd and Henry Thoreau, Mark Twain and Willa Cather, these are the rustic American aristocrats, able to educate themselves in the woods, like their more privileged and titled European counterparts, the Darwins and the Lubbocks on their baronial English estates, about things like the bees inside the wild irises, and a phenomenal migration of hawks.

Meadowlark Farm

Meadowlark Farm sits in the lee of a high, north-facing hill above the Village of Lake Leelanau. Established in the spring of 1996 by Traverse City natives Jenny Tutlis and Jon Watts, Meadowlark is reputedly Northern Michigan's first experiment in subscription agriculture, a farm where people pay a monthly fee to get fresh, high-nutrient, organic vegetables.

Community Supported Agriculture, or CSAs as they are called in the plural, is nothing more than small, family-owned farms or farm cooperatives, an historic informal tradition going back thousands of years. This ancient tradition began to slowly go out of fashion about 70 years ago with the advent of corporate industrial agriculture.

A revival of support for small family-owned farms began in the 1960s in Germany, Japan, and Switzerland; people there began to question the safety of chemical fertilizers and pesticides, especially as they learned about the connection between these toxins and cancer. People were also worried about their compromised immune systems as they became aware of the harmful effects of antibiotics and hormones, routinely added to the feed of farm animals, which they were unwittingly consuming in their meat and milk.

Major food scares around the globe—from the salmonella outbreak in U.S. chicken factories in 2010, to the Mad Cow disease in Britain in the 1990s, to the toxic fire retardant accidentally added to cattle feed in Michigan in the 1970s—caused people to become concerned about food safety. The term "Community Supported Agriculture" was coined by

Swiss intellectual Jan Vander Tuin who brought the CSA movement to the United States in 1984.

According to figures from the United States Department of Agriculture, the number of CSAs is approximately 15,000— and increasing all the time—especially around major urban centers such as San Francisco, Atlanta, Chicago, Seattle, New York City, Boston, Washington, D.C., and Miami where the demand for local food is increasing. Leelanau County has seen an increase in CSAs since the 1980s and, counting Meadowlark, there are now more than a dozen.

Over the course of the last seven decades, as I've been watching and thinking about the Leelanau Peninsula, it seems I can feel the beginnings, the glimmerings, of a small microculture coming into existence on this tiny spit of land, arising out of the hopes and dreams, or maybe just the circumstances, of people's lives. I think it'll be slow in taking shape, as these things usually are, but I think I can feel it coming, like a change in the weather across the lake.

A place becomes itself, slowly over time, like a person. Geography has something to do with this. The caliber of people who are attracted to a beautiful place like the Leelanau Peninsula, where they know there are few ways to make a living, has something to do with it. Simply by being there they have chosen nature and beauty over money and power and, as more and more people have done this, it has created a small group of people in a small, out of the way place with a way of seeing the world that is based less in the material than in the spiritual. Some of these people who now live on the Leelanau Peninsula are people who came as children in the summer. Some are Native people whose ancestors were always here. Some are world travelers who feel they have found the last, best place on earth. Some are people like me, people who had grown up on the peninsula, left for parts unknown, and returned to stay. In the aggregate, there are more people trying to make a difference for the better in this one small place than I've encountered almost anywhere. The beauty of the land, which drew them in the first place, seems to inspire them.

Tutlis and Watts started thinking about how to create a community supported farm when they were still in the Peace Corps in Papua, New Guinea in the 1990s. When they came back from their Peace Corps service in Indonesia, they worked on a farm in the southeastern U.S. before returning to Northern Michigan and renting the first Meadowlark farm on Leelanau County's French Road. "We wanted to test the market," Watts says, "test ourselves," adding that they knew it would be extremely hard work with little profit and they wanted to make sure they could do it. They have become solid and successful and Jenny says that, "Maybe when we're in our 70s or 80s, we'll go back to the Peace Corps." She laughs, "But that's in the future."

For several years, in addition to their farm labors, the pair worked outside jobs, waitressing for Jenny and construction for Jon, to make ends meet. Finally, they were able to buy the land where they are now, along with an abandoned farmhouse, a barn, and a few outbuildings. They've made the farmhouse livable, restored the other buildings and added hoop houses—rudimentary greenhouses. They produce all of their own fruits and vegetables but purchase unadulterated milk from Shetler's Dairy and natural meat from the Amish in Manton.

Like any small farm, Watts says, they have a staggering amount of overhead, starting with the mortgage. Labor and equipment are expensive. If one of them should become sick or injured, it would be perilous for the whole venture. They feel lucky every year to have escaped natural disaster and to have stayed ahead of their bills.

The couple belongs to no formal international movement or any stateside farm organizations, and neither do most of the CSAs in the United States. However, the farming enterprise at Meadowlark falls loosely under the umbrella of what's called the Slow Food Movement, a movement started by Carlo Petrini in Italy in 1986 to preserve regional foods and traditional farming practices. Italian people, proud of their cuisine, knew that traditional methods of cooking and farming took more time, but they felt traditional farming produced better food and was less destructive of community. They wanted to counteract "fast food" chains such as McDonalds, Kentucky Fried Chicken, and Burger King (then making inroads into Europe), and keep and support their old-fashioned family farms and farmers.

"Traditional farming retains soil structure, but intensive modern farming practice does not," according to Barbara Kingsolver, writing in the *Washington Post* in 2007. Kingsolver, the daughter of a country doctor who stressed the connection between good food and good health, became famous in 1998 for her best-selling novel, *The Poisonwood Bible*, about cultural conflict in the Belgian Congo. She began to advocate for local, organic agriculture soon after and wrote a book, *Animal, Vegetable, Miracle*, in 2007, a non-fiction account of her own family's year-long efforts to eat only what they or their neighbors had grown. "Since the 1970s," Kingsolver continues in the *Washington Post* article, "while global grain production has tripled, an estimated 30 percent of the world's farmland has become too damaged to use" from the results of the chemical pesticides and fertilizers used in industrial farming.

Tutlis and Watts are part of the global return to traditional, labor-intensive, organic farming. "I think the thing that holds it all together," Tutlis says, sorting through bushels of just-picked, dew-speckled, green kohlrabi, "is that we're growing food that's good for the community, that's creating healthy humans."

Tutlis, dressed in farmer coveralls, sweaty from field work, without any makeup, bears an uncanny resemblance to the iconic American women in Charles Dana Gibson's portraits from the 1890s. Europeans, captivated by the combination of beauty and independence in these women, asked Gibson where he found them, to which he answered, "all over America." Gibson said he found the women in the fields, in the streets, in the drawing rooms. The portraits became associated with what Europeans saw as the freedom and progress exemplified by the New World.

"Feeding people," Tutlis says after a moment's reflection, "feeds me." Meadowlark supplies local restaurants, including Red Ginger in Traverse City, Fig's in Lake Leelanau, as well as grocery stores, such as the Leland Mercantile, Hansen's in Suttons Bay, Anderson's in Glen Arbor, and Oryana in Traverse City. Their fresh cut flowers are sold in beautiful bouquets in all of those places and in Burritt's on Front Street in Traverse City.

Watts, a pleasantly serious man in fisherman's waders, is washing lettuce in big tubs. The sound in the background is the washing machine that is "drying" the lettuce on spin cycle. Approximately 150 households are subscribers, according to Watts, who says that it's about "shared risk, shared reward." Jenny says, "We don't advertise. We can do what we do because we're efficient, but we don't want to grow beyond where we are. We're as big as we can be on 20 acres." The subscribers keep the farm alive through the lean winter months, when the farm provides lettuce from the greenhouses and root vegetables from the root cellars, and then they reap the bounty in the summer when there's not only a seemingly endless abundance of vegetables, but also the world's most delicious strawberries.

Watts says that his and Jenny's retired parents fully support their commitment to the farm, give lots of encouragement, and often come out from nearby Traverse City and help with the work. The people who work for vegetables and the paying subscribers all unabashedly praise the farm and the way it's managed.

One subscribing family, physicians Curtis Cummins and Paula Colombo and their children from Traverse City, have come to pick up their own boxes of vegetables. "It's a ton of work," Cummins says, explaining why he and his wife are subscribers. "We trust them. We see how hard they work. We know the food is excellent. We could never replicate what they're doing."

Colombo supplies other reasons. "It's local. It gives jobs to local people. It cuts down on the damage to the environment caused by unnecessary transportation. We know what we're getting: no toxins, no genetically modified seeds. It's grown in organic soil using organic compost."

The couple's two children play on the swing and roam among the lettuce sorters and kohlrabi pickers. Cummins explains that, as physicians, they are aware that "you can reduce your risk for a lot of illnesses by eating well," adding that the peace of mind in doing so is worth as much as the food.

Beyond the swing, several workers are washing lettuce and, despite the warm day, they say that keeping their hands in cold water requires the extra layers of sweatshirts and even wool hats. For a few moments, the farm's fields and surrounding hills, the people out weeding the rows, the people carrying baskets of vegetables up to the tanks, the people washing the vegetables, and the people packing the boxes, even right down to the clothes and the expressions on their faces, is a panorama wonderfully reminiscent of Brueghel's painting, *The Harvesters,* from the 1500s. Timeless.

Elizabeth Och, a worker on the farm, is a graduate of Northwestern University in Chicago. She'll graduate from the University of Michigan Law School in Ann Arbor and go on to a career as a lawyer in Denver. Och, when asked that summer why she works on the farm, laughs and says, "Eight dollars an hour and lettuce. Great lettuce." Most of the several full-time and part-time workers, as well as the people who work in exchange for vegetables, have college degrees received from universities in places as far away as New Hampshire and California and as close as Kalamazoo.

Och says that growing up in Leelanau County she's worked all kinds of minimum wage jobs. The Leelanau Peninsula is increasingly a destination for the wealthy and famous from all over the globe, several of whom have well-protected, multimillion-dollar, lakeside mansions. Local people recognize that they're lucky to have the chance to work in the wine industry, the hotel and restaurant business, to work as private house cleaners and child care providers and grounds keepers, to facilitate in art galleries, to clerk in clothing boutiques and gift shops, and to have the opportunity to provide all the kinds of services to which sophisticated travelers and wealthy summer residents have become accustomed in their busy and demanding lives.

Och's been at Meadowlark for the last three years and says the work is qualitatively different from most peninsula summer jobs and also has some intangible, nonmonetary rewards. "You're supporting the ideals of healthy food, so you feel good about that. I like the conversations. We talk when we're weeding. We talk when we're filling the boxes. The time just flies by. I know some of the customers personally," so she says that, too, is fun and makes the work meaningful.

It's also, she admits, a nice change from endless hours studying, sitting motionless under the fluorescent lights of the university's law library during the school year. "It's outdoors," Och gestures around at the green fields and blue sky, "I'm moving." She says she loves the rhythms of the work, the cool of the morning when she's dressed in layers, the late afternoon when it's hot and she's in shorts. But most of all it's the camaraderie, the human connections. "By the middle of the summer everyone who works here is like family."

Tutlis and Watts have two, almost-grown children, Ella and Eli. In the summer they do the planting and harvesting along with their parents and the crews of college kids, "learning all the time," Tutlis says. In 2018 Ella will enter a program to get her Masters in social work and Eli will begin his first year in college.

Watts says they are "maxed out" in terms of growing any more food on their 20 acres. He sees them "just doing what we're doing" for a long time to come. The hardest part of the job, Watts says, is crop failure. "One summer it was late blight. It's not a fungus. It's not algae. It's in between. It's a devastating one. It wiped out our tomatoes. It got into our potatoes. I cried." He felt he had let down his subscribers, he said, although none of them abandoned him. "The biggest factor in good food," he says, "is the fertility of the soil. And that's not all about the size [of the vegetables]. It's about taste."

Carol Waters, a weaver, and Alison Heins, a horticulturalist, come to Meadowlark to work in exchange for produce. Both say that the taste of the food is the way they remember it from childhood. Writer Marcel Proust, who made the French cookie, the madeleine, famous for being capable of evoking the entire world of his childhood, was ahead of his time; now neuroscientists say that the memories of tastes and smells stored in the hippocampus are part of who we are, of our sense of identity, without which, we don't exist in any meaningful way. It reflects well on the farm's management that many of the people there, like Waters and Heins, have been contributing their time and energy, in exchange for wages or vegetables or both, for years.

Every Friday, gourmet cook, Nancy Allen, comes to Meadowlark to whip up a lunch for everyone. That's what she does in exchange for her vegetables. In 2014 Allen published a 900-page textbook, *Discovering Global Cuisines*, a decades-long project based on years of traveling and cooking—and, finally, recipe-testing at Meadowlark Farm. Allen, the daughter of immigrants, grew up in a Detroit community made up of immigrants from all over the world. The church cookbooks all across America have cabbage rolls from Romania, lasagna from Italy, Greek salad from Greece, alongside the Betty Crocker and Fannie Farmer standards of meatloaf and macaroni and cheese. But now, Allen says, all those previously foreign foods are foreign no longer. Allen didn't make this happen, she recognized that it had happened, and codified it in a textbook.

"Nancy's created a community around the farm food and the cooking," says Tutlis. "People love to come for Friday meals. We were so lucky to be a part of her process."

Allen is working in a rustic cookhouse behind the lettuce bins and packing tables. Her assistant today is Maureen Suelzer, a wonderful singer, a woman who survived the bombing of London when she was a small child, a time she recalls now with some amazement after having lived in America for years, as she remembers her taciturn fellow Londoners behaving in typically British fashion: going about their business, having tea, and taking the tram as if everything was normal. No drama.

"I'm a convert," Suelzer says in her lilting British accent, while rinsing potatoes. "We went through a phase in society where people were doing the box mix—quick and easy. In the old days I never made a casserole that didn't have Campbell's soup in it." But Suelzer goes on to say that she began to develop allergies and migraines, "Now I do everything from scratch. Everything fresh. Everything organic. No white sugar. No health problems."

"In Finland they call it [white sugar] the white death," Allen comments, adding that diabetes, arthritis and heart problems have been attributed to consuming large quantities of bleached white flour and white sugar and other overly processed foods containing unnecessary additives and preservatives. "My parents came from Eastern Europe. We always had a big garden [down in the Detroit area]." She gestures around at all the tables and counters heaped with fresh vegetables, "This is normal for me. This is the way I grew up."

Allen says the nutrient value of the food, which is in turn derived directly from the quality of the soil, creates the taste. "I don't think people are stupid," Allen says, pausing with her knife over her parsley. "I think if you give someone an organic carrot and a chemical carrot, they'll prefer the organic one hundred percent of the time. It tastes better."

The people are starting to come in from the fields. They're washing their hands outside at the spigot and taking off their rubber jumpers. They're starting or continuing conversations with each other. Potato soup is on the menu today. And they're hungry.

North Manitou Island

North Manitou is the island I saw out our front window when I was growing up in the 1950s above Sleeping Bear Bay. It was out in Lake Michigan, directly opposite our house, about 10 miles north out in the water that's always changing color. *Manitou* is the Ottawa word for holy. I always thought of North Manitou as *that holy island*.

I always thought that I would go there someday. I imagined I would see the mainland from North Manitou. I imagined I would sleep a night on that shore. I'd been to the adjacent South Manitou Island, several times, because my father had a logging operation on South Manitou, and so South Manitou held few mysteries. North Manitou was the great unknown.

When I was a young woman living in a high-rise apartment on Manhattan's Upper West Side, I had a dream about North Manitou. All the water was gone from the lake. I was walking from the Glen Arbor shore across a damp lake bottom strewn with boulders.

Another time I dreamed there were giant bridges connecting the islands to each other and to the mainland. The water was still there. The dream of bridges connecting everything was probably my way of trying to make Manhattan and the Manitou Islands more similar.

Sometimes in the winter when I was a kid, we could see the ice out in Lake Michigan. On some occasions it froze all the way to the islands. I wanted to walk to the islands, but knew the lake sometimes only appeared to be frozen, and I might be walking on a thick and solid piece of ice, far from the shore, only to discover the ice was moving.

One spring day I looked through the telescope on our dining room table and saw deer on the North Manitou shore, eating something. Later I learned that the deer were eating the shad on the beach. Deer don't ordinarily eat fish, but that year there were so many deer that they were willing to eat anything to stay alive.

Another time, late at night, I awoke for some reason and went into the living room. There, out over the lake, the sky was filled with strange lights rising from the horizon: green, blue, pink. I would not learn for some long time that those were the northern lights, the aurora borealis.

There is some debate about when the first Native people began to visit the area around the Manitou Islands. It might have been as long as 35,000 years ago, but if it was, their campsites and artifacts would be under water now. There are artifacts on North Manitou from 6,000 years ago. This was documented in 1966 by Charles Cleland, curator of anthropology at Michigan State University and later, in 1984, confirmed by William Lovis in an Archeological Survey for the National Park Service.

Andrew Blackbird, the last chief of Harbor Springs wrote about his childhood on the shores of Lake Michigan in the early 1800s, when they used to spend summers in the north and winters down near Chicago, moving the whole tribe, using large birchbark cargo canoes to make the trip. Blackbird writes, "These canoes were very light, out of white birch bark, and with a fair wind they could skip very lightly over the waters, going very fast, and could stand quite a heavy sea. In one day, they could sail quite a long distance along the coast of Lake Michigan." My youngest daughter's grandmother, Mary Elizabeth Pyant Johnson, born in 1887, a granddaughter of Andrew Blackbird, grew up in Harbor Springs where she lived as a child in what is now the Andrew Blackbird Museum, a tiny house near the water, and she

could remember as a small child those fall and spring migra-
tions, the excitement of getting ready for the trip.

Blackbird described the whole coast as "perfumed with
the smell of ripe fruit." He thought his people inhabited a perfect place, with plenty of fish and game and maple sugar.
They could, and did, go everywhere around the Great Lakes.
Anywhere their canoe could go, they could go, too. The coast
was theirs. The woods were theirs. They were free and life
was beautiful. "When night overtook them," he writes, "they
would land and make wigwams with light poles of cedar
which they always carried in their canoes. These wigwams
were covered with mats made for that purpose out of prepared marsh reeds sewn together, which made good shelter
from rain and wind, and were warm after making fires inside
them."

The tribes of the Great Lakes were water travelers. The
lakes and rivers were their highways and they knew them
well. They had expertise with canoes and with navigation.
When the first European explorers came to the area, the Native people were indispensable because of their knowledge of
the weather and the water. The canoes generally travelled
the shore, but if they struck out across open water, they
planned for it, and tried to go when the weather was favor-
able.

One of the first French explorers to see the Great Lakes
was Samuel de Champlain in 1603 travelling with a free
black translator, Mathieu da Costa, who knew several Algonquin languages. One can only try to imagine where da Costa
came from or how he learned all those languages. Another
French explorer, Jean Nicolet, crossed Lake Michigan in
1634, looking for China, so convinced he would find it that he
donned the silk robes of a Chinese mandarin to go ashore in
Wisconsin. Louis Jolliet, born on an island in the St.
Lawrence in 1645 and raised among Native people, traveled

with the Jesuit priest, Jacques Marquette, to show him the source of the Mississippi.

Jesuit explorer, Pierre Charlevoix, came along the northwest coast of Michigan in 1721. Charlevoix, from a family of minor nobility in Saint-Quentin, a town in the north of France near Belgium, about 170 miles from the English Channel, was sent to Canada first sometime between 1705 and 1709 as part of his Jesuitical training. He returned to teach in France where, to put things in historical context, one of his students was the philosopher, Voltaire (an early advocate of civil liberties who would be imprisoned and exiled for his beliefs). Charlevoix was sent again to North America in 1720 with the express purpose, according to his journals, of finding a passage to the Pacific, "but still give the impression of being no more than a traveler or missionary."

To imagine Charlevoix's journey along the coast, first picture his mode of travel: the birchbark canoe. These canoes, described in 1812 by a United States Senator from New York, Gouverneur (his first name, not a title) Morris, were marvels of ingenuity. In an address before the New York Historical Society, Morris said, "Its slender and elegant form, its rapid movement, its capacity to bear burdens, and to resist the rage of billows and torrents, excited no small degree of admiration for the skill by which it was constructed."

The birchbark canoe was also admired by Henry Schoolcraft, an explorer for the United States Department of War, who came through in 1822 by canoe with Native guides. Schoolcraft wrote, "These [canoes] are fabricated with an astonishing degree of lightness, strength, and elegance. Those of the largest size are 35 feet in length and six feet in width, at the widest part, tapering gradually toward the bow and stern. They are constructed of the bark of the white birch, which is peeled from the tree in large sheets, and bent over a slender frame of cedar ribs ... around these the bark is sewed, by the slender and flexible roots of the young spruce, so the

gunwales resemble the rim of a [Native] basket ... The join-
ings are rendered water-tight by a coat of pine pitch." These
canoes could carry up to four tons, were equally well-suited
to lakes and large rivers, and were light enough for every
portage. All materials for repairs were carried in the canoes,
including a small pan in which to heat pine pitch.

The Native canoers had vital knowledge of the lakes, the
currents, and the vagaries of the weather. Managing canoes,
or any seaworthy vessel, on the Great Lakes was not a job for
novices or weekend hobbyists. Melville wrote about this in
Moby Dick and how sailors, like one named Steelkilt, knew
the storms on the Great Lakes could be more ferocious than
on the ocean. The reason for this, as it was explained to me,
is that on the Great Lakes, being smaller than the oceans,
the wind can whip up huge waves in a short time, and sailors
don't have a chance to batten down the hatches and get to
shore.

Native guides doubled as hunters and fishermen. Fish
could be speared and game could be shot with guns or bows,
but you had to be seriously expert to do it while making good
time up and down the Great Lakes. There are photos, before
the locks were built, of Native fishermen standing in canoes
in the St. Mary's Rapids at Sault Ste. Marie, with spears
poised. It boggles the mind as to how anyone, without capsiz-
ing, could stand in a moving canoe, and at the same time, be
balanced enough, and move slightly enough and deftly
enough, to spear a moving fish in the rapids. When the Native
guides stopped and pitched camp for the night, they needed
to find animals and shoot them, and do so quickly, in time for
supper.

Another thing Native guides did at each campsite, according to Schoolcraft, is leave a message for others who might
be coming along the same way. He writes: "On quitting our
encampment this morning, the guides left a memorial of our
journey inscribed upon bark, for the information of such of

their tribe as should happen to fall upon our track. This we find to be a common custom among them. It is done by tracing, either with paint or with their knives upon birch bark, a number of figures and hieroglyphics." The message was then put on a pole and the pole pointed in the direction of travel. "The entire party," Schoolcraft writes, "was represented in a manner that was perfectly intelligible." The Native guides also made maps, in the same manner, as to where they had been and where they were going. Before computers and Google Translate, the Native peoples of North America, because they travelled all over the continent, had a symbolic, written, universal language of graphic symbols that transcended dialect or tribal language; they had hand sign language that did the same thing.

By the time the French nobleman Alexis de Tocqueville came to Michigan in 1831, having been told by people in New England when he'd first arrived several months earlier that this was where he could see real wilderness and real Native people, he had trouble finding either. "Not only have these tribes receded, but they are destroyed; and as they give way or perish, an immense and increasing people fill their place," he wrote in *Democracy in America*, "There is no instance upon record of so prodigious a growth or so rapid a destruction."

In 1843 writer Margaret Fuller, New England abolitionist and friend of Ralph Waldo Emerson, was one of the first tourists to visit Michigan. James Fennimore Cooper, author of several novels with wilderness settings and characters, also visited Michigan during this time. Once the Erie and Welland Canals were dug and boats could get around Niagara Falls, the rest was easy. The Great Lakes were a good highway and Michigan's shores and islands were benign and accessible, park-like because the canopy of the big trees prevented underbrush. The French explorer and founder of Fort Ponchartrain at Detroit in 1701, Antoine de la Mothe Cadillac, described Michigan as "so temperate, so fertile and so beautiful that it may justly be called the earthly Paradise of North America."

At one point, stopping to get out of the rain, in her travel by steamboat up Lake Michigan to Mackinac Island, Fuller found a small group of Native families on the shore. "We reached them just as the rain began to fall in torrents, and we had to take refuge in their lodges," she writes. "We crowded the occupants much, among whom were several sick, on the damp ground. But they showed all the gentle courtesy which marks them toward the stranger, who stands in any need."

Margaret Fuller's boat stopped to refuel at the offshore islands. "In the afternoon we went ashore at the Manitou Islands, where the boat stops to wood," she writes, "on this most beautiful beach of smooth white pebbles, interspersed with agates and cornelians."

On July 31, 1846, William Cullen Bryant, editor of the *New York Evening Post*, came ashore on North Manitou. "About an hour before sunset, stopped to take in wood at the upper Maneto Island where we landed, and strolled into the forest. Part of the island is high, but this, where we were on shore, consisted of hillocks. They were covered with a growth of enormous trees which must have stood for centuries."

Michigan islands, like North Manitou and South Manitou, were some of the first places immigrants landed. Early Leelanau pioneer families like the Schaubs and the Dechows landed on the islands and then later came to the mainland. Some immigrants stayed permanently out on the water; there were ten applications for homesteads on North Manitou. On the islands, at least initially, there was money to be made cutting wood for the steamers, a good way to supplement the subsistence farming.

Some Native people in the Leland area earned money showing immigrants to the best plots of land. One Ottawa

man called Big Joe John, according to Brad Houdek, helped
his Houdek forebears find an excellent homestead, one with
an artesian well and fertile soil. Theresa Schaub said some
of her German ancestors from Alsace-Lorraine lived for a year
on South Manitou before coming to Leland. They were looking for high hills near water with good air drainage, for vineyards. They were shown to their place near the Lake
Leelanau Narrows by an Ottawa man who brought them by
canoe. Ms. Schaub said her family had suffered excessive conscription during the Napoleonic Wars, and came from Europe
to escape a repeat of that. Paul Dechow, head of a department
at Texas A & M and a member of a family of early immigrants
to Leelanau County, chatting outside the bookstore in Leland
in the summer of 2016, said, "There were no opportunities in
Europe." He said that the people who worked for the noblemen were not able to earn enough to own land or become educated. Ordinary people couldn't legally hunt or fish. The
laws benefited the gentry. Wave after wave of immigrants
came seeking a better life for their children, and the freedom
they had heard was available in America. Chicago, which had
been wilderness in 1800, would have a million-and-a half people by 1898, the fastest growing city in the history of the
world.

North Manitou, with 15,000 square acres, is the second
largest Lake Michigan island after Beaver Island. In its heyday in the 1880s there were 50 families and, according to government records, 269 people, many of whom were day
laborers who worked in the timber and fishing industries.
Some of the names of the first families on North Manitou can
be found in today's Leelanau phone book. The Stormers, a
German family who had a sawmill on North Manitou in the
1860s, moved to Empire eventually, as did the McClarys, the
Alysworths and the Fredericksons. Other islanders, people in
the Deegan, Dexter, and Dalton families, came over and settled in the Leland area. The Nels and Sophia Carlson family

came in 1880 from a Swedish fishing village to North Manitou. The Carlsons thrived on North Manitou but after a particularly hard winter in 1903, crossed on the ice, with their twelve children and belongings to Leland, a crossing that took eight hours, and an unimaginable amount of fortitude.

Della Paetschow, from a Danish fishing family on North Manitou, married Tracy Grosvenor, the son of a sawyer at the island's mill. Tracy would eventually take over his wife's family's mail-run and boat service. Tracy Grosvenor piloted the ferry between the island and the mainland from 1917 to 1952. At some point the Grosvenors built a home in Leland, but they kept their first home on North Manitou until the 1960s. Great-grandchildren of Tracy Grosvenor are still operating the ferry between Leland and the islands. When the timber was gone and there began to be more opportunities on the mainland than on the island, many families left. The Maleski family, the last family to leave North Manitou, came over to Leland in 1940.

In the mid-1920s, at the end of the Gilded Age and just prior to the Great Depression, a private men's club, the Manitou Island Association, was established on North Manitou. They brought deer over in 1926 or 1927 to start a herd. In the late 1930s the management of the club was taken over by William Robert Angell, president of Continental Motors in Detroit. During the next few decades the club flourished and many famous people came to the island, including the entertainer and television star, Arthur Godfrey. Every November, men would fly in from all over the country for the annual deer hunt.

Ruth Hadra and her husband Jack Hadra, about six months after the United States entered the Second World War, decided on the spur of the moment to become the island managers of the club. "It was late in the day," Ruth Hadra writes about her first visit to the island in the summer of

1942, "Tracy Grosvenor, Captain of the Manitou, started the engine and eased away from the dock and into the eddy below the dam. Using the current, he made a complete circle and steered through the narrow passage lined on either side by a fleet of fishing tugs. Tracy skillfully maneuvered the Manitou, gliding within inches of the other boats and within minutes cleared the Leland Harbor and set our course for North Manitou Island. As the only passenger on board, I was grateful for Tracy's good humor and conversation during this first trip."

Ruth, a young woman who had lived in New York City where her husband entertained business associates and friends, had been accustomed to a sophisticated and urbane existence: museums, concerts, art galleries, plays, movie theaters, dining out in French restaurants, Bloomingdales, Swiss chocolates, Chinese laundries, the New York City Public Library with the stone lions on Fifth Avenue at 42nd Street, Jewish delicatessens, bookstores everywhere, and Sunday walks in Central Park.

Jack Hadra's decision to accept Angell's offer to work for the Manitou Island Association was made over a July weekend in Detroit, a scant few days before Ruth got on the ferry in Leland to go and prepare their island lodgings. She and her husband would go on to manage the Manitou Island Club during the economic boom in the years after WWII. Ruth would fall in love with North Manitou, but she had no inkling of that on the day she arrived in Leland, a few days ahead of her husband, and got on the ferry in a tailored suit, high-heeled pumps and sheer stockings, realizing instantly that one of the first things she would need to do was order island-appropriate clothes.

The next year, when Ruth was pregnant with her first child, it was Tracy Grosvenor who managed to come through fog and ice to take her to the mainland. Grosvenor used a special boat in the winter. Ruth writes that she and her husband shouted to let Tracy know where they were. "Tracy was without benefit of two-way radio, depth finders or radar, but armed with unerring instinct, years of experience and more than one man's share of courage, he made his way through." Ruth met the boat at the edge of the ice sheet off the island and negotiated a slippery and precarious climb into the boat. Once they reached the mainland, five-and-a-half hours behind schedule, Tracy Grosvenor "plowed back and forth through the ice . . . and kept the boat in motion . . . even though we were far off course. Everyone understood that if Tracy could not make his way through the ice, no one could get through to help us."

No one goes to an island without a boat and, starting in the early 1900s, transportation to and from North Manitou has been provided by someone in the Grosvenor family. First it was Tracy Grosvenor, then his son, George, then George's son Mike, and now Mike's children and grandchildren. Knowing intuitively how to pilot a boat, "is something that comes up through the bottoms of your feet from the boat," Mike Grosvenor is quoted as saying in Laurie Kay Sommers' book, *Fishtown: Leland, Michigan's Historic Fishery.*

Archie Miller, an Ottawa man who grew up in Peshawbestown and worked in his later years for the Manitou Island Association on North Manitou, told a story of a trip from the island with George Grosvenor, Tracy's son, as pilot. Archie was a good story teller. It was November and they crossed in a storm that included high seas, fierce winds, snow, and rain. When they finally made it to shore, Archie said it took two hours of swapping stories about other close calls, around a woodstove, before they thawed out and regained their composure.

Many years later, after Archie had gone to his final resting place, George Grosvenor died at the age of 86 in 2008, having undoubtedly survived many a harrowing journey across the water. George was celebrated by everyone who ever rode the ferry or watched him bring in the boat. Like Tracy Grosvenor, his father, George was courageous and careful. Ann Weber, writing in an online remembrance blog, wrote, "My fondest memory of the Captain is one day when a sudden severe storm blew in over the lake and we all stood in awe watching him bring the passengers from the Manitous, slipping by a sailboat stuck in the harbor entrance, in 90-mile-an-hour winds, the waves so high, you could not see the boat in between the waves. He made it in, as everyone said, "'Only George could have done that!'"

North Manitou is now part of the federally owned and managed Sleeping Bear Dunes National Lakeshore. This national park includes both North and South Manitou Islands and about 55,000 acres on the mainland shore stretching approximately from Frankfort in the south to Leland in the north.

One day when the weather was very fine, I took the ferry over to North Manitou. Knowing I would be spending the night, I took an old Army sleeping bag, a plastic tarp in case of rain, some cheese and crackers, some cucumbers and a little salt, some apricots, and some water in a Mason jar. I wanted to travel light. But just in case the weather turned, I took some mittens, some extra socks, a scarf and hat, and a disposable rain poncho. I took a book of Jim Harrison's poetry because he'd recently died and I wanted to read his writing again.

The people on the boat are city people, all kitted-out with fancy camping gear. One gentleman on the boat is dressed like a young Ernest Hemingway, right down to the brown leather, lace-up, high-top boots with brass hooks at the top, boots that looked like they must have cost a thousand dollars, and the 1920s Gatsby-style haircut, and a newsboy flat hat.

He's wearing pressed, cotton, khaki shorts and shirt—not the tweed knickers and tweed jacket with leather elbow patches; too hot for that; but he has everything else, even the way he's standing with his arm on the rail, very still, and looking into what writers call "the middle distance," almost as if he expects someone to take his picture. Did he study early photos and copy them? I'm wearing a kind of smock over baggy cotton pants, old clothes that are probably stained (I never checked), and instead of hiking boots, well-worn canvas sandals I'd had since the Peace Corps in Thailand. A man near me says, "You aren't from here, are you?"

I smile. I know what he's thinking. "I'm from exactly here," I say, and point across the water toward the dunes. "I grew up *there*." Then I say, "But I've never been to North Manitou."

At the dock I learn I cannot bring a bag on casters because of the risk of bringing in invasive plants. Fortunately, the ferry has already left, otherwise I think the rangers would have liked to put me back on the boat. There are two rangers, one old, fit, polite, and calm; and one bulky, middle-aged, less fit, less polite, and visibly beside himself that I am not like the other campers. I don't have a water bottle on a hook at my waist. Also, I'm not as young as the other campers and I limp. The older ranger figures it out. He picks up my bag— too heavy for me, but not for him—so it doesn't roll on the ground and bring in spotted knapweed or garlic mustard. He decides, without consulting me or his befuddled and twitching fellow ranger, that the best place for me will be the empty shoreside boathouse. This ancient structure is open at both ends. The big, sliding doors are open on the shore side and the little door on the land side is ajar; not their usual set up for campers but reasonable under the circumstances. The boathouse appears to have a minimal number of spiders and wasps, perhaps because of the swallows in the eves. There's a through-breeze and a view of the lake.

Once on the island, after all the other passengers have faded into the woods, I can hear no sound but the rhythmic slapping of the water on the shore and the slight hum of a good east wind. There are some gulls calling occasionally. The mainland's not too far away and I can make out Sugar Loaf south of Leland and the clay bluffs north of Leland. The island itself, although described in the national park literature as "a managed wilderness," is scarcely wilderness at all. There are open meadows around the dock. There are old roads that are easy for walking. The beach is like an ad for the Bahamas in a travel magazine. The clouds over the lake, constantly changing as the day goes on, from cirrus to cirrostratus to cumulonimbus, are endlessly fascinating. The water is milky blue-green near the shore and then a blue like a blue crayon in the Crayola box, and then dark blue with small whitecaps farther out still.

I walk over to Cottage Row, where the men from the Manitou Island Association used to stay. I think about Ruth Hadra. Her first husband, Jack Hadra, died in 1964. She married Ken Rusco in 1966 and together they continued to manage the property for the Manitou Island Association. Ken Rusco died in 1988 and Ruth Hadra Rusco moved to Muskegon, returning to North Manitou as often as she could until her death in 2011. Now her children and grandchildren visit, staying in the family cottage. Ruth Hadra Rusco loved North Manitou Island, something that's clear from the book she wrote, *North Manitou Island: Between Sunrise to Sunset*, available on Amazon. She loved all the seasons. She loved the quiet. She loved the boat that brought her to and from the island. A place may legally belong to a governmental bureaucracy, a corporation, or a private individual, but it belongs most to the people who love it most.

The night, when it comes about ten that evening, is glorious. The stars are so many and so bright I can't pick out the constellations. The stars feel friendly, not just beautiful, but beautiful in a joyful way.

Thinking about Ruth and her almost fifty years on North Manitou, I remember the story, *Island of the Blue Dolphins*, by Scott O'Dell that I used to read to my children, about a Native girl stranded on an island off the coast of California. We were fascinated by the way she made a cloak of feathers to stay warm and found sea urchins to eat. The story was supposedly true, but whether true or not, what is true is that to know the rhythms of a place, day after day, year after year, through times of joy and times of sadness, to know the changing colors of the water, and the way the different kinds of clouds move across the sky, is to find solace in the land and the elements in a way that creates a deep and mysterious bond. The people in the British Isles wrote love songs to islands. "Over the Sea to Skye" is one of the songs, and there are countless others.

Islands are, by definition, finite. The mainland feels, by comparison, infinite. It's not, but it feels that way because it would take you a long time of walking to go in one direction and come back to the spot you'd left. Our existential loneliness is also part of a human being's fascination with islands. Maybe we could survive alone, like the girl in the book, but it would be hard both physically and emotionally and impossible of course, all alone, short of a miracle, to create the next generation. But there's a pull there, too, to be alone, truly alone, at least for a while. We want to be totally self-sufficient, or to imagine that we are, to live closer to the bone. And maybe we actually want to be lonely. My old friend Archie Miller, the man who had worked on North Manitou when he was young, always wanted to go to an island alone. Every fall, without fail, he'd show up talking about it. I think now he wanted to die, and the talk of going off to the island was the metaphor. Or maybe he just wanted to imagine being there, so he could talk himself into staying on the mainland. Like Jim Harrison, Archie'd had some hard times in his life, and imagining his death maybe gave him the emotional wherewithal to go on living.

I didn't understand this at the time, because I was young, but now that I'm old, I think I see where Archie was coming from. I live in an apartment building where people die. It's a senior living place and so it's to be expected. At first, I thought it would make me crazy, but in fact it makes me sane. It's like the line from *The Book of Common Prayer*, the one: *in the midst of life we are in death*. Or, the Latin: *Media vita in morte sumus*. I laugh to myself thinking about the first week I moved into my senior housing complex, when I thought I should get to know some of the people and so I baked an apple pie and took it down to the community room. I offer it to everyone, a gesture of friendship, and sit down casually in the sitting area. Someone mentions that a resident had "passed" and that at the time, sitting with their friend, they saw the silver coil. Everyone nods knowingly. Really? I'm living in a place where people all seem to know about something called the silver coil? There are four people there, besides me. I've never heard of the silver coil, and so I ask. "The silver coil," I'm told by an elderly lady, "is the soul leaving the body. It looks like tinsel." Another person says it looks like "a puff of purple smoke." Still another says it isn't visible, but has a sound, like faint music. Thinking back to that, I fall asleep in the boathouse, with a sky full of stars out over the lake, laughing.

The next day, the sun is bright above the water. "The earth is almost round," Harrison's poem about nature begins, "The seas are curved and hug the earth, both ends are crowned with ice." When you're on North Manitou, you can't help but think like this and also, if you're me, wonder why the almost-round earth's waters don't fall out of the giant lakes and splash out into space.

"September was a time of preparation," Ruth Hadra Rusco writes about autumn on the island. "School was back in session. There was the canning and freezing of fruit and vegetables to last through the winter. The island boat was to begin to haul supplies of fuel oil and deer feed. An island deer hunt was special in those days." A restaurant in New York City took some of the venison. "Late October brought the first snow. Lake Michigan changed color from the deep blue of summer to steel gray. Waves smashing over the dock left layers of ice." Winter, when people lived on North Manitou, was a time of quiet, of snow and peace. Spring break-up of the ice brought the summer visitors back again.

Today the Sleeping Bear Dunes National Lakeshore administers the routines on North Manitou. In November they allow permits to deer hunters who come and cull the herd. And by mid-December the island reverts to its prehistoric self—with a quiet in the short winter days and long winter nights, and the snow blanketing everything—a timeless seasonal stillness that must be the very essence of peacefulness.

Fall

Living on the Narrows

At dawn on the Lake Leelanau Narrows the mist can be so thick sometimes there is no other world. Strange sounds—well, strange to those who don't hear them every day—come from the marshes. There's a bird somewhere in the distance, maybe a dove, with a sound like a kid blowing air over a Coke bottle, a kind of low, breathy, Peruvian flute sound. There are the red-winged blackbirds with their high-pitched trill rending the air, as if they think they won't be heard except at the peak of shrill. They skim low through the cattails and sometimes perch there, too, sideways like a parrot, and swaying slightly; perhaps they like the feeling of swinging.

Nancy Priest has watched and listened to the wildlife, from where she's lived on the Lake Leelanau Narrows, for almost fifty years. "One day I saw a wolf crossing on the ice," she says, still amazed by the memory, glancing reflexively out her picture window as though she might see the wolf again, reliving for a moment the awe she felt at that singular event and the sheer otherness of the wolf. "It was winter. He was crouching low. He was large. His fur was black-brown, rippling in the light. A magnificent creature, very handsome. He disappeared into the hills. I called the sheriff's department. I said, 'I have just seen a wolf.' He said 'I believe you. We've received a few calls.' This was about six years after Don died." Don Priest, her husband of many decades, died in 2011.

"We had two male swans who got in a fight," Mrs. Priest says, looking out at the water, remembering. "They're very territorial. My husband rowed out and broke it up. They would have killed each other. We had a female swan, Regina, she lost her mate. He hit an electrical wire. They had two signets. She mourned up and down the Narrows for years." Swans mate for life. And contrary to their name, mute swans do make a sound, although rarely, a little cough or slight, low quack that's not very audible.

Mrs. Priest, born Nancy Howard, grew up in the woods at the edge of a marsh about a mile west of the village of Lake Leelanau. The village sits in the center of the Leelanau Peninsula, just where the long lake narrows through an extended marshy area. Hidden springs dot the hills. The St. Mary School and the adjacent St. Mary Church are here, the oldest institutions in the village and around which the community revolves. The village's first cemetery, originally a Native cemetery, according to the old-timers, used to be in the yard around the school and church, but had to be moved because the water table was too high and the caskets were being pushed up out of the ground.

To my surprise, Mrs. Priest grew up in the same house I lived in for 36 years, until recently, back near Provemont Pond, adjacent to 80 acres of Township recreational land. We know the land there. We know the surround sound of the frogs in the spring around that old Leelanau homestead, the hammering of the woodpeckers in the distance, the roar of Lake Michigan from the top of almost any hill when the wind is strong; this is music with which we are both familiar. A small creek runs across that yard, coming out of a land too hilly and too marshy to farm. In the winter when the ground is frozen this tiny creek sounds like a Caribbean barrel drum song. Beyond the house itself, other than some logging of hardwoods in the 1880s and again in the 1950s, the place has been almost-wilderness since time immemorial, rarely visited by people other than the long ago Anishinaabe, the original people, who were once everywhere on the peninsula. Sometimes in the spring, morel mushroom hunters will come to this untrammeled forest, but even then, usually only people who have grown up there as children and know where to find the delicious mushrooms.

"My brother, Bob, and his wife, Sharon," Mrs. Priest says, "were back in there, finding morels, about three years ago. They saw two cougar babies on the forest floor. Bob said, 'Don't look up. If we make eye contact with the mother, she *will* attack.'" They moved, as unobtrusively as possible, back to the old logging trail through the woods. That woods, part hilly forest and part spring-fed stream and marsh, would be a safe place for a shy and wild creature like a cougar.

Animals seldom seen on the Leelanau Peninsula in the last 100 years, animals like bears, cougars, wolves, coyotes and bobcats, are now moving into areas where people live because development is pushing them out of their usual habitat. This is happening all over the world, according to *The Guardian* in May 20, 2017 and corroborated by many articles ranging from the *New York Times* to the *Denver Post* over the past 10 years. In some places such wild animals are being sighted even in urban areas and suburbs. A raccoon was found in June 2018 on the 12th floor ledge of a St. Paul, Minnesota skyscraper. Raccoons are really good climbers.

The woods in the spring ring with the singing of songbirds. They come north and build their nests, calling to their mates, a symphony of sound. The cardinal calls, "Teacher, teacher, teacher," and the oriole, "I'll be home for dinner, sweetie," and the robin, "Cheery-up, Cheery-up, Cheery-up," and the wood thrush, with its squeaky-teeter-totter sound, high-and-sweet-and-meek-all-at-the-same-time, but with such reach, "East, oh, with the sweet, the sweet, and to me, sweetest dream." How many of our aboriginal musician-ancestors were first inspired to count beats and find the right note, the exact tone, by listening to the birds in the spring or the high-pitched, tinny sound of a creek in winter? Robins, I learn on Google, have such acute hearing, they actually listen for the worm under the soil, and that's why they tilt their heads, cocking an ear toward breakfast.

"Don tamed a red-tailed hawk," Mrs. Priest says. "It would fly into the maple tree and Don would say, '*Monsieur, Le Hawk* is here for his supper.' He'd take raw chicken out to the porch and the hawk would come. The hawk seemed to sense that we would feed him." Hawks and other raptors have been tamed by people all over the world for millennia, often to catch small game since they are naturally birds of prey. Falconry has traditionally been a sport for noblemen in Europe. In Outer Mongolia eagles are still used to help with hunting.

"The foxes could feed themselves," Mrs. Priest says. "The gray foxes had their babies here and they would play. They would come right up to us. They were not afraid because they were acquainted. Our children were grown. We didn't have cats, dogs, gerbils, all those things you have when you have children. The wild animals and birds were our pets."

Don and Nancy Priest grew up as readers of nature, finding layers within layers of meaning in the sights and sounds of the woods, the changes in weather, the tracks of animals that revealed their unseen movements, the subtle changes in light from dawn to dusk, the way the air smells in winter off the lake, like cucumbers, and the way it smells in late fall, with the slightly winey sweetness of the autumn leaves. Any child who has ever watched a squirrel build a nest high in the trees, carrying leaves and branches, and shaping the lining of the nest by lying in it and turning around, would choose that over TV. The marshlands around Lake Leelanau are not only filled with wildlife of all kinds, but filter the water that goes into the lake, keeping it clean. The marshes are the most remote and untouched part of nature we still have. In winter, when everything freezes, one can visit these wild places, usually on snowshoes or even walking if things are safely frozen.

"Every year in June," Mrs. Priest says, "five to seven big turtles come ashore and dig big holes. And then along comes the skunk and digs out some of the eggs. Then in late July, the baby turtles hatch and your yard in September is full of turtles. Then they go to the water. The deer just come. There are coyotes. We hear them in the hills. We know ancient people lived here. We've found arrowheads." This house on the lake, surrounded by wildlife, is still recent enough, in terms of the history of settlers, that the presence of Native people and their tenure on the land is still in evidence.

"This past year, I've had a hawk. He comes and sits in that tree by the water. That was Don's tree. Then maybe I don't see him for a few days, then he goes away. Then he comes again. There was a connection between Don and the hawk. That was Don's hawk." She pauses and looks out at the lake where nature speaks a special language, of seasons and changing light, and something inexplicable and deeply mysterious, and says, "There's something more to all this than what you can learn in books."

She pauses again. "Don was my prince. He was a loving and generous man. He was fabulous." They met at a dance in the early 1950s, she says, "and we just kept dancing." They were among the lucky ones, with love for each other and love for the beauty of nature all around them. The first frozen grass in the fall, the first red partridge berries in the spring, a world where, in the words of Walt Whitman, "a mouse is miracle enough to stagger sextillions of infidels."

They got married at St. Michael's Church in Suttons Bay in 1953. The 1950s were generally a good time to raise a family. The Great Depression was a thing of the past, the Second World War was over, the economy was booming. It was possible for one person to support the family while the other stayed home and saw to the house and the kids. Blue Cross Blue Shield Health Insurance was provided with Don's job; some kind of health insurance was available to most people and the terrors of economic ruin seemed to be at bay. The community was close and, because families had intermarried over the generations, many of the families in and around the village

were related to each other. Life revolved around the church
and the school. Birthdays, baptisms, funerals and weddings
were celebrated with family and community, as were all the
major holidays. Basketball games kept people entertained in
the winter.

"We used to be able to catch panfish for supper. We'd send
the kids out in a rowboat," Mrs. Priest says. "Bluegill, sun
fish, bass, perch. But then the Michigan Department of Natural Resources planted walleye. Walleye eat the smaller fish.
Walleye are more fun to catch, I suppose, so that's why they
do it."

Her generation was a frugal generation. Their parents
had gone through the Depression and they had grown up
learning how to live with less. They'd acquired their parents'
house-holding skills. Men knew basic carpentry and mechan-
ical repairs and women knew how to cook, clean, and sew.
People canned everything they could from their vegetable
gardens, plus apples, peaches, cherries, raspberries and
strawberries that they bought from farmers, doing the picking themselves to save money. There were wild blackberries
and wild blueberries. Fishing and hunting supplemented the
food from the grocery store. No one spent money on fancy
cars, brand name clothes, or long vacations. The Leelanau
Peninsula was clean and safe. Ordinary people could fish,
swim, ride bikes and enjoy the beautiful green hills and deep
blue waters of Lake Leelanau, and the ever-changing colors
of the water—from dark-blue to pale-turquoise to gimlet-
green—of the surrounding Lake Michigan. Those who've
grown up on the peninsula, even today, know the different
shades of the water and the weather that goes along with
them. It's a good feeling, this feeling of intimate knowledge
of something vast and beautiful.

The house in which Nancy Priest lives, right on Lake Leelanau, is a modern ranch, built when her husband became
sick, when they needed a home on one level with no stairs,

and doorways that could accommodate a wheelchair. Their first house, a hundred feet up the slope and a few hundred feet from St. Mary's Church and School on Lake Leelanau Drive, was sold when they moved closer to the lake. "Before the wealthy people came and bought up all the land, we had the run of the place, when we first moved here in 1963," Mrs. Priest says. "It was a different world 70 years ago—it was a totally different world 80 years ago. We were outside all the time.

"Don always made sure that he took the kids to the beach. We took them sledding up on the hills. Don's father died when he was four months old. His mother didn't have time for him. It must have been very hard for her. It was the Depression. She had to work to feed her family. There were three older brothers, but they were busy with their own lives. What he had was the out-of-doors. He always loved nature. It sustained him. His life was not different from that of other boys. No one had wealth. People here came from Europe with the clothes on their backs. The out-of-doors was what they had."

Nancy Priest's family, the Howards, came from a long line of American pioneers, mainly English, with an admixture of other European nationalities, the exact lineage erased by time. Don's family, the Priests, were German and came in the 1840s, when people were leaving Germany to escape war and unrest and to escape the feudal existence generally. On Don's mother's side, they were French-Canadian, in America for centuries, with one of the great-grandfathers having a Native wife, finally coming down out of Canada to the United States. Nancy has heard stories of sod houses, dirt floors, large families in cramped quarters saying, "Florence Lamie, 12 children. They came from Canada. They went back to Canada. In the winter, they put boards over the windows, to keep out the cold, and lived in the dark." She herself lived in the house near Provemont Pond when there was only wood heat, no electricity and no indoor plumbing. A pump at the kitchen

sink brought water from a hand dug well. "We had a chande-
lier," she says, smiling. "It was beautiful. It took kerosene. It
was seldom actually used. We went to bed when it got dark."

In the early 1900s most of the people in America were
farmers and there were many people, like Nancy and her husband Don, who grew up on small farms. "We didn't have anything," she says, "in those times. So, we had nature. You're
born here. You belong to the soil. There was no TV, all you've
got is nature, which is maybe why I'm the way I am. I would
go out and dig out the pretty little stones in the hills. And
when my Uncle Joe died, I would go out and bury stones, as
we had buried him. Something simple. God, how I loved that
man. He would carry us around. Make ice cream with us."

Nancy and Don Priest grew up when the wide out-of-doors
was their playground and refuge and they shared a reverence
for the creatures of the wild. "We just fell in love with the
wildlife: deer, muskrat, weasels, foxes, coyotes, otters. The otters come up out of the water and play. They run around and
jump over each other, like little kids."

Don, who worked for Michigan Bell Telephone for 36 years
until he retired, a few years after Michigan Bell became a
subsidiary of AT&T in 1984, was known to his customers as
"Pa Bell" for his wealth of knowledge and expertise. Mrs.
Priest was a stay-at-home housewife, raising six children
(three boys and three girls) and teaching Sunday school. "I
was a catechist," she says. I taught catechism, the stories in
the Bible." Through that work she had the opportunity to
travel to the Holy Land and work on archeological sites in Is-
rael, travelling with Catholic church groups in Europe as she
went to and from the Middle East. Stop here, and think for a
minute: a girl who grew up without running water, on a little
homestead in Lake Leelanau, eventually became a world
traveler. That's how fast things have changed.

"I visited the site of ancient Troy, in Turkey, on the shores
of the Mediterranean," she says. "I fell in love with Turkey. A
crippled woman on the street, I touched her and she gave me

a talisman. It was a blessing. There was a current of energy that went between us. No words. We didn't speak each other's languages. I could feel it. She could feel it. I've never gotten over it. One person to another, in a strange place." Many of the European people Nancy met became friends, visiting her home in America. Tragically, several members of a Belgian family to whom she became close, people she had visited in Belgium and who had visited her in Lake Leelanau, people she imagined knowing all her life, died in a one-in-a-million traffic accident in Egypt.

Mrs. Priest returned to the Middle East for several summers. "We found pottery, weapons, hidden jewels. We proved scripture. Who lived there, how they lived. Don paid for my tours. He didn't want to go. He'd travelled in the military. He wanted to stay where he could hunt and fish. My children were here and could help him with whatever he needed. His children adored him. Then when he got sick, I took care of him. We built this house. I thought I'd go back to the Holy Land, but I'm too old now." Nancy Priest is in her 80s, but looks and acts at least two decades younger. She can still shovel snow. "It's very hot there," she says, "over 113 degrees in the shade. So, my time is here now and that's fine. This is what's meant to be." She's written a book about her life, *One Leelanau Girl,* which she hopes her grandchildren might read someday.

Esther and Ralph Cordes live on the Lake Leelanau Narrows, right on the Narrows, almost at the epicenter, in a brick house that belonged to Ted Grant, Esther's father. Ted Grant was from the large Grant family who farmed further south on Lake Leelanau. The Grants came from Scotland in the 1800s; there's a Grant castle there, according to a young relative who has seen it. Esther's mother was a Hahnenberg, Germans farmers in the first generation and now in the second and third generations teachers and nurses, musicians and priests, the extended family numbering in the hundreds.

Esther and Ralph attended the Catholic school together in the village of Lake Leelanau and met and fell in love there. Ralph Cordes hails from a German family in Leland. His family established the Leland Mercantile in the mid-1800s, when it was an all-purpose general store, supplying goods to the islands, North and South Manitou, when those islands had more people than the mainland. Ralph Cordes grew up at the northwesterly end of Lake Leelanau, where the Leland River flows into Lake Michigan.

Esther grew up six miles south of Leland, straight down the lake at the Lake Leelanau Narrows, where they live now. Ralph Cordes became an accountant and they travelled and worked all across the United States before finally returning to Lake Leelanau. Their home faces north. There are many majestic, old trees to the west and east and a long sloping lawn to the water where there's a narrow dock. There's an extensive cattail marsh across the way, off limits to all but the shyest and wildest animals.

One day a bear swam across the Narrows, Mrs. Cordes says, and disappeared into that marsh. Deer have several times been seen swimming across. Muskrat, beaver, otter, fox, and squirrels have from time to time appeared in the yard. In the waterway itself ducks and swans swim happily. They nest in the marsh. A sandhill crane once stood on the end of their dock. A sandhill crane is such an odd-looking bird, with those long legs and the little red topknot.

"We used to fish off the dock," Mrs. Cordes says. "when we were kids. We caught bluegills, sunfish, perch." The world was smaller then, a world within the mist rising from the Narrows.

The marshland opposite the Cordes home, considered one of the most beautiful and complex on the lake, has been preserved by the Leugers family with a donation to the Leelanau Conservancy. In 1937 George and Louise Leugers came from Cincinnati and established what would become a 10-cottage family complex about a mile south of the Narrows, opposite Fountain Point. Wetlands are essential habitat for spawning fish. Waterfowl nest in the safety and privacy of the marsh. The rich wildlife at the Narrows, enriches the lives of the people there.

Esther and Ralph Cordes have not only traveled all across America, but they go frequently to Hong Kong where their son and grandson live. The grandson sometimes visits them in Lake Leelanau. "At first, he was afraid," Mrs. Cordes says, "But then he learned there was no danger [from the wild animals]." Their family has global connections and, in a way, the village of Lake Leelanau does, too. The local grocery store, which belonged to the French-Canadian Plamondon family for three generations, is now owned by a Hindu family from India, famous for the fresh, homemade samosas that come hot from the oven every day at noon. The Postmaster's family originated in Mexico and his assistant has a mother from the Philippines. Investment broker Paul Sutherland, brother to Bob Sutherland who has Cherry Republic, sends his adopted African children to the Lake Leelanau Catholic School. Jeremy Evans, a star student at Glen Lake in the 1980s, who married his male partner in the early 2000s because they wanted to make a public commitment and because they wanted to become foster parents, is now the music and theater teacher at the Leland Public School where he puts on performances that would rival anything on Broadway and he does it with students who would otherwise not know a thing about singing, dancing, and acting out a story. The Leland Public School has several foreign exchange students and offers an International Baccalaureate Degree. The village of Lake Leelanau, once so insular that everyone seemed to be related, is now multicultural. People are from everywhere.

In the 1960s and 70s the Leelanau Peninsula, as did many places in the country, experienced the back-to-the-land movement. It was a time of worry about bombs dropping and water and air becoming polluted. People wanted to escape the confines of the cities, where they felt they'd be trapped in case of war or environmental disaster. In this movement, in these people, was the dawning of ecological awareness. They wanted clean air for themselves and their children because they were afraid of the diseases—asthma and lung cancer foremost among them, but there were also a host of other lethal diseases that they might get from breathing bad air. They wanted to grow their own food because that way they would know where it came from and what was in it. They wanted to have a clean source of water even if they had to haul it from a hand-dug well up a hill on a sled in the middle of winter. These were people with college degrees, many of them, and yet they were willing to work as carpenters and waitresses, school bus drivers and bar tenders, tree trimmers and cleaning ladies, in order to try to create wholesome lives for themselves and their children.

The back-to-the land people—creative problem solvers, environmentalists, risk-takers, social entrepreneurs—taught themselves how to grow vegetables organically, without pesticides or chemical fertilizers. They heated with wood. They learned how to compost, something revolutionary in the 1960s but now done everywhere. Some learned how to hunt and fish. Some became midwives. The home births that were controversial in the 1960s are today so commonplace that hospitals, always competitive, now offer natural birth options. Some back-to-the-land folks home-schooled their children. None of this was happening in isolation, just on the Leelanau Peninsula, but was happening across the country: in Oregon, Washington State, California, Vermont, New Hampshire, North Carolina, Colorado, and a dozen other places, usually rural places, and usually beautiful places. It was hard work, all of it, and some of those back-to-the-land people left for better jobs or a place where they didn't have to haul water up a hill on a sled in the winter. However, many stayed. They had children, children who are now adults with families of their own, some of whom live on the Leelanau Peninsula, almost all of them with electricity, running water, and good educations.

The peninsula always had a few trust fund babies, people who didn't really need to earn a living and dabbled in the arts. Some of those people stayed and became real artists. They became determined, just like Van Gogh, Picasso and Leonardo De Vinci before them, to make good art on their own terms, no matter what people thought. They established art associations. They created new and interesting businesses: artisanal bread, breweries, wineries, rustic furniture, felted wool garments from recycled wool, and an authentic Italian restaurant, exactly like one in Florence.

The beauty of the Leelanau Peninsula brings people. Those who stay year-round often forego wealth to be here. Yes, there are people of wealth here, but their money was made elsewhere. Most of the wealthy are retirees with good pensions and good investment portfolios. Some have inherited wealth. For some their Leelanau Peninsula home is one of several. These people make Leelanau County the second wealthiest in Michigan (after Oakland County). And they have not, so far, dominated the culture. There was a rich man in Glen Arbor who tried to swap his not-so-great-land for national park land so he could put in a big golf course along a river, but local people, and their lawyers, stopped him because the golf course would have destroyed wildlife habitat and the chemicals from the golf course would have ruined the river. There was a billionaire who came to Leland and bought a prime piece of real estate on the lake, tore down all the trees, put up a garish mansion, and then had an equally garish, extremely loud, all-night-long, fireworks display. His blue-blooded, old-money neighbors tried to dissuade him from these tasteless ventures, but with little success. They waited, however, and when their moment came, they did not let him join the country club; perhaps the cruelest cut, at least for him. Yes, it's true, a culture can be wiped out overnight by war, drought, famine or simply a monstrous person, like Hitler or Nero, rising like Grendel from the swamp to terrorize people and stalk the land, coming nightly to devour the most talented and beautiful young people, but so far, at least, it hasn't happened on the Leelanau Peninsula and even if it does, thousands of years of recorded history indicate that it won't last, because bad things like that never do. The struggle for freedom and dignity will never stop, will always come again, as long as people are people. It's who we are, like monarch butterflies flying 3,000 miles at five miles an hour from Michigan to Mexico.

Computers and the Internet in the 1990s changed everything, not just on the Leelanau Peninsula but in the world. People could now telecommute to Chicago, Manhattan, San Francisco, London, Shanghai. Many in the various Leelanau Peninsula groups—back-to-the-landers, summer people, Native people, trust funders, telecommuters—had children and some of those children married each other. A measure of how times have changed is that it's now a greater mark of distinction to say you are married to someone local, hopefully someone whose family homesteaded on the Peninsula in the 1850s, than to say that your father was a General Motors executive in Detroit and that you grew up in Bloomfield Hills. Fishermen with mostly only high school educations have married women with advanced university degrees. Hippies have married farmers. The son of an African American migrant family on the Peninsula became a great teacher and married his high school sweetheart, the lovely, fair-skinned daughter of a local businessman and they have two, wonderful sons. The tall, beautiful, blonde, college-educated daughter of the former head of the county road commission, a woman with a great sense of humor, like her grandfather who had only a fourth-grade education, married a black man from a southern state and he was welcomed up north by her family. A man who owned a funeral home brought home a wife from Japan. A restaurant owner fell in love with and married someone from Mexico. A Thai family opened a restaurant in Suttons Bay. Catholics have married Protestants. Germans have married Poles. Republicans have married Democrats. And Native Americans have married everybody. We are the melting pot— and it's working.

In a fragment of Abraham Lincoln's writing about the great American experiment, which I just came across in Jill Lepore's new book, *These Truths: A History of the United States*, Lincoln wrote, "They said some men are too ignorant, and vicious, to share in government. Possibly so, said we; and by your system, you would always keep them ignorant, and vicious. We proposed to give all a chance; and we expected the weak to grow stronger, the ignorant wiser; and all better, and happier together. We made the experiment, and the fruit is before us." I'm from this experimental place. I'm from America, specifically the Leelanau Peninsula. Even now that I've moved to a senior residential community in nearby Traverse City, I'm still from the place that has made me, that has informed my sense of the world, that taught me who I am, who I think I am, that has given me my ideas and my core self. I'm from the Sleeping Bear Dunes and the wind from the west that created them. Most days, anyway, the wind is from the west, coming across the vast expanse of Lake Michigan. I'm from the place where we can smell the rain or snow on the wind before it reaches us. We all need to be from somewhere, and I'm from the Leelanau Peninsula, even if I'm no longer there. Luckily the natural world in Leelanau County, to which those of us who call it home are emotionally connected, has to a fair extent, remained unchanged.

Owls hunt here on the Narrows, with their binocular eyes. Owls have big legs and claws. Owls have incredible hearing, allowing them to "locate their prey in total darkness," according to Robert Paxton, in the *New York Review of Books* in May 2017, who writes, "In some owls, one ear is larger than the other and located higher on the head, so they can locate rustling mice by aural triangulation."

Swans swim up and down the Narrows and, in the spring, swim trailed by the baby swans. "The snapping turtles get the baby swans," Mrs. Cordes says, "They come under the water and grab their legs." Snapping turtles are cute when they're babies, like all baby creatures, but dinosaur-like when they are older with their hoary heads and armor plating. They can live to be over 100 years old. Their necks are deceptively long, capable of reaching all the way back to their hind legs.

"We don't put out bird feeders," Mrs. Cordes says, "because of the bears." They have many hummingbirds. They can see them in their flower garden. A ruby-throated hummingbird "can burn up to a third of its tiny body weight crossing the Gulf of Mexico," according to a *National Geographic* article on "Why Birds Matter," in January 2018. Poet Emily Dickinson said, "Hope is that thing with feathers," which is all birds; which is why we love them. Hope in the air.

Across the way a red-winged blackbird perches on a cattail, sideways, the way they do, and then literally floats down into the marsh, like a soap bubble, or a dandelion fluff. Birds have air pockets in their bones. They're light, and strong, built for flight.

"In the summer," Mrs. Cordes says, "the water lilies, white and yellow, are so beautiful, and the white ones are so fragrant, almost like a gardenia." We're sitting, facing east, the place of the morning's gathering light. Robins, orioles, bluebirds, warblers, canaries and indigo buntings, flit through their yard. The Cordeses will hear the oriole's high-pitched call and then see a flash of orange. "This is our entertainment," Mrs. Cordes says. "We sit out here and feel at peace."

Kehl Lake

Geologic time is palpable at Kehl Lake. This small lake in the center of a wide, low, rangy marsh—like a sheet cake that hasn't cooked in the middle—is a reminder of the days when the waters of Lake Nipissing covered the land after the last glacier receded about 4,500 years ago.

Kehl Lake is an embayment. This means that it was a bay of Lake Michigan for hundreds of years before finally becoming an inland lake connected to the big lake by a small stream. A few more centuries and the stream itself began to blend into the wetlands. But you can still see the outlines of the stream and feel that slow, almost eerie, incremental but inevitable, passage of time and changes to the land.

Lake Leelanau and Glen Lake are also inland lakes that were once bays of Lake Michigan. Those two lakes still have viable connecting waterways. Lake Leelanau has the Leland River emptying into the Leland Harbor and Lake Michigan. Glen Lake has the Crystal River flowing into Sleeping Bear Bay and Lake Michigan. Everywhere you look there's evidence of a previous geological period. It's part of the personality of the peninsula.

Kehl Lake is small compared to Glen Lake and Lake Leelanau, but is similar in formation. And like those other bays of Lake Michigan which, over time, became inland lakes, it would have been a natural campsite for Native people: an easy stop on their lake route, first with a canoe right up the stream and when the stream became narrower and, in the case of Kehl Lake, disappeared, then with a portage.

Driving up to Kehl Lake one day, I stop at 9 Bean Rows on East Duck Lake Road (M-204). This is a little bakery with butter croissants that are like the ones I used to get at a French pastry shop on the Upper East Side in New York City. Jen and Nic Welty have been doing this bakery and Community Shared Agriculture for a few years. They also do an upscale restaurant in Suttons Bay where some friends took me for an amazing meal of an octopus appetizer, lamb chops, and a Manhattan, all firsts for me. I told Jen later that I thought the food was delicious, even though I'd never eaten anything like it before, but I thought the Manhattan tasted like mouthwash, like Scope. She nods, "A grown-up drink." I loved that evening. I loved the generosity of my friends taking me to dinner at a fancy restaurant and encouraging me to order new foods. I loved their duet-telling of the story of how they fell in love, with first her telling how she was on the verge of tears because skiing was new to her. And then he tells how he was skiing up the mountain backwards. And then she tells of how he was telling her stories to keep her in forward motion. "And I could see he was a really nice guy," she says. And he says, "And I could ski uphill backwards."

Truth: I'm especially fond of 9 Bean Rows because I know the Yeats' poem, "The Lake Isle of Innisfree" for which it is named: "I will arise and go now and go to Innisfree . . . nine bean-rows will I have there, and a hive for the honey-bee." And that poem, now also a song, "Innisfree" is why Jen and Nic came to the Leelanau Peninsula. They were romantics, like Yeats, and thought they could do it, and they did. They were also hardworking and knew how to cook. And so, with a dream, good culinary skills, good gardening aptitude, and hard work, they succeeded.

The Ottawa name for Kehl Lake was Midassagan, meaning "legging" an article of clothing made of deerskin. The name may have been given to the lake because it was here that the Native women could soak the deerskins for the leggings. The shape of the lake is also that of a legging. On the shore is a quite large, old pine marker tree, the kind of tree Native people bent to mark a spot, a tree now falling into decay but still visibly a marker tree. Oral history indicates that the site was used as recently as the 1930s for Native gatherings.

Ottawa people typically went south in the fall and then back north again in the spring, travelling by canoe along the coast, making several stops along the way. Various sites offered fishing opportunities or plant-gathering opportunities and presumably a site like Kehl Lake would have offered both. The sheer number of indigenous plants used for medicine, crafts, or charms, suggests that some of the plants may have been deliberately brought to Kehl Lake and nurtured by prehistoric botanists. Today, fishermen can catch small-mouth bass and northern pike in the lake.

To picture how to get to Kehl Lake, first imagine the Leelanau Peninsula, an isosceles triangle with a scribbly shore, about 30 miles wide at its base and about 40 miles up each side to the tip. Go a few miles beyond Northport, the last village on the peninsula, and you will find Kehl Lake, a short distance northwest of Woolsey Airport. During the Algonquin epoch, when Lake Michigan was higher, much of the northern one-third of the peninsula was a sandbar under water. Kehl Lake would have been a depression in the sandbar.

Unlike those other bays of Lake Michigan that became inland lakes, Kehl Lake is observable in its entirety because it has escaped development. Because of the water table always having been so high at this lake, even now, the trees were relatively small and undesirable when the peninsula was first timbered off in the 1870s; and so, for that reason, it was left alone.

Going to Northport along M-22, the road that follows the coast, I stop just south of Omena at Carolyn Faught's U-Pick flower garden. It is late in the season, but amazingly there are still dahlias blooming. They have survived a mild frost or two. There are some that are almost-white, translucent, with lavender centers. They will be like Van Gogh's *The Starry Night* in my tiny apartment kitchen as they open. I put them in a jar of water in my car. Fresh flowers and a candle can make any place in the world not only homey but beautiful.

Kehl Lake is about four miles north of the village of Northport. If you visit in the fall and spring, you'll have a front row seat from which to observe birds migrating in the north-south flyway. In 1982 the Michigan Nature Conservancy compiled a species list of more than 200 birds here, including the hermit thrush and the common loon. The hermit thrush, often called the American nightingale, is, true to its name, reclusive. It is brown, rather nondescript, about the size of a robin, but if you are quiet in the woods, you may be fortunate enough to hear those liquid, dulcet tones. The loon, an ancient species dating back 20 million years, has a haunting call that in the mists of early morning, out over the water, seems a cry from another world. Their sleek, black-and-white checked backs and striped bands at the neck make them look like nattily dressed Wall Street bankers. The *Wilson Journal of Ornithology* reports that loons can dive up to 200 feet: their heart rate slows so they can conserve oxygen.

The three-foot-high, breath-takingly gorgeous groupings of the delicate cardinal flowers, like a red haze in the distance, are here. Cardinal flowers used to grow in the wet ditches along the Leelanau back roads because they like their feet in water but their heads in sunlight, but are now rarely seen there because they are sensitive to the exhaust from cars and the spraying with herbicides. The glorious red cardinal flowers can still be found in abundance at Kehl Lake, from sometime in July, depending on the kind of weather, through August and even into September or early October. Other plants now rarely seen, such as the pink lady's slipper and bloodroot, bloom here in the spring. Mushroom hunter Curt

Cluckey of Glen Arbor says the edible boletus mushrooms grow here under the trees. The tracks of bear and bobcat have been seen here. In November 2016 there was a beaver lodge on the south shore of the lake.

Kehl Lake takes its present name from the first European immigrants who homesteaded here in 1849. John Kehl and his wife Elizabeth (Bosch) Kehl, both the offspring of German immigrants, came from Buffalo, New York. John's father, Albert, had been a bugle boy in Napoleon's Army. Like many European immigrants in the early 1800s, the Kehl family came to America in order to escape conscription in the Napoleonic Wars in which an estimated six million people died, half of them soldiers and about half of them civilians.

Old pear and apple trees from the Kehl homestead can be found at the beginning of the trail out to the lake. The trail is easy walking and not long, maybe a thousand feet. Kayaking is allowed. Dogs are allowed but must be kept on a leash since the loons and some of the other birds have their nests on the ground. The presence of loons at Kehl Lake is a testament to the purity of the water, since loons dive for their prey and can't see to do that in dirty water. Two hundred acres of wetlands, nature's ingenious water-filter system, surround the lake and contribute to the excellent water quality.

Elizabeth Kehl ran the farm with her five sons and two daughters while her husband often left in order to find work, notably in the shipyards of Wisconsin. Northport was the first town on the Leelanau Peninsula, according to Will Thomas, 92 years old when we spoke to each other in 2016 at the museum. Thomas, who would die a year or two later, said he was a Northport descendant of the Kehls on his mother's side. John Kehl was a veteran of the Civil War, one of several soldiers from Northport, and one of the few who survived.

Many Native people from Michigan also fought and died in the Civil War. Payson Wolfe, a sharpshooter in the Civil War with an all-Native company, also from Northport, also

survived. Wolfe was married to Mary Smith, the daughter of
Reverend George Smith, the first missionary to Northport. In
1839 Smith established Waukazooville with a band of Ottawa
from the Kalamazoo area. Waukazooville, on the southern
edge of the current village, is now part of larger Northport.

The Kehls moved from their homestead into the village of
Northport in 1889. Will Thomas told me his grandfather built
several houses for the Kehl family. Many of the descendants
of John and Elizabeth Kehl are married to people who still
live in Northport.

The Kehl Lake Natural Area was being eyed for a golf
course or some other development when, in 1990, a 100-acre
portion was purchased by the Leelanau Conservancy with donations from several hundred local families and businesses.
More acreage was added over the next few years until the current site of 279 acres was established.

One of the best things about the Kehl Lake Natural Area
is that it combines ease of access with the opportunity to see
an abundant variety of rare birds and wild flowers. Like the
vast and storied rooms of the Metropolitan Museum of Art on
Fifth Avenue in Manhattan, you could visit every day for the
rest of your life and see something new every time.

Pierce Stocking, Park Maker

We would get up at 4 a.m., eat breakfast, leave Cadillac, and drive about an hour west, turn at Thompsonville and cut across on an angle, going another hour north-by-northwest. We'd arrive at the Mill Pond at the west end of Little Glen Lake about 6:30 where, almost without fail, I'd wake up and need to "up-chuck"—his phrase—because of the two hours breathing exhaust fumes in the old car. My father would get out, come around, wipe my mouth with his large, blue-and-gray-plaid handkerchief, and we'd get back in and go on. This happened every day for years. He never complained, never commented.

Like a lot of men in that generation, he was not one to overreact. He'd grown up on a pioneer homestead in Hoxeyville, near Cadillac, working on the farm and in the timber industry as his father had. When the Great Depression came along, after he'd been arrested for poaching deer, he joined the Civilian Conservation Corps (CCC). The CCC was the program instituted by President Franklin Roosevelt to get idle and reckless young men off the streets or, in my father's case, out of the woods. The $30 a month he earned cutting trails and planting pines enabled him to help his parents pay their property taxes and keep their farm. All the Stockings were woodsmen. Stocking means a measure of timber ready for harvest; the name was recorded in the Domesday book in 1086, the first census in England.

My father's mother had four sons: Pierce, Deck, Hale, and Rod. Think about those names for a minute and think about her calling them to her aid in a time of danger, names that were both an incantation and a warning, names that were an extension of herself, her domain, and her fierceness. If she'd had four more sons, she could have named them: Ream, Crush, Sleet, and Stab. My father's mother, my grandmother, was a woman who could read, breastfeed, and knit all at the same time. In the backwoods, where people had few books, she had hundreds. She was a genius, everyone said. She could play the flute. Her chickens produced the best eggs and her cows the best cream. She was a compendium of abilities, but more than that, she loved her children, and her grandchildren, with a deathless love.

My father was at first just a lumberman and eventually, as the timbered-off parcels accumulated, a land speculator. He bought up the whole south side of Little Glen Lake in 1948 when there was nothing there but wildflowers.

We spent hours together every day in the woods. When he was supervising the men cutting trees, he would put his black-and-red buffalo-plaid, wool over-shirt on the ground, place me on it and tell me to stay there. I'd wait for the shout, "Timber!" followed by a huge, earth-shaking thud, and then feel myself being lifted up into his arms again. He carried me when there were too many tree-falls for short legs but in places where they weren't cutting, it was clear enough for me to walk.

One day I was holding onto his hand as we were walking through the woods in early spring—before the leaves were on, but it was hot—and I stepped on a nest of baby snakes. Startled, I leapt into his arms. He looked down and, after a minute or two, put me back down again and said, "Nothing happened to you." And then, after another pause, "Nothing happened to *them*." I don't know how old I was, but I've never forgotten the "*them*".

My father and I were alike, and not alike, as parents and children usually are. In addition to his being an adult and my being a child, he was naturally athletic and I was naturally uncoordinated. He had excellent balance, and I didn't. His innate sense of spatial relations was something I didn't inherit. He was a good map maker and map reader; it's something that still challenges me. He had an incredible sense of direction and never got lost in the woods; I would get lost even with a compass. If we crossed on a log over a small stream, he always made it to the other side and, more often than not, I fell in. If there was a mosquito or deer fly within a hundred miles, it found me. They were not interested in him. Children have a higher body temperature, is the reason for this, so I've heard, but it meant that I was often a welter of bites. The bug spray made me sick to my stomach and so we gave up on it. Following his example, I never complained. If we were near where it grew, he would crush the stems of the golden jewelweed and put it on me, as a poultice. What my father and I had that was similar was an ability to observe and remember things in detail. Like him, I was hyperaware of sights, sounds, moods, smells; because we had seen and remembered, we anticipated based on previous knowledge, and seemed to know things in advance that other people didn't. My sisters and my mother saw me as too sensitive, a lot of bother and probably not normal, but he was fine with the way I was, and so was my grandmother, his mother.

His time in the backwoods buying timber from farmers and his time in the courthouse filing quit claim deeds made him aware in the mid-1950s, before anyone else, that federal surveyors were in the Glen Lake area. He saw their stakes. He would've seen their crews and asked what they were doing and, as just another guy in the woods, he would have been told. Quietly, little by little, he began buying up land in the dunes—cheap, worthless land, just sand—even some from the State of Michigan.

In 1962 when Senator Phillip Hart first introduced a bill in Congress for the Sleeping Bear Dunes National Park, my father owned more land in the area than any other individual, an estimated 10,000 acres or more, gambling on a big payout from Uncle Sam. What a good, slow joke on the government bureaucrats. Where else would he find a single buyer for so much real estate? Some of it previously considered worthless?

He'd figured a lot of angles but what he hadn't figured was it taking 20 years from surveyor stakes in the 1950s to Congressional approval of the new national park in 1970, and then another six years for the adjudication of the value of all his sandy and hilly acres. He understood land values, he understood gambling on land values, but he didn't understand dealing with Uncle. If the United States couldn't get his land cheap with their first offer, through eminent domain, they could take it for nothing, if he was unable to pay his property taxes. They had him boxed in. You don't want to do business with the government, as a rule, because they have more financial resources, more lawyers, and will always outlive you. He hadn't figured that out, but of course he would.

Mortgage payments on all that land regularly came due, as mortgage payments always do. As the years rolled inexorably by, he had to try to generate cash flow—beyond cutting trees and selling lake lots—doing things he hadn't done since he was a young man, like being a hunting and fishing guide at his cabin in Kalkaska.

Finally, running out of ways to create ready cash, and with property taxes on all that land due and overdue, he convinced the township to rezone his land in the dunes as recreational land and built a park where the national park was slated to be. He already had the work crews and heavy equipment because of his lumbering. He knew how to make roads in the woods; he'd been doing it for years to get the lumber out. It would be deemed "compatible use" unlike all the other property he owned which he could neither sell nor develop since it was slated to become part of the national park. It wasn't just that the taxes were killing him, it was that he couldn't sell anything to pay them.

He had always, for years, whenever he logged off a piece of land that had a beautiful stream, or a high hill with a view of a lake, set up a picnic table and a refuse barrel. He did this instinctively, naturally. He wanted people to see and enjoy the beauty that he saw and enjoyed. He was on a date with the world. "Hey, look at this. Isn't it amazing? Don't you love it? Aren't you glad to see it?" He already had the logging road; the table and barrel were easy to add. Sometimes people were untidy and left garbage and he would have to clean up after them. Sometimes they were reckless. Once someone used a picnic table to build a fire, apparently not knowing how to get dead branches out of the woods. He was taking the chance that someone might burn down the whole forest, but he took that chance because he wanted people to feel the kind of awe and inspiration and joy that he felt in the presence of amazing natural beauty. The odds were on his side; by and large there were only one or two idiots among all the visitors to his beautiful places in the woods, not a majority of them. So now, after more than five decades of making little remote picnic areas in the backwoods, for which he never charged, he was going to build an entire park and make enough to pay his property taxes.

He put in eight or more miles of roads through the dunes, installed picnic areas and overlooks, created an entranceway with a replica of the Great Lakes surrounded by rose gardens. He did it in six months and then charged $2.00 admission per car. People with taste were offended by his crass materialism.

Meanwhile, his other cash enterprises were not going well. People had changed since he'd first started guiding. By the 1970s, everyone had pretty much grown up in cities and, unlike their fathers and grandfathers, didn't actually know anything about hunting and fishing. My father had trout ponds where he charged to let people fish. A motorcycle gang came to his trout ponds in Kalkaska one day while he was there.

They began to fish, and pretty soon they began to drink, and after a while they began to vandalize. The young man working the fish ponds, the humble and noble Robbie Dunham, quietly slipped away to call a friend at the sheriff's department. My father asked the motorcycle men to leave. This was a large group and they were drunk, and also angry at being asked to leave. Some began quietly to leave, but others, when they jumped on their Harleys, threw their still-full beer cans at my father's head, wanting to see him try to duck. One clipped him, causing a nasty bruise.

That fall a party of wealthy Ohio hunters came for deer season. Some of them behaved badly in the woods, drinking while hunting and shooting squirrels and other small animals just for the fun of killing; my father called them to task. Even in the era before video games made killing something unrelated to death or suffering, they had lost all notion of the seriousness of taking a life. My father thought you could choose to believe that life is sacred everywhere, or not at all; he chose the first and thought anyone who didn't was less than a man. These were educated men, Harvard men some of them, but the part of their education where they would have learned to value life, was missing.

The next morning, as my father made one of his famous lumberjack breakfasts for them—pancakes, bacon and sausage, fruit and sour cream, maple syrup, three kinds of eggs, coffee and orange juice—one of the hunters regaled the others with an account of how he had seen my father in his deer blind the day before, describing everything in detail.

My father turned from the stove and asked, "How did you see all that?" The man answered, "Through my scope." For readers unfamiliar with guns, in order for the man to have seen my father through the scope on his rifle, he would have had to have been pointing the gun at my father; and to have seen his every move over a period of time, he would have had to have been doing it deliberately. The first lesson any hunter or gun owner is given, is to never point a gun at someone. The gun might be loaded, even if you think it isn't; it could go off accidentally. Only children who don't know any better, poor fools who can't learn, or psychopaths with bad ideas ever point a loaded gun at someone.

My father waited until the hunting party had finished breakfast and had gathered, ready for him to take them out in the woods. As they stood, he refunded their money one by one, slowly and deliberately peeling the cash from the wad he always carried. He told them to pack and go back to Cincinnati. And that was the end of his late-life guide work.

He'd bet the house and he was losing.

"I'm slowing down," he admitted to his workers one day in 1975 when I was running the park for him. He'd had prostate surgery the year before and his eyesight was going, something he never mentioned, and something I wouldn't have known except that when he arrived at my house at the base of the dunes, he would ask me to look up phone numbers and, if it was a local call, dial for him. He could not see the small print in the phone book, obviously, but also, more surprisingly, did not want to use his limited energy to dial the number. He was saving his energy, something unimaginable in a person who had always seemed to be indefatigable.

His log rolling days for big lumber companies, jumping from log to log with a cant hook to break up log jams on the Manistee River, were long over. His time in the Civilian Conservation Corps, where he'd received a certificate of excellence for his skill in operating heavy equipment—his greatest academic achievement, maybe his only one; he kept the certificate his whole life—was far in the past. His years traipsing up and down hills over tree falls, estimating board feet of hardwoods by the acre, were mostly over. But he had discovered what he loved to do. He loved to design parks. He had no engineering or landscaping background. He was a dyslexic with a backwoods education. An autodidact, his approach was seat-of-the-pants intuitive.

After the first hoots of derision about my father's effrontery in putting a private park where the public one should have been, people started changing their tune. He knew a lot about how to handle city people in the woods; he'd been doing it for years. He himself loved the most remote, hard-to-get-to swamp, but he knew most people didn't want to get out of their cars—which was good in this instance: the roads kept the people corralled so they couldn't wreak havoc with the dunes, which were not as indestructible as they looked; plus, rescuing people from places they shouldn't have gone anyway was a headache. People loved the rose garden and the drive through the dunes and the views over Lake Michigan.

All summer long in 1975, and again in 1976, I went to court hearings down in Grand Rapids before Federal Judge Noel Fox, where my father was fighting the federal government for fair value for his land. If you were playing craps at the casino, Judge Fox would be the Pit Boss, the one everyone has to bow to after the deal has been called—and disputed.

Judge Fox was a wise and kind man with whom I would later discuss Native fishing rights, when I was a reporter for the *Traverse City Record-Eagle* newspaper in the late 1970s. I was 32 and Fox was 68, an age that seemed ancient to me at the time and, as these things go, no longer seems so. He was guileless, genuine, with an easy, loping mind, the natural sweetness you sometimes find in exceptionally intelligent and compassionate people, the kind of person where, if they like you, if you can make them laugh, it's a good and memorable thing that'll last the rest of your life.

Fox knew, I think, that although we were ostensibly talking about Native rights, we were also talking in a kind of code about my father's recent case before him, about basic fairness. And he said, "There are many miscarriages of justice, but not a multitude of them."

He also told me that when his daughter, a single parent, was dying of cancer, he adopted her children so they wouldn't be orphans. He knew we were talking about justice in a much larger sense than the cases that came before him. We were talking about justice as an outgrowth of our compassion for others. We were talking about our humanity and how one should live in this world.

I was reminded of this the other day when I came across something made famous by the Reverend Dr. Martin Luther King Jr. during the Civil Rights movement of the 1960s, an otherwise obscure passage written in 1857 and attributed to New England minister Theodore Parker, *"I do not pretend to understand the moral universe, the arc is a long one, my eye reaches but a little ways; I cannot calculate the curve and complete the figure by the experience of sight; I can divine it by conscience and, from what I see, I am sure it bends toward justice."*

That summer of 1976, before I started working for the *Traverse City Record-Eagle*, my father's legal dispute with the government was, finally, coming to a close. My father planned, once he got his money, to build another park over at Jaxson Creek near Kingsley, where there were two lakes, a stream, a large log lodge, and many rare wildflowers and birds.

He'd set it up with his lawyers to put his money in trust with Michigan State University so the money wouldn't go for taxes and so there would be educational programs about the flora and fauna. People said no one would pay good money to go see a forest when there were forests everywhere. He said, "The woods are not always going to be here." No one believed this. People said the woods near Kingsley weren't as dramatically beautiful as the dunes. "Each is beautiful in a different way," he said. "You just have to stay long enough to see it."

My father died September 3, 1976, the day after he got his three-and-a-half-million-dollar settlement from the federal government and the day after his 68th birthday. His wife cashed the check immediately. Six weeks later, she left for

Sun City, Arizona, their home burning down behind her as she drove away. The furnace in the home had mysteriously blown up, setting the house ablaze, when she was only about a half hour south on I-75. It burned to the ground before the fire trucks could get there.

My sisters and I had only seen my father's second wife on rare occasions. She had never wanted anything to do with his five daughters from his first marriage. Her obligatory Christmas presents to us, tattered yard sale items poorly wrapped, were a family joke. A lot of stepmothers, just like in the fairy tales, don't like their stepchildren. They might not even like their husbands, the fathers of those stepchildren. The world has never been an easy place in which to survive. This second wife had never shared my father's passion for parks and didn't care much for winter, either. She'd almost certainly hated the idea of his putting all his money in trust with Michigan State University in order to finance the Jaxson Creek Park, something that never transpired because of his untimely and unexpected death. All I ever knew about this second wife, because it was public information, was her large contributions to the Reagan and Bush campaigns. Shortly after my father's death, oil and gas were discovered on some of his 50,000 acres in Kalkaska, Grand Traverse, Antrim, Manistee, and Wexford Counties. The income from mineral royalties on all this land, land which had been in my father's name and which became my stepmother's land upon his death, was annually in the several millions during the oil boom of the 1970s and 80s. This stepmother, she-of-the-cheesy-Christmas-presents, eventually died herself, at the age of 98, still in Arizona, in 2011.

Did my father lose his bet?

After all the hard years cutting trees and all the crass years buying up whole sides of lakes—like sides of beef—and carving delicate beauty up into "lots" with roads throughout, he had discovered he liked to make parks. Worse things can happen to someone than discovering their heart's desire in their last decade.

Watching the arc of his transformation makes me realize that change is slow. We evolve in our awareness as individuals, over a lifetime, if we're lucky. And we evolve in our awareness as nations, and as a species, as the individual members do, and that can take several, accumulated lifetimes.

The Sleeping Bear Dunes National Lakeshore is but a metaphor for how we should value all land, not only the dramatically beautiful but also the softer, sometimes more gentle and obscure beauty that is all around us; not just the Grand Canyon, but the small pine in our backyard and the robin's nest; not just the Boardman River when it wasn't polluted, but the Boardman River as our responsibility to make sure that it's clean again.

We're all of a piece with our human and natural environment, and whatever happens to the smallest part, happens to us all. It's been said before but it can be said again: the land belongs not just to us now, but to future generations; not just to private property owners, but to itself, as an intrinsic entity that subsumes and transcends anyone's possession of it. It's our honorable obligation to take care of it all, whether rivers, or people, or baby snakes. We can't let anything bad happen to *"the them"* beneath our feet.

Becky Thatcher, Artist

Sometimes someone notices something, and out of that noticing and the inspiration it provides, makes something no one's ever seen before. It's called "making art". Becky Thatcher does it all the time.

Her inspiration is nature and her art form is jewelry. It started back in the 1970s with stones from the Lake Michigan shore, and gradually through the 1980s and 90s, involved world travel and gem-buying trips, incorporating carved jade from Thailand, pearls from Tahiti, turquoise from the southwest, and opals from Australia.

A lot of people notice beauty and are inspired to make art, but only a few people do it every day in a way that leaves others in awe. The artist is the intermediary between nature and art, between the stones in the water—we're talking Thatcher's jewelry here—and the piece of jewelry a person can't get out of her mind after she leaves the jewelry store. The artist has to see, with an extraordinary kind of seeing, and then she has to make something with an extraordinary kind of skill.

Vision is a gift one is born with, like perfect pitch, and if acknowledged and cultivated, over time it can be developed to a high level. Craft is acquired through years of application to the work. Vision without craft is nice but it can't be easily shared. Craft without vision is simply craft. Only when vision and craft combine does something, in this case a piece of jewelry, become art. Art is what the artist creates out of love and offers up to others out of love. Art and love are the same.

The French have an expression for how this coming together of what's in a person and what's in the world occurs. It's called "lorsque le travail entre l'homme" or, loosely translated, "when the work enters the man," or "when a person and their work become one." Thatcher is one with her work.

Along with her artistry, Thatcher has two other gifts: a lot of common sense about making money and a ferocious work ethic. Anyone who's been around for a while can remember her first studio, where her Glen Arbor store is now on Lake Street, between M-22 and Lake Michigan. It had gray asphalt shingles over old, weathered-board walls. It was the kind of house that in the 1950s would have had fish nets drying in front of it. She went in on it with two other people, Tim Nichols who now has the Riverfront Pizza on Western Avenue and Rob Rader, known for the history of Glen Arbor Township which he wrote in 1977 and whose parents started the landmark Totem Shoppe (now Shop) in the late 1930s. The trio bought the place for $32,000 on a land contract in 1983 and remodeled it together. Rader slept there at night in one of the initial phases and during the daytime Thatcher sold Rader's antiques and her jewelry out of the house. It was heated with a woodstove in such a way that when the fire was hot it felt dangerous. Eventually Thatcher bought out her partners and the place became her home, studio, and store. It's still there. It's her flagship store. Now she has three others as well.

Thatcher's story begins in Maumee, Ohio, where she grew up, and continues with summers up north on Sleeping Bear Bay, looking out at the Manitou Islands. Artist Midge Obata, a Glen Arbor neighbor, says, "Becky's work is fabulous, always has been. She looks around, she appreciates what she sees: the shapes in the water, the flowing design on the dunes, the brilliant changing colors." Thatcher's color sense is second to none. Obata goes on to describe the way the land influences an artist, Becky's ability to connect to the sky, the waves, the healing beauty of nature and how she was able to bring that into her work. "She knows a lot about semiprecious gems, too," Obata says, "and I think that helps."

Thatcher no longer sleeps in her studio. She designs the jewelry but has a staff to polish and make it. Her store in Glen Arbor is not quite as down-home as it once was, but it's low-key, as she is. She treats everyone—the fabulously wealthy and the waitress from down the street—the same. Thatcher herself was once a waitress.

Thatcher worked in Virginia as a hostess in the elegant, upscale Red Fox Inn—the oldest continuously operating Inn in the country—where she really wanted to be a waitress because that's where the most money could be made. One Mother's Day event, while still in her hostess job at the Red Fox, she was wearing the requisite high heels, as every hostess at a fancy restaurant would have in the 1970s. "It wasn't a dress code," she explains. "No one told me to wear high heels. It was just what you knew you had to do." That day she moved tables for hours in those high heels and says she "lost the feeling in my toes for a year." Thatcher was also the one who did the flower arrangements for the private dining room. C. Z. Guest, the socialite and horsewoman somehow related to English royalty and Winston Churchill, who sometimes hosted large events at the Red Fox, had advised Thatcher that all bouquets should have roadside flowers in order to avoid a stiff, funereal look. Thatcher, good at her job, obliged. One day the manager's brother came into the dining room and said, "The tables look nice, Becky. Are you allergic to poison ivy?" Every bouquet had poison ivy in it. Thatcher says, "It was the perfect color, too, just turning red." But she took it all out; it might have sent the wrong message to the guests. "He probably saved my job," she says of the manager's brother. She later moved on to a waitress job in metropolitan Washington, D.C., at The Magic Pan, which allowed more time for craft shows, because she now could earn more money, and left her days free for making jewelry.

Before the restaurant jobs, Thatcher had worked in a tack shop. She'd essentially run away from high school in Ohio. "I had enough credits to graduate, so I just left," she says. She did receive her diploma. Thatcher loved horses and worked her way through a six-month riding school course by grooming horses and mucking out stalls. She still loves horses. Her Icelandic pony, Uggi, is ensconced behind her Glen Arbor studio every summer. Thatcher, on the back of Uggi, has logged over 1,800 hours as a trail steward for the Sleeping Bear Dunes National Lakeshore.

On Thatcher's lucky, exhilarating and sometimes rocky road to success, there were a lot of part-time jobs, and more than a few times when she travelled to craft shows and couldn't afford a motel and had to sleep in the parking lot of a safe-looking marina or a well-lit Denny's. During her first attempt to live in Glen Arbor, Thatcher baby-sat for Bette Bach, wife of Richard Bach, best-selling author of one of the first self-help books, *Johnathan Livingston Seagull*, while Mrs. Bach made art. Richard Bach became very rich and very famous and married three more times. "Bette was an inspiration," Thatcher says, because in the teeth of marital shipwreck and trying to raise six children alone, Bette just kept making art. Thatcher also worked making stained glass in Suttons Bay during that first, failed attempt to live in Glen Arbor when, she says, "I starved-out."

Somewhere along the way Thatcher got in a semester of summer school at Bowling Green, receiving excellent grades in art and psychology. "My SAT scores weren't high enough for the regular fall and winter semesters," she says ruefully. She confides that she only passed high school algebra because her teacher was kind and without his kindness, she wouldn't have qualified for summer school at Bowling Green. She says, "I've always wanted to find him and thank him." She adds that she was good at geometry, however, because geometry, unlike algebra, was three-dimensional, like jewelry.

While in high school, Thatcher says she took several classes at the Toledo Artists' Club. "Fine instruction," she says, from a teaching assistant from Bowling Green University. Her brother took her to an art fair in Ann Arbor, long before art fairs were ubiquitous, and she had "the first inkling" of the possibilities for her own work. One summer up north she learned how to make macramé from Midge Obata's daughter, Nori, now a ceramicist and glass bead maker with a studio in the Lake Street Gallery in Glen Arbor. That fall when Thatcher returned to high school in Ohio, she made macramé plant holders and sold them at school. "I could make one macramé plant holder a night," she says, "and so I could make $25 a week," and finance more jewelry classes. She entered a few, small, craft shows in Toledo while in high school.

Thatcher entered her first big craft show in Maryland in 1974, still living hand-to-mouth, she says, "just going full-time with my jewelry making." Meanwhile, she says, "There was a craft renaissance in Washington, D.C.," as there was in scattered places across the nation, places like San Francisco, Ann Arbor, and Asheville, N.C. Each time it happened, in each place, there was a shocked 'this can't be happening here' kind of response, followed very quickly by a ripple effect. Remember Ben and Jerry's ice cream and their 1970s start in an old, abandoned gas station in Burlington, Vermont? A summer project that everyone thought would never last? The Ben and Jerry's that now has stores in Copenhagen and Singapore? That kind of thing was happening all across America in the 1970s.

"Rosalynn Carter went out and got hand-woven cloth for chairs in the Whitehouse and she found people who made hand-thrown plates [for state dinners]." As a result of Rosalynn Carter's influence, all of Washington and the surrounding area became fascinated with handmade American crafts. "I rode the wave [for this renaissance], right into the Philadelphia Museum Craft Show," one of Thatcher's first juried shows, a benchmark in her career because it was an honor to be accepted. If it hadn't been for that renaissance, she says she doesn't know where she'd be now. She acknowledges that there's a mysterious bit of synergy between the artist and her society. The artist has her finger on the pulse of what's happening and, albeit unconsciously, responds.

Craft shows began to be lucrative, allowing Thatcher to give up waitressing and mucking out stalls, and eventually she saved enough money to move back to Glen Arbor and purchase the gray-shingled house and become a fulltime artist. The house is in a quiet place with swaying pines against a backdrop of the ever-changing colors of Lake Michigan. In those days, the upscale restaurant, Blu, and all the other tony shops on Lake Street, which ends at the Lake Michigan shore, were nonexistent.

In June of 1983 she began to sell jewelry out of the front room. In 1984 she was able to hire someone part-time to help with the jewelry making. Thatcher continued to attend craft shows and at one of them met and fell in love with a gem dealer from Atlanta, married in 1985 and had her son, Devin. The marriage didn't last; as a single mom, she continued to live in Glen Arbor and make jewelry.

The difference between an artist and a business person is that the business person makes art in order to make money and the artist makes money in order to keep making art. Thatcher is the latter, a genuine artist. Not only does she have vision and skill, she has guts, an ability to take risks, confidence, courage and an absolute indifference to public opinion when it comes to her jewelry. She doesn't set out to make what she hopes people will buy; she makes what she loves and believes when people see it, they will love it, too.

Photographer Kathleen Dodge Buhler, known for her model-good-looks (tall, patrician, gracious, prepossessing), says that one dull winter day when she was living in Glen

Arbor, Thatcher called and said, "Do you want to go to Bangkok?" She needed someone to accompany her on a gem-buying trip across Asia. "So, there we were at the lapidary company in Bangkok because the order they had sent to the U. S. had many broken pieces. Then we're having lunch with these five, 30-year-old Chinese executives, impressing them with our expert use of chopsticks. We were so good with the chopsticks, we could pick up a peanut.

"It was all very social and friendly," Dodge-Buhler says, "but they did not want to credit Becky for the damaged pieces." Unofficially Dodge-Buhler was there as the kind of ersatz female companion Agatha Christie's heroines always had to buy train tickets and double-check the security of the luggage and notice the number of spoonfuls of something or other going into the tea. "Everything was very smiley and happy and I said to them with a big smile on my face, showing them my big, white American teeth, perfectly straight from braces, 'You don't want to mess with Becky.'" She laughs. "They corrected their error." These days Thatcher attends the winter gem shows in Tucson, Arizona, the world's largest international show, held in 40 locations all over the city, accompanied by several members of her staff.

In 1993, after 10 years in business in her Glen Arbor studio, Thatcher began to host her now-famous Tuesday teas, "Tea at 3 in the garden." One day a chemistry professor, David Watt, showed up, escorted by his sister who was trying to get him a date, stayed for tea, and by the end of the summer, David and Becky were married. Watt now does the gem talks at the garden teas on Tuesdays.

In retrospect Thatcher sees that her jewelry-making may have begun as early as her first jewelry-making class at Camp Kohahna near Pyramid Point on the Leelanau Peninsula when, too young to work with metal, she sat mesmerized for hours watching an older camper, Julia Flowers, make a silver apple with a worm, enthralled with the sawing, filing, soldering and polishing that produced a piece of jewelry. Flowers, now retired from management with Neiman Marcus's fine jewelry department, says that, "In my early years all the camp awards were silver charms made by the counselors and older campers. It was a very special part of Camp Kohahna," and for a young Thatcher, would have made an indelible connection between the bonds of friendship and jewelry, between community and keepsake.

Thatcher says she also thinks that two Glen Arbor neighbors she knew as a young girl in the summers, Mary and Franke Schimpff, a mother and daughter who made jewelry and won prizes at the DeBeers' diamond competition, were also early mentors, unawares. The Schimpff studio was behind the old general store, next to where Cherry Republic is now, in a refurbished train depot that had been moved there from Copemish, and Thatcher visited often. It was owned by Virginia Hinton, a teacher at the Leelanau School, the first woman to graduate from the Gemological Institute of America, an institute established in 1931 to teach jewelers how to evaluate gems and semiprecious stones. Hinton was "an amazing woman," Thatcher says, a leader and path-maker for women, another influence. But a lot of us have made jewelry at a summer camp when we were kids, and most of us have met one or two amazing pathfinders, and a few of us have met prizewinning jewelers as well, and we didn't become jewelers, so there's got to be more. Perhaps it's the confluence of all those different coincidences and chance encounters, all combining to create a gravitational pull toward jewelry making.

One thing about Thatcher is that she doesn't stop changing and growing as an artist or a person. A walk in the woods two or three years ago, where she saw where a woodpecker had made a hole in a tree and left pieces of the tree on the forest floor, inspired a new jewelry line. Thatcher felt sorry for the tree and tried to make a patch for it, a kind of arboreal skin graft of copper. Then she went back in a year and saw that the tree had healed itself and didn't need her, but the idea of things on the forest floor, including mushroom spores, intrigued her and she made a whole line of jewelry with that theme. She began reading about trees and how they "communicate" with each other and with the soil. She began reading about things under the soil. She became interested in mushrooms. She also made paper with forest ingredients to wrap the jewelry in; that's the kind of thing she does.

At Martha's Leelanau Table in Suttons Bay, Thatcher and a few others are dining on excellent crab cakes, like the best in Baltimore where they've been doing it for 400 years and have the know-how to prove it. It's a beautiful evening. Owner and chef, Martha Ryan, comes out from the kitchen to join the conversation about art, food and a migrant family in Lake Leelanau, the target of a recent raid by the government looking for illegal aliens. At the time he was put in jail, the man's home was under construction and vulnerable to the elements. Several builders and carpenters offered to come finish the house, but he had too much pride to accept their help. One of the man's citizen-relatives works for Martha and Martha was trying to give the woman extra hours so the woman could help keep her family afloat. The gathered Leelanau artists, and the artist-chef who's standing there with us, see their communities, whether the forest floor or the Hispanic window washer down the road, as part of a whole and they respond with their art, whether cooking or jewelry, music or painting. Art is not separate from community but connected to it, both the community of nature and the community of people. We are all one.

Jewelry is ancient, as old as humanity. We know this because beads of jade and jasper and other indestructible substances are found with the bones of cave dwellers, in the dust where their necks would have been. Jewelry lasts. It doesn't rot when we do. Jewelry is worn for decoration, for status, to commemorate a major life event, and as keepsakes. Thatcher's jewelry is unusual in that, in addition to all of the above, it's talismanic of nature. It gives the wearer a special connection to a place, so that when she wears those gold and opal and tourmaline and turquoise dangling earrings, while she works in a cubicle in some infinite office complex, for example, or as a volunteer in the children's intensive care unit, reading stories, she can be thinking about the blue-green waters of Lake Michigan, the dark green islands, and the golden-rose dunes, and the sparkling light above the Manitou Passage, images that stay with the wearer, wherever she goes, like an aura. And the other office workers and the children love to see the colors, too.

On the plane home from their Asian adventure, Dodge-Buhler asked Thatcher if she wasn't worried about people stealing her design ideas. Thatcher said, "No, I'll just come up with more." Nature is infinite and so, for Thatcher, for whom nature is a vital source of inspiration, she'll never need to worry about running out of ideas.

Native Wild Rice and the Fall Harvest

When the leaves start to turn those exhilarating fire shades of crimson, gold, sunset-orange, scarlet, vermillion and blaze-yellow—with edge colors of green and dark blue—and a hundred other hues, this is the time of year the wild rice harvest traditionally takes place on the quiet lakes and streams of the Upper Midwest. Native people go through with canoes, usually the man at the push pole and the woman with small sticks to knock the grains of rice into the canoe.

These are those mid-September days of cool mornings with heavy dew and gossamer mists, and hot afternoons with a beating sun and sometimes cold, clear nights with lots of stars. These are the days with a sharp, cake-like scent in the air, a combined odor of apples, autumn leaves, and the sweet hay-in-the-barn smell of the blazing midday sun on dry grass. There's almost an hour and a half less daylight than there was in mid-summer and our internal clocks tick louder, telling us winter is coming, even when the sun during the day seems to shine more warmly and more directly than it did in July.

Michigan used to have wild rice everywhere. Saginaw Bay and the surrounding streams had miles and miles of wild rice, all destroyed by logging, dams, and industrialization. Wild rice is a grain, not a rice, an aquatic grass native to the Great Lakes. It has superior nutrient value, according to Richard La Fortune, author of *Wild Rice Revolution*. This grain is highly prized by gourmet cooks the world over for its delicious taste, but its health benefits are just beginning to be recognized. Like quinoa, the super-cereal from the mountains in the Andes, the wild rice of the Great Lakes is the next new thing for good health.

The Grand Traverse Band (GTB) of Ottawa and Chippewa Indians, employing the knowledge and efforts of Brad McClellan, Tina Frankenberger, and Gerald Luskey, among others, is participating in a statewide indigenous effort to replant wild rice. The wild rice planters are going to be working with the naturalists in the GTB Natural Resources Department, State of Michigan botanists, and rangers from the Sleeping Bear Dunes National Lakeshore. Deer Lake, on the western edge of the national park—more of a swamp than a lake and not on most readily available maps—if the conditions are right for wild rice, may be one of the replanting sites.

Tucker Lake off Westman Road near Glen Arbor, Shell Lake near Pyramid Point, Lake Manitou on North Manitou Island, and Lake Florence on South Manitou Island, are four, small lakes within the boundaries of the Sleeping Bear Dunes National Lakeshore, which might also be suitable as potential wild rice places.

It takes two or three weeks to harvest the rice since it ripens gradually from the top of the long stem to the bottom. It requires several passes through the rice beds to gather the seeds just as they become ready. This is a labor-intensive but joyful endeavor and the reward is a highly nutritious, tasty grain called *manoomin* (pronounced *man-OH-min*) by Native peoples.

Wild rice is considered a "spirit food" by the indigenous people, according to McClellan who says, "It kept us alive." It is often the first solid food given to babies and the last solid food given to elders. It has a slightly nutty taste and so many trace minerals, amino acids, enzymes, vitamins, and proteins that it can sustain an entire tribe through tough times. When parched, it has an indefinite shelf life.

Wild rice harvested in the traditional way is expensive, $20 a pound, but it is also available in a less expensive form from commercial growers. Whether you buy the most expensive, hand-harvested, organic wild rice or the least expensive commercially grown wild rice where pesticides and chemical fertilizers have been used, it still has a great taste and a nutritional value comparable to quinoa. Wild rice takes about 45 minutes to cook but the cooked rice freezes extremely well. Wild rice—combined with a handful of giblets that have been cooked for three hours in broth and finely chopped, another handful of roasted pine-nuts, and all seasoned with onion, celery, thyme and rosemary—makes a delicious stuffing for turkey. A simple lunch can be made with two-thirds wild rice, a small amount of sautéed green onions, a handful of small pecan pieces—served in a half-avocado with a dollop of peach and ginger chutney.

There's increasing awareness in American culture of the importance of good food to promote health. In 2017 Traverse City hosted its first Culinary Medicine Conference at the Northwestern Michigan College Great Lakes Culinary Institute. Harvard Medical School launched a similar event in 2007 and there have been many others, too, along similar lines, across the world. The conference in Traverse City brought together physicians, nutritionists, and chefs.

Locally, Brad McClellan and Tina Frankenberger, two Native young people with hands-on expertise as well as academic training in the study of Native gardens and wild foods, are trying to bring back the cultivation of wild rice. Frankenberger's first interest was in bringing back Native gardens with indigenous seeds, and she is now equally committed to the restoration of wild rice.

Wild rice grew all over Northwest Michigan 200 years ago, according to Frankenberger, and can still be found in a few places, such as Ellis Lake, between Grawn and Interlochen off U.S. 31, and also, nearby, the north end of Big

Platte Lake in Benzie County. It used to grow in the shallows and shoals of Lake Leelanau, she says. Most of the wild rice beds in Michigan have been destroyed by development and will have to be re-planted in quiet, clean bodies of water. Wild rice is sensitive to the disruptions caused by power boats and people on water-skis. This highly nutritious Native grass requires a lake, stream, or marsh with alluvial soil, soil carried by flowing water and deposited where the flowing water slows down.

McClellan says there's an Ojibway migration legend, about how a tribal group on the Atlantic coast more than a thousand years ago, using cowrie shells for divination, made their way over many years to the Great Lakes. "A woman had a vision," he says. "In it she was told her tribe should go west until they came to the place where the food grows on the water and where they would find the sacred miigis (also spelled "megis") shells or white shells." Wild rice is the food that grows on the water. There's a place in Manitoba in Canada called White River where there are white shells which are regarded as sacred. The Native name for wild rice, *manoomin*, means *good seed*. "I like to use the original Ottawa words," McClellan says as he produces a wild rice worksheet with the words in English and Ottawa.

At the time Frankenberger met McClellan, she had been trying for three years to interest her tribal government in a Native agriculture program. She said she was on the verge of giving up when McClellan encouraged her to keep going and told her about the wild rice restoration program in which he was involved. Over the next several months they became friends. Frankenberger is vivacious, relaxed, with a quick laugh and lilting speech. McClellen is quiet, serious, reserved, with a soft voice. He talks slowly and his speech is largely uninflected.

The goals for the agricultural project dovetail with the wild rice restoration, they both say. "The goal," Frankenberger says, "is to be able to feed all the local Native people within three years." They do not want to use heavy chemicals or pesticides. The Grand Traverse Band of Ottawa and Chippewa Indians has tribal members in the counties of Antrim, Benzie, Charlevoix, Leelanau, Grand Traverse, and Manistee. They have planted gardens and wild rice in five of the six counties, Frankenberger says. Her mother, Debra, is the sister of well-known and well-regarded tribal commercial fisherman, Ed John of Peshawbestown. Frankenberger grew up in a farming family in mid-Michigan and graduated from Michigan State University with a degree in wildlife and fisheries biology.

Food gathering, food growing, food sharing—consuming a meal together—is at the core of community, according to Frankenberger. It's a communion with each other and with the earth. If you stop and think about it for a minute, this seems true: we don't go to those pancake breakfasts in the village because we want the pancakes so much, but because we want fellowship. We want to see our neighbors, eat with them, and have tangible reassurance that we're all living in together in peace and harmony in the same small place.

"Native culture is a sharing culture, especially with food," Frankenberger says. "Monsanto wants to patent all seeds, but we feel seeds are for everyone. Food is for everyone. We don't want to make a profit by selling the seeds, and by keeping them from other people. We want to share our seeds not just with the Native community but with all the people in our immediate area and even in the world."

Frankenberger is not alone in having a passion for saving seeds. The Svalbard Global Seed Vault in Norway has been gathering seeds from around the world for a decade. A new book, *Seeds on Ice* by Cary Fowler, a visiting professor at Stanford University, presents a history of this, with photos. The Russians during World War II had a similar seed bank in Saint Petersburg (then called Leningrad). Under siege for two years, nine of their scientists starved to death rather than eat their seeds.

"They knew it was important," McClellan says. The global importance of maintaining food sources is obvious to almost any thinking person. No one needs to have a vision to get to this level of understanding, although with McClellan and Frankenberger, like many other young farmers and promoters of good food who are willing to do the back-breaking work knowing that they will never make much money doing it, there seems to be a visionary and spiritual quality imbuing their drive and determination.

"It is extraordinary," writes British naturalist Michael McCarthy, in *The Moth Snowstorm*, his most recent book, "We are wrecking the earth, as burglars will sometimes wantonly wreck a house. . . We who ourselves depend upon it utterly are wrecking our home." He talks about the intense love of the natural world. "I believe the bond is at the very heart of what it means to be human; that the natural world where we evolved is no mere neutral background, but at the deepest psychological level it remains our home, with all the intense emotional attachment which that implies—passionate feelings of belonging, of yearning and of love." Something of that awareness is under the surface in the huge amount of work, presumably fueled by the dream of restoring the indigenous food, culture, and wild rice, that Frankenberger and McClellan have undertaken.

McClellan, also a member of the Grand Traverse Band of Ottawa and Chippewa Indians, became interested in Native culture when he was a teenager and attended the tribal high school of the Little River Band in Manistee County. A flooring specialist by trade, he also took classes in wild rice restoration at the Saginaw-Chippewa Tribal College in Mount Pleasant. "Native culture is respectful of nature. We cherish wild rice as a food," McClellan says. "We respect it because it helped us stay alive. Traditionally we would carry about 40 days of wild rice on us when traveling, but would store enough for one to two years, depending on the harvest yield, for either tribal use or for trade."

On a bright, sunny Saturday at the tribal Eyaawing—pronounced Aye-yah-wing; it means "Who We Are"—Museum and Cultural Center in Peshawbestown, McClellan and Frankenberger are conducting a Wild Rice Workshop: how to plant it, how to grow it, how to harvest it, complete with all the raw materials gathered from tribal lands and their instructions on how to make the tools. There are 10-foot cedar saplings to be made into push poles. There are forked hardwood pieces that look like large slingshots for the pushing end of the pole. McClellan will show people how to attach the two pieces of the push pole, notching and affixing the pieces with twine.

Frankenberger has brought a wild rice casserole and a birch tea drink; another tribal member has brought Sloppy Joes. This is food for the 25 or more people who are in the room. People seem happy and social but also seriously ready for the work. A man who identifies himself as Tom, and says he's the interim tribal doctor, is there. Young John Petoskey, son of the Native attorney by the same name, home from law school at the University of Michigan, is there. There are several babies in the room being passed from one pair of loving arms to another. Jerry Luskey, a tribal elder, stands and says a prayer in Ottawa, giving thanks for the food and the project. The caring and respectful expressions on the faces of the people in the room are enough to give anyone hope for a better world.

According to early explorers, missionaries and ethnographers—Pierre de Charlevoix, Father Marquette, Frances Densmore and others—the Native culture was one that used dreams and visions for guidance. As part of cultivating a person's ability to feel safe enough and spiritually strong enough to do that, children were doted on and never beaten, given infinite love and protection but also, after they became teenagers, given infinite freedom to make their own choices. The lack of physical punishment, the lack of regimentation provided to children and the freedom given to them to make their own decisions, although now widely recognized in America as sound upbringing practices if one wants to have highly intelligent, socially responsible, and creative children, at the time of contact with early European visitors and immigrants to America, these ways of raising children were seen by the Europeans as overly indulgent and they thought it wasn't right.

Bringing back the original Native culture is not easy. Relearning the language, as Luskey avers, is hard. The culture, unlike the European culture, was not primarily a materialistic or desperately survival-oriented culture. European peasants, at the mercy of feudal lords, were routinely conscripted against their will and, in years when the crops were not plentiful, the peasants were reduced to a starvation diet of oatcakes and not much more. Native people, on the other hand, had access to a lot of game and other food, either foraged or cultivated in gardens. Food was plentiful and they lived in such a way that they had a lot of leisure time, time for thought, and this probably made a difference in the way they saw the world.

"One thing with respect to which the Native people are never forgetful, let them be in ever so great an extremity," writes Charlevoix in 1720, "is whereas, amongst us, it's the living who are enriched by the spoils of the dead, the Native people on the contrary, not only carry along with them to the grave everything that belonged to them, but also receive presents of their relations." Native people had enough of the things of this world that they not only buried personal belongings with their deceased loved ones but found additional items to put in the graves as well. The cultures were at odds from the start, but here's a thought to ponder: it's possible that one of the best parts of America might not be its nuclear arsenal, but the mountains and prairies, the lakes and trees, and the people who understood them.

Wild rice, as was noted in the textbook, *Wild Rice and the Ojibway People,* by Thomas Vennum, Jr., was one of the things frequently put in the graves as food for the journey. Everything, on some level, was sacred. The material value of something was eclipsed by its spiritual value. The children, the most spiritual part of the tribe, could only be capable of dreams and visions if they were nourished, not only physically with food and exercise, but also intellectually and emotionally, by all members of their tribe. Such an upbringing produced a people where all the senses, including the sixth sense, were developed. Unconditional love and hands-on learning created highly intelligent, resilient, and thoughtful adults, according to early European explorers and missionaries. Charlevoix noted the physical strength of Native peoples as well as their articulateness and quick-witted repartee. Many Jesuit missionaries (see: *The Collected Letters of the Jesuits,* edited by Reuben Gold Thwaites) noted that the Native children learned much faster than the non-Native children.

Rediscovering, retaining, and transmitting the increasingly fragile, ancient knowledge, whether with growing and harvesting wild rice, raising children, or relearning the language, requires a lot of workshops, a lot of casseroles, a lot of carting around of the materials, a lot of the setting up of chairs, and a lot of simply "showing up" in the basements of tribal museums. Native people are bringing back their culture, one wild rice bed, one carefully nurtured child, and one reclaimed Anishinaabe word at a time. It's the culture that's important, not who is and who isn't one hundred percent biologically Native, according to Frankenberger. And this time the cultural exchange is going the other way, and they are consciously bringing the Native culture to the larger society. The restoration of wild rice, one piece of the cultural revival, is the work that McClellan and Frankenberger have embraced.

McClellan and Frankenberger had so many interests in common that it was only natural that they would want to work together. "She's one of the few women I've met," McClellan says, "who really likes to be outdoors." Frankenberger nods in agreement. Coincidentally, each of them is part-German and part-Ottawa. Frankenberger's father is German and McClellan's mother is German. Both are eager to work, not just with the Native community, but with all sectors of the population. They want to forge good relationships with farmers and other food-growing members of the community as well as any supportive governmental agricultural or nonprofit entities.

They believe that food cultivation and food preservation are important to survival, not just for the tribes, but for all people. "We want to work across cultural and ethnic lines," Frankenberger says. And McClellan adds that as part of that they want to work with people from the Michigan Department of Natural Resources as well as botanists from the National Park Service. Recently, working in conjunction with the Leelanau Conservancy, they have established an edible forest at the DeYoung Natural Area at the southerly end of Leelanau County. This effort to be inclusive is something that is happening in Native communities across Canada and the United States and is part of what many Native people regard as a Native Renaissance.

"It is astonishing the extent to which Aboriginal peoples still engage in intercultural dialogue with generosity, understanding, and goodwill," writes Adrienne Clarkson, the former Governor General of Canada in the foreword to a 2004 Random House collection of Native stories from Canada. "I have always marveled at how measured, wise, yet impassioned *their* statement of their being is—the way in which they want to include the rest of us."

The workshops conducted by McClellan and others explain the various tools and stages in harvesting wild rice: the push pole used for moving the canoe through the rice beds, the mortar used in pounding rice, the parching of the rice, the baskets used for winnowing. There are special moccasins worn for "jigging" the rice or dancing on it to loosen the hulls. Children like this part of preparing the rice, especially when there's drum music to help them "dance" the rice.

Another thing that is helping the culture of Native food come back to the tribe is the close association with their Ottawa relatives from Canada. Hiawatha Osawamick, a young Ottawa woman from Manitoulin Island in Canada, is an award-winning chef and gourmet cook. She has frequently catered the Language Conference in Peshawbestown, usually held right after the Powwow.

Osawamick started out, while still a teenager, working in her aunt's restaurant on the island of Manitoulin: washing dishes, bussing tables, chopping onions, and finally cooking. She had a passion for cooking and was interested in the color, texture, and flavor of the food she served. Osawamick says that there are not many caterers, or even restaurants, that serve indigenous food. These foods are much higher in vitamins and enzymes than processed foods. Maple syrup, for example, has potassium which helps the heart and other muscles; white sugar, on the other hand, has nothing but calories and chemicals. Wild rice has twice as much lysine, necessary for a healthy immune system, as white rice, and twice the protein.

"She has a niche," says Cheryl Recollet, the director of sustainable development at Wahnapitae First Nation north of Sudbudy, who has used Osawamick's catering service on several occasions. "Indigenous sustainability calls for the use of indigenous knowledge," according to their website. Recollet had Osawamick cater a five-course meal for Aboriginal Affairs Minister, David Zimmer, and the minister said he'd never been fed that well. "As soon as everybody knows Hiawatha's catering," Recollet says, "they all go 'Yes!'"

The thing one notices immediately about the regal Ms. Osawamick, six feet tall and broad-shouldered, is her commanding physical presence. She, in and of herself, could be the poster for Native resurgence. She has, without doubt, Olympic-athlete-level strength and stamina. She needs it as a caterer. She recently catered an event for 2,600 people in Toronto, the World's Indigenous People's Conference on Education (WIPCE). She managed an impromptu staff of 30 to provide food for the opening ceremony, made 2,600 box lunches for tours, and provided a seven-course dinner for 2,600 people for the closing ceremony.

Osawamick usually recruits her staff from the Native community wherever she caters an event and buys the produce and other things, to the extent that she can, from local organic farms. Her organizational skills are equal to her cooking skills. She appears to be tireless. This is a person who answers her own phone and responds to emails promptly. In Toronto, she and some of her staff went two days without sleep to serve the 2,600 WIPCE conference-goers from Hawaii, New Zealand, Australia and from across North America.

"The sauces, the salads," says Minnie Wabanimkee who attended an Osawamick-catered event hosted by the Grand Traverse Band last year in Peshawbestown. "All the food was just so fresh and delicious."

Osawamick is focused on providing not just food that looks great and tastes great but also food that is healthy. Many people today have illnesses, such as heart problems, cancer and diabetes, which can be traced to what they eat. Osawamick's father has cancer. "The tumors feed on sugar," she says. "He loves his ice cream." White sugar, white flour, and chemicals take a heavy toll on aboriginal people who for countless millennia had natural food. But good food is often expensive, preparation is a luxury for busy people, and heavily processed foods, with low nutritional value, are temptingly inexpensive, and so readily available everywhere that they're hard to avoid.

As a child growing up on Manitoulin, Hiawatha Osawamick, one of six children, says she liked to be outdoors and doing things, whether helping her grandparents on their farm or playing hockey. Her family fished, hunted, and foraged every day. Her grandmother routinely took all 15 of her grandchildren sledding on the high hills behind the village of Wikwemikong. The family is close and when she caters the GTB language workshop, her mom and aunt will help her. One of her brothers, Quentin Osawamick, who lives in Warren, Michigan, will also come north to help. Like his sister, he can taste the food and knows when it tastes right.

Manitoulin Island bears a striking resemblance to the Leelanau Peninsula. Although rockier, it has high hills with panoramic views of the blue waters of Lake Huron. Inland, the rolling meadows, small lakes, and beautiful streams extend between villages. The majestic hills and water vistas give the island the feel of Michigan's Leelanau Peninsula. Wikwemikong itself, called "Wiki" for short, is a tiny village, with curving dirt streets ranging over the hills above a bay of Lake Huron on the east side of the island.

The Native people on Manitoulin are closely connected, both culturally and through their extended families, to the Native people in Peshawbestown. Several people have relatives in both places. When the United States government removed Michigan indigenous people from their traditional lands in the 1830s, many returned to their ancestral home on Manitoulin, the largest freshwater island in the world, and the only unceded territory in North America. The Ottawa language, largely lost on the Leelanau Peninsula, was never lost on Manitoulin and is now being relearned in such things as the Native language conference being held in Peshawbestown. Osawamick says she stays at the Grand Traverse Band Hotel when she comes to Peshawbestown. She recruits workers from the local tribe to help her.

Rice harvesting was always a social event, according to Frances Densmore, an American anthropologist and ethnographer born in 1867 in Red Lake, Minnesota. She writes, "Driving through the rice country late one afternoon [I] came upon a camp of three or four tipis. The rice gatherers had returned from the fields, and the men [who had been doing the strenuous work of poling the canoes through the marsh] were sitting on rush mats and smoking while two younger women were parching rice, and an older woman tossed a winnowing tray. At a fire one woman was preparing the evening meal and at a distance another was seen chopping wood. Dogs and little children were running about, and the scene with its background of pines and shining lake was one of pleasure and activity."

Densmore's work is respected by Native peoples, an indication of which is that it is sometimes used as a reference because of her thorough and careful documentation of herbs, food, crafts, tools, and customs. Densmore, a musician educated at Oberlin before she began her ethnographic work, recorded Native music 130 years ago, including that of musicians who were ventriloquists; this music is now archived at the Smithsonian and the Library of Congress. She was preserving the culture at a time that the federal and state governments, in both Canada and the United States, were aggressively doing the reverse and pushing assimilation, to the great detriment of the indigenous peoples. Although many ethnographers and anthropologists have been accused of exploiting or misrepresenting Native people, Densmore's work has escaped this criticism because she was both scrupulous and respectful.

On a recent Saturday, Frankenberger and McClellan are out in a canoe on tiny Deer Lake, slightly inland from the shore of Lake Michigan north of Empire, in the Sleeping Bear

Dunes National Lakeshore. He's poling through the water, trying to assess the feasibility of planting the lake with wild rice. When they return to the shore, he takes a pinch of tobacco from a pouch around his neck and puts it gently down into the soil at the edge of the lake.

"Prayers," Frankenberger says. "Lots of prayers and songs—and hard work. And people helping. That's how we'll bring back the growing of rice here, the growing of other foods, and the traditional Native way of doing it."

"I like to teach the craft," McClellan says as he hauls the canoe up on the shore. "I like seeing people learning about their heritage and reclaiming it."

Out in the black, mirror-like waters of the small lake we can see the reflections of the soft white clouds and the blue sky.

Winter

Orchards and Orphans

They met in the summer of 2012. Still in college, she had come north from a suburb of Detroit to take a job as a waitress at the Cove in Leland. He was managing The Cyclery in Glen Arbor and beginning to think about ways to create a high-density apple orchard in the hills above Lake Michigan, land his family has farmed since they came from Bohemia in the mid-1800s.

They had friends in common. Her best friend, Bradi Pasch, from college, is the sister of one of his best friends, Dave Pasch, a young man who's his partner in the orchard enterprise. He is Brad Houdek. She is Gina Wymore.

He says, "Initially I thought she would want nothing to do with me—she being from West Bloomfield and me being the son of a farmer from up north. The first few times we spent together within the same group of mutual friends, I chose to not go out of my way at all to get to know her. She was only up north for the summer, she would be leaving soon, and I must be of no interest to her. I realize now I was making assumptions. It was also a stressful time for me, only two years after my dad's passing, concerned about the future of the farm, and I wasn't concerned with making too many new friends."

She says, "He was so different from other guys I had known. He never put himself forward or tried to impress me. He was self-assured, but not egotistical. He has such depth of awareness and sensitivity. When we picked apples in his orchard, I was wearing his old, stained coveralls, several sizes too big. He just kept saying how beautiful I was."

He says, "Gina has a huge heart and would do anything to help someone. Over time I realized my assumptions about Gina being a city girl were nothing more than assumptions. She started to catch my attention as a very selfless, kind, and upbeat person, with whom I had a lot in common. She was a great partner in every way, whether it was emotionally or doing a project together. She was someone I truly enjoyed being around."

The friendship grew over time. Then in the spring of 2016, Gina left for Haiti to work in an orphanage.

There are perhaps no two places on the planet as different from each other as Haiti and Michigan's northern Leelanau Peninsula. Only two thousand miles apart physically, in almost all other ways they are millions of miles apart.

Haiti is the poorest country in the western hemisphere. It has a colonial history of unrivaled greed. The Native people all died in the first hundred years from the diseases of their conquerors and the vicissitudes of slavery. The African slaves were next and most died in their first year under the lash in the cotton and sugar fields. The indifferent use of the people by the colonial owners was exceeded only by their reckless use of the land. Much of Haiti's soil washed into the sea.

Leelanau County is the second wealthiest county in Michigan after Oakland County near Detroit, but, unlike Oakland, has no factories and only 20,000 people as compared to Oakland's population of 1.2 million. The Leelanau Peninsula includes 71,000 acres of the Sleeping Bear Dunes National Lakeshore, 34,000 acres of natural areas and conservation easements preserved by the Leelanau Conservancy, and 500 acres owned by the Grand Traverse Band of Ottawa and Chippewa Indians.

Haiti is 10,714 square miles, roughly the size of New Hampshire, with 10 times as many people as New Hampshire and 500,000 times as many people as the Leelanau Peninsula. It has as many people as Manhattan with minimal sewage facilities: only one person in four has access to a toilet. It was forested over sixty percent as recently as 1923 but now is forested only over thirty percent, based on 2016 satellite images from the publication, *EnviroSociety*. Haiti sits on fault lines that make it prone to earthquakes. It's in the path of hurricanes. Eighty percent of the population in Haiti lives below the poverty line. Only a little more than half the people have a rudimentary ability to read and write. Skill levels for anything beyond manual labor are low. Parents have to pay to have their children educated since there is no public education.

The Leelanau Peninsula isn't in the path of anything. This narrow land of lakes and orchards juts out into western Lake Michigan about 300 miles north of Chicago. There's 2,532 square miles in Leelanau county, of which 347-square-miles is land, including four off-shore islands; 2,185-square-miles is water, much of it in the part of Lake Michigan surrounding the peninsula that is mapped as part of the county, and some of it on inland lakes and streams. This is, above all, a literate community with four public schools, three private schools, one Montessori School and dozens of children being expertly homeschooled. There are four public libraries, four bookstores, and two newspapers. Leelanau County had the highest voter turnout in Michigan in the 2018 November election, 71%. Don't ask anyone what they think unless you are fully prepared to have them to tell you—for the next hour.

Similarly, where Gina Wymore grew up in West Bloomfield was worlds away from Haiti. Gina says where she went to school in Bloomfield Hills, "The parking lot at school was filled with Hummers and Audis. I grew up in a bubble. I didn't know that everyone else didn't live like this until I left home."

While studying to be an English teacher at Central Michigan University, she visited Haiti with a mission group. This was right after the earthquake of 2010 where millions were left without homes and many thousands died. "She came home profoundly changed," says her mother, Colleen Wymore.

"I returned home depressed, anxious, feeling incredibly guilty," Gina says. "How could I be handed such an easy existence when others suffered so intensely? I had seen crippled babies abandoned in the streets. Starving children begging us for food. A pastor encouraged me to channel my depression into something good. I formed a club at my university called World Changers. We educated other students about abandoned, abused, and orphaned children. Exposing myself to so much need has prompted me to help others. Surrounding myself with compassionate people, also helped to build compassion in me."

Brad Houdek stands in a field next to his orchard under blue skies with whimsical white clouds. Flashy orange berries hang from the mountain laurel. "Brought by birds," he says of the mountain laurel; he didn't plant it. The bushes of the autumn olives are covered with bee-bee-sized dark red berries. "I made fruit leather out of it," he says, laughing. "It took forever because of all the moisture." I put one of the berries in my mouth. "Chalky," Brad says as he sees me make a face, "Not ripe. Try another one."

There's a strangely marked caterpillar on the ground, "A sphinx moth caterpillar," Brad says. "I think."

Brad says he and Gina stay in touch through email and Skype.

"Brad has been so much support," Gina says. "I couldn't do this without him."

Brad says he admires what Gina is doing and understands that Haiti is a cautionary tale about what happens when the environment is degraded and people have bad government. Later he writes in an email, "As a species, we have done terrible things, especially the "developed" countries, as far as I can tell. At this point in human history there seem to be so many problems that need solving—problems with the environment, society, and the economy—that everyone who's able should focus on doing their part to help, in whatever way they can. The days of selfishly worrying only about having a fancy car, a big house, and an even bigger bank account are past."

Brad Houdek and Gina Wymore are doing what young people all over the world do at their age: trying to understand their values, form a relationship, and create a life path. They're questioning what they've been taught and talking things over with each other. They're trying to find a way through the uncharted, newly borderless world created by the Internet, a world racked with mind-bending environmental degradation creating, in turn, horrible social challenges.

"From my understanding," Brad says, "a person can do their part in one of two ways: in the present sense, by helping people in need here and now, and in the future sense, by devising and implementing new ways to solve our basic needs, without further compromising our future." He's interested in the philosophy of bioregionalism which promotes the deliberate restoration and maintenance of local natural systems.

In his beautiful orchard Brad can hear the Honeycrisp— big red apples—hitting the ground. He can hear them in his sleep. Every apple that hits the ground is a loss. He and his friend and partner, Dave Pasch, recently hired a team of migrants and paid them $14 an hour to pick the apples before there was any more loss. "Migrants are hard workers." Brad says. "They know how not to bruise the fruit. It's about eye-hand coordination, speed and stamina."

Gina's parents, Colleen and Greg Wymore came to pick apples, too. And Al Skeba, Brad's uncle on his mother's side. And Grandmother Delores Houdek made lunch for them. Delores Houdek is famous for her cooking, especially her soups and potato dumplings. Potato dumplings, deceptively simple in terms of the ingredients, are made delicious only by someone with a gift for cooking. Vicki Houdek, Brad's mother, is here. She's taken a day off from her office job to help. They all say they love being out in the orchard: the sunlight is golden, the skies are blue, and the apples are a mouth-watering red.

Brad's read Tracy Kidder's book, *Mountains Beyond Mountains* about Paul Farmer's work in Haiti. Paul Farmer is the Harvard professor and McArthur award-winner who, like Gina, went to Haiti when he was still in college and decided "the only nation is humanity" and he could do something in Haiti to make a difference for the better. Farmer met a girl in Haiti, the writer Roald Dahl's daughter, Ophelia, and fell in love with her. The romantic relationship didn't last but they remained lifelong friends. Haiti is hard on romance.

The Danish philosopher Søren Kierkegaard was engaged to be married in the 1800s to a beautiful young woman named Regine, when he decided one must choose between a secular life and a religious life and broke off the engagement. George Lucaks, quoted in the *New York Review of Books* in November 2016, suggested that Kierkegaards's entire philosophy, summed up in his pseudonymous (published under the name *Victor Eremita*, Victorious Hermit), two-volume book, *Either/Or*, could be found in his separation from Regine. When he died Kierkegaard left all his money to Regine; she had long since married someone else. Kierkigaard was a Lutheran, but Catholics at the time felt much the same way about the necessity to separate human love from religious devotion. Mother Theresa, now officially a saint, never even considered marriage.

The mystic Simone Weil (pronounced Vey), living and writing in France in the years right before the Nazi invasion, wanted only to eat what the poor French factory workers could afford to eat and she wanted to harvest grapes with the grape pickers so she would have work as physically hard as theirs. Her friend Gustave Thibon, who saw to it that her philosophical endeavors were published posthumously, after

Weil's early death, writes, "Simone Weil's conception of the universe brings vertigo; man sees himself hanging there, without ladders or bridges, suspended between necessity and good—between the abyss of gravity and the abyss of grace."

That's where Brad Houdek and Gina Wymore are, suspended between gravity and grace. They are somewhat like the religious acolytes of a previous time, with two important exceptions: they want to do together what those earlier religious devotees thought they could only do alone and they are true Americans and thus eternally optimistic. American writer Nathaniel Hawthorne has a character in *The Marble Faun* in 1860, Hilda, who has this to say about the proverbial misty chasm, "If there be such a chasm, let us bridge it over with good thoughts and deeds, and we shall tread safely to the other side."

Hurricane Matthew came and pummeled Haiti on October 8, 2016. Gina wrote that high winds battered the orphanage all night accompanied by torrential rains. Cholera, which is carried by dirty water, swept through the island in the wake of the hurricane, causing misery and death.

The closest thing the Leelanau Peninsula has come to a hurricane is the wind storm in the summer of 2015. Gina says, "I was working at the Cove during that storm, and that was nothing like the hurricane in Haiti." The wind on the Leelanau might have gusted up to 100 miles an hour, but the entire storm lasted only 30 minutes. Trees came down, but people didn't lose their homes. No one got cholera. The Hurricane in Haiti lasted for hours and the rains that came with it lasted for days.

"Sometimes I feel a massive disconnect from everyone back home," Gina says. "No one understands. I try not to let it drive me away from my loved ones. I've prepared myself for the possibility that this distance and misunderstanding could cause tension between Brad and me. But he's very patient and down to earth and I'm thankful he's so accepting of my

doing this. I need him to visit, but with the farm and fi-
nances, it's hard for him."

Brad and Gina talk all the time. When Gina was recently
nursing an 18-year-old boy with cholera at the orphanage—
trying to get him to drink fluids and knowing that it is physically painful to drink with this disease and also knowing he
might die if he didn't—and not wanting to tell him because it
might alarm him, Brad said, "You have to tell him." And she
did. And the kid drank something and lived.

Brad's Grandmother, Delores (Korson) Houdek, who still
lives on the family homestead says she met her husband
Julius, a distant cousin, when they were in high school together. "We went to the same school. We went to the same
church. His family knew my family. We lived down the road
from each other our whole lives."

This is a different generation.

"Marriage has become harder," says writer Stephanie
Coontz in a recent interview in *The Sun*, "not because people
did it better in the past, but because we have higher expecta-
tions of what a marriage should be."

Both Brad and Gina share a similar devotion to others
and a lack of materialistic goals. "I think there exists a universal force that binds us all together," Brad says. "For me,
this is felt when things are done in harmony with the universe. This is done by doing good for others, helping those in
need, and taking care of the environment in a responsible
way that benefits us all." When he was studying science at
Grand Valley University, Brad says he went through a period
of feeling that "all life was random . . . and the laws of science,
factually backed as they were, left no voids." Now, however,
like Einstein who believed that 'something deeply mysterious
is behind all this', he feels that "nature has a strong connection to heaven."

Gina is going to visit her parents over the 10-day winter
break; she plans to return to Haiti to teach until July when

she'll take another break to visit Michigan and then in August she'll go back to the orphanage for her second year. She'll stay in Haiti this year until December 26 so she can help the children celebrate. "Christmas is for kids," she says. She's hoping Brad will be able to come to Haiti for Christmas. "He can be Santa Claus." Her conversation at any moment is filled with his name and references to things he's said. It's clear he's never far from her thoughts.

"Brad is constantly giving me information about how I should build and maintain our garden. The kids ask me almost every day about Brad. They call him, 'Mr. Bread.' At night when I tuck them in they ask me to describe him. He's a role model for these kids and they've never even met him. He feels like family to them. When we built our raised beds, one youngster complained he was hot. I gave him water and told him to take a breather until he felt that he could tackle another task. Another responded, 'Mr. Bread built his all on his own and there's 30 of us. We can do it!' He's a model of hard work, respect, modesty, simplicity and ambition."

Gina had a blog, *Songs of Haiti,* in which she wrote about how her faith has sustained her there. "It seems like Haiti has a way of strengthening my faith."

When Gina's mother, Colleen, visited she said, "The poverty left me reeling." She described the sewage system as "right down the middle of the street."

"Naturally I miss home like crazy," Gina says. "Mostly, I miss seeing Brad and my family. I miss being able to walk down the street without fear. I miss warm showers. I miss bike rides, hikes, and personal space." Then she says, "I teach children. But what the children are teaching me is far greater."

Brad is in the hills above Lake Michigan on a day the clouds are blue and gray and roiling. "My dad grew gourds here," Brad says. He's cutting wood for the winter. "I didn't like it when I was a kid. It was just work to me. My plan was to go to grad school. Then in the early spring of 2010, my father died." He pauses. "I felt I should do something with the land." A bird flies over and Brad says it's a northern flicker.

"The land has so much meaning to me. I'm the fourth generation." He shows me the small house by the creek where his great-grandparents used to live: no running water, no electricity. But so, so beautiful. Somewhat like Haiti, perhaps, when Haiti was first seen by Christopher Columbus, a place the intrepid explorer described in his maritime journals as a paradise of "beautiful beaches, groves of trees, all loaded with fruit ..." Columbus was invited inside a home that was made entirely of shells and thought he was "in a temple."

Gina and Brad see that the Leelanau paradise could become like Haiti if care isn't taken to protect the land and nourish the people. Their utopian dream is to somehow combine orphans and orchards. "I don't tell everyone this," Brad confesses. "I'm afraid they'd laugh at me." Utopian ideas, once considered naïve and unrealistic, are coming back into vogue. Erik Reese, an environmental journalist quoted by writer Akash Kapur in *The New Yorker* in October 2016, says, "Things will only get worse if we *don't* engage in some serious utopian thinking."

Gina, asked how she and Brad were going to be able to combine an orphanage with an orchard, laughs and says. "I have no idea. God will show us the way."

Meanwhile, back on the Leelanau Peninsula, Brad's trying to find a proper Santa Claus outfit. "The kids wouldn't want a Santa Claus from up north," he says, "to show up in a t-shirt, shorts, and flipflops."

Hank Bailey, a Part of the Place

About a block up the road from the old Cannery down on the shore in Glen Haven, Henry "Hank" Bailey gets out of a white Lexus in front of an abandoned, turn-of-the-century building that looks like it used to be a store. The whole village is deserted. Glen Haven today is a shoreside ghost town, treeless and bleak in the bright sunlight. The National Park Service cut the black locust trees, which they consider invasive, and has not replanted. There's no tree canopy.

Hank is a Native man in his late 60s, recently retired from the Department of Natural Resources at the Grand Traverse Band of Ottawa and Chippewa Indians. He moves easily, smoothly, sure of himself, but somehow humble, too, without arrogance. "This is what I want to show you," he says when we reach each other.

He points to a trail behind the building, now marked with national park signs. "My mother's family lived down this trail." It's cold suddenly, with a gust of wind off the lake and we instinctively turn that way to look at the water. Lake Michigan is blue-green close to shore and dark blue further out. There are high waves. The temperature today, out of the wind, might be 40 degrees, but with the wind coming off the water, like invisible darts, it feels a lot colder. I pull my coat closed.

"I knew you grew up around here," Hank says, "so I wanted to start here." I tell him I used to walk that trail looking for arbutus. I'd heard there had been a Native camp in the former D. H. Day State Park, now part of the Sleeping Bear Dunes National Lakeshore.

Hank explains that relatives on his mother's side of the family, people with the last name of Jackson, would have worked in Day's lumber business. D.H. Day came to Glen Haven in the late 1800s. "My people were here," Hank says. "We've always been here. We're still here, and hopefully will always be here."

I've heard of the Jackson family. The Jacksons were friends with Frank Fradd in Empire. Fradd recounted visits to the campsite of the man called Indian Jackson, no first name, in the early 1900s in an area on the north side of Empire, near a little stream. This is now a Natural Area called Chippewa Run, with a small parking lot and some trails, owned by the non-profit Leelanau Conservancy, a land preservation group in Leland, and is open to the public.

When the man called "Indian Jackson" by the white people died, he was very old. The age listed on his death certificate was 115. When Mr. Jackson was buried in the woods out behind the Maple Grove Cemetery, Fradd was dismayed, not only because he'd been friends of the family, but because it seemed to be such an unnecessary and mean-spirited snub. In the Empire Museum's collection of oral histories, Fradd was recorded as saying, "No matter how poor, every white and nine black people buried there were always furnished a grave in a lot, and a casket to be buried in, and the cost was paid by someone. But [the Native people] were buried in the woods [in what] was called Potter's Field. Webster's dictionary says, 'This means a burial ground for a person who dies poor or unknown.' But who knows? All of [their] ancestors were buried in the open land, so maybe they would prefer it that way."

In its heyday, the timber mills of the late 1800s and early 1900s in Glen Haven and Empire required as many men as they could get to do the work. Michigan's trees rebuilt Chicago after the big fire in the fall of 1871.

"The women would have cooked for their men," Hank says. "Probably they cooked for the people who worked at the mill. It would have been cold on the shore, but they were back in this little valley, with the dune between them and the lake, and it would have been warmer."

Hank says, "I have another place to show you," and tells me to follow him in my car. He stops at the corner, where M-109 turns to go up the hill toward Empire. He gets out of his car and comes to my window and points to the northeast corner, "A school used to be there." Hank's Great Uncle, Antoine Jackson, attended the school there for a time when he was young. "Antoine also matured into the logging industry," Hank says. Hank looks up toward the ridge and makes a sweeping gesture. "All through here," he says, "there's burnt rock from ancient campfires. Our ancestors were here for centuries."

Hank wants to show me a place, on Westman Road, the road that runs between the Homestead on Lake Michigan and Dunn's Farm Road along Glen Lake. Mrs. Westman, the sister of Hank's great-grandmother, lived on the road. "If you look," Hank says, getting out of his car after we turn off M-22 near the Homestead, "You can see the dip where they had a root cellar."

Glen Arbor Native people escaped being force-marched west during Andrew Jackson's Indian Removal, but government policies, imbued with the racism that justifies dominance, can encourage otherwise decent and ordinary citizens to do wrong things. Native villages, both those that were well-established and those that were impromptu, were often burned down by white settlers who laid claim to the land. Those white settlers felt justified in doing this and were never called to account in the courts. Sometimes white settlers said the land had been sold to them, and they had title to it, and other times they claimed the land had been lost through back taxes. The Unites States government's rules regarding Native people were an ever-changing checkerboard: as noncitizens, they were sometimes told they couldn't own land; other times they were told they didn't have to pay taxes since the land had been reserved to them by treaty, but then this idea changed, and the land was seized for back taxes. Even without broken treaty promises, the rules kept morphing. Hank's father, Henry Bailey, born in 1917, was not considered an American citizen until 1924.

On French Road in Leelanau County, an Ottawa village was burned one night in 1881. In Vonda Belanger's book, *Heritage of Provemont*, the people who lived there are named: Keduenachgud, Kewayguiscum, Louis O-Kin-pewan-O, NeChquay, Jos. Shema Kaw, Saw ne quay, C. L. O'Kinwan, Way Waysemah, An naw no quay, F. Kimp Wano, Say hego bay, Ne Bahne geshik, Mutch wetah, Eliz Muskotass uqua, Wah be mingo, and Etowe gezhick. "The combined properties of this group," Belanger writes, "totaled about 1,160 acres." On October 15, 1900, during the day, the Ottawa village at Burt Lake in Cheboygan County, was burned down by a sheriff's posse, reportedly because the Native people hadn't paid any taxes.

Another way the white settlers had of pushing Native people off the land was by creating a state park where they were living; this is true not only of state parks in the United States but is also often the case with the Provincial Parks in Canada. In Canada today, some National Parks, like the Pukaskwa on Lake Superior, are to this day, cheek-by-jowl with tribal encampments. Pukaskwa has been variously interpreted as meaning "safe harbor" or "place of fish eaters." As recently as the 1980s, when my Ottawa husband and I camped with our kids up in Canada, because the tribal campground was adjacent, we could hear their music at night, and Native kids would come over to play with our kids. At South Bay National Park, the Native kids amused our family by alternately imitating Michael Jackson doing the moonwalk and by perfectly imitating the cry of the loons.

In Leelanau County the town dumps were sometimes placed where Native people had made their homes in order to make the site as unpleasant as possible. Westman Road used to be where the Glen Arbor town dump was located, and the same was true of the area near the Ottawa village on French Road.

Native people in Leelanau County, starting from the time of the Civil War, served in the United States armed forces but they were not allowed to go to school, according to Robert Rader's book, *Beautiful Glen Arbor Township*, until 1920, when Harry Dumbrille became the county's Superintendent of Schools. Technically, Native people were allowed to vote in 1924, but often only if they gave up their tribal status. Native citizenship, which could affect everything from the right to buy property to being able to get an education, was sometimes absolutely required and, perversely, sometimes absolutely not allowed, so that full citizenship and the attendant rights thereof, wafted this way and that through shifting laws and the fogs of policy, with the result that legal barriers to voting by Native people were not removed until 1947.

In Leelanau County indigenous people became largely invisible until 1980 when the Grand Traverse Band of Ottawa and Chippewa Indians received federal recognition for being part of a sovereign nation with treaty rights, and they then established a permanent community on land they purchased in Peshawbestown. The Grand Traverse Band of Ottawa and Chippewa Indians, according to an article in the *Leelanau Enterprise* on June 21, 2018, claims that 87,000 acres in Leelanau County were taken illegally. In the case of the village on French Road, it would seem some of the land may have also been seized criminally. John Petoskey, tribal attorney quoted in the *Leelanau Enterprise* article, says that the tribe wouldn't ask for the land itself to be returned, but for reparations ranging from $30 million to $300 million.

Hank sits down on the ground with his back to a log, "My great-grandmother's sister married a Westman." He points across the road to the east. "There was a crippled guy in a nearby house and they took care of him."

Some of the most desirable places to live in the Glen Arbor area—at the mouth of the Crystal River which is now the Homestead, the big meadow at Dunn's Farm on Big Glen Lake, and the tree-shaded clearing on Little Glen Lake in what is now the Dorsey Trailer Park—were traditional Ottawa campsites. At the Homestead, they came every spring to fish and make reed sleeping mats. At Dunn's Farm, they were there all summer. Michigan State University anthropologists have found burned wild rice seeds at Dunn's Farm dating back 4,000 years, and Mike Dow (not the Mike Dow from Midland), whose family has a 100-year-old cottage nearby, said he has found arrowheads. The Dorsey Trailer Park, according to Jim Dorsey, was shown to his great-grandfather, John Dorsey, by an Ottawa friend who thought it one of the most beautiful and peaceful places on Glen Lake. Nan Helm, writing in the 1940s, recalled Native people coming in the 1920s and 30s to sell baskets at her father's Burdickville general store. As recently as the 1930s, summer people could remember Ottawa women going by canoe around Glen Lake, selling baskets to the houses on the shore. In the 1950s, Ottawa women were still coming to sell baskets to Mary Rader, owner with her husband, Jack, of the Totem Shoppe (now Shop) in Glen Arbor.

It's warm out of the wind. There are no insects. "My grandmother and her sister were great Basket Makers," Hank says. "There's a photo of them. The hills [in the photo] were bare." The entire peninsula had been clear-cut by then. "It might have been here." He looks north and east as if trying to see the hills here and recall the ones in the photo. He could be talking about the rooms of his house.

Sitting at the edge of Westman Road where some of his mother's relatives once made baskets and took care of a crippled man, Hank says that the source of his spiritual strength is his relationship to the land. "I see people who come to this country. They don't care about the land. They don't know who they are. I know who I am so strongly. I'm part of this. I'm black wolf clan. A wolf is a natural hunter." A hunter is a problem solver. A hunter works with reality, with complexity, with contradiction. And must correlate, compare, and cross-reference countless pieces of information: about the weather, the color of the sky, the way the wind is blowing, the animal signs, the endless scents, the seasonal habits of all creatures, the sounds, the lack of sounds. A hunter is patient, able to wait, and can act in a flash.

"As a young kid, out in the woods alone, I felt right at home," Hank says. "When I was in public, I knew I wasn't looked at in a good way [by white people]. But in the woods, I knew I was good. When you feel the [natural] environment around you, and know you are a part of it—when you feel that, you know you aren't more, or less, and you know you're just part of it—that's a good thing." The earth is an extension of his own being and he is an extension of the earth; to foolishly or wantonly, to deliberately hurt the earth would be to wound and possibly destroy himself, and that would be a sacrilege.

"Let's step back a few years," Hank says. "President Jackson signed the Indian Removal Act of the 1830s. Everyone knows about the Trail of Tears. But no one knows about the Trail of Death [down through southern Michigan]. So, we were running and hiding, just hiding out in the forests. This was going on for years." Some Native people retreated to the areas back in the swamps and dunes, land the Europeans didn't want because it couldn't be farmed, some went north to Canada and stayed with relatives on Manitoulin Island.

"The Jackson family, all my relatives, they really didn't have any place to work, so taking out the trees, was the only work they had. My mother grew up on Craker Road near Northport. This would have been a little bit of a trip in those days [for members of her family], but I'm sure this is where they were because this is where the work was."

The Treaty of Washington in 1836, Hank says, in which the Ottawa people, with their backs against the wall because of the Indian Removal Act, were forced into ceding their land, allowed Michigan to legally become part of the United States' Northwest Territory in 1837. Chief Andrew Blackbird of Harbor Springs was one of the Ottawa leaders who signed the treaty. Hank's great-grandfather on his father's side, Cobmoosa from the Little River Band of Ottawa, was a signatory to the treaty. Cobmoosa died at the age of 98 near Lowell. In old age he lived with one of his daughters who had a husband named Joe Bailey, one of Hank Bailey's relatives on his father's side. Fifty-four Ottawa and Chippewa chiefs were involved in the 1836 treaty. The Ottawa and Chippewa tribes are related and they overlap, geographically and through marriage; they speak dialects of the same language.

The cutting of the virgin timber, which began as soon as the treaty of 1836 was signed, made Michigan one the richest states in the union. The clear-cutting destroyed the fish, the game, the rivers, the forests. That treaty, theoretically, gave Native people the right to stay in the state, but like many treaties it was more honored in the breach than in the observance. According to a May 2018 program on National Public Radio, 500 treaties with the Native people were made, and broken; this is corroborated by several other sources.

"We never got any of the things they said we were going to get," Hank says. There was supposed to be approximately $540,000 in cash, but most of that went to white negotiators. Henry Schoolcraft, one of the negotiators, was accused by the United States government of absconding with funds but was never prosecuted. During this period, Schoolcraft, who had been married to a Chippewa woman from a prominent family at the Soo, daughter of an Irish nobleman and the daughter of a Chippewa leader, changed his name to Colcraft (in what today would be recognized as an identity crisis), and moved back to New York State, marrying a southern spinster who was wealthy from selling her slaves. His second wife, Mary Schoolcraft, wrote a thinly fictionalized account of her husband's first marriage to "his Pocahontas," something foolish that he did "in a burst of ethnographic enthusiasm," an account that veers off into various psychotic, racist screeds that purport to be arguments for slavery; like the mice in the cookhouse, she goes wherever she wants. The book, *The Black Gauntlet*, is available on Amazon.

Native people in America, according to a study conducted by J. David Hacker and Michael R. Haines in the Department of History in Binghamton University, New York in 2005, were reduced from a population of an estimated 7 million in the 1600s to an estimated 240,000 by the early 1900s, an 85 percent loss. War, disease, displacement, having their villages where they thought they owned the land burned to the ground and government removal policies created deep damage. There's an old trick in war, "poisoning the well", that was done psychologically to Native children. The government of the United States, either on purpose or by default, had policies that seemed designed to destroy the hearts and souls of Native children. They not only took indigenous people from their lands but put their children in government orphanages where they were beaten for speaking their language, punished for their spiritual beliefs, subjected to physical abuse and sometimes sexual abuse—all this childhood trauma becoming imbedded in the psyches of the children and carried back to the tribes where it created and was further compounded by the resultant waves of alcoholism, poverty, violence, malnutrition, diabetes, and suicides—making it almost impossible for people to survive.

Native writer Sherman Alexie, speaking on *National Public Radio* in 2017, said, "Children on reservations have the same degree of post-traumatic stress as combat veterans." Life expectancy for indigenous people in America in 1976, according to the Unites States Indian Health Service, was 48 years, while for other Americans it was 72. Life expectancy for Native people has increased since the 1980s and is now at 73, five years below that of other Americans, but much better than it was.

"We lost everything," Hank says about the previous century and the broken treaties. He doesn't enumerate. He's quiet for a while, then says, "Hitler did what he did in a short time. What happened to Natives happened over a long time." Native children were taken from their parents who loved them and put in boarding schools where they were constantly devalued as people. "My father ran away three times [from the boarding schools where Native children were placed after being taken from their parents]. He survived by escaping into alcohol. My parents both spoke the Ottawa language. The language stopped—in one generation, my parents' generation." He pauses, "I think it's just human nature [the genocide of Native people]. It's a cruel world out there."

Writer Jim Harrison, in a *Detroit Free Press* interview in 1988, said, "This nation has a history, but it also has a soul history. Our original sin in this country was the desecration of Indians, followed by the importation of slaves. Underlying all this is greed. But if you think a BMW is what works for you, just go look at LA. Those people are living and dying in a shit monsoon. Because without moral vision there is no future. Without vision, you die." In his 1988 novel *Dalva*, which would be made into a movie by the same name, one starring Brad Pitt, Harrison has one of the characters, a history professor named Michael, describe reservations as "concentration camps" and the exterminators of Native people as "pack-rat little Nazis." Harrison at the time of the interview lived on the outskirts of Lake Leelanau, on French Road, near where the Ottawa village had been burned down in 1881. In Harrison's *Dalva* novel, his character, Michael, says, "If the Nazis had won the war, the Holocaust, finally, would have been set to music, just as our victorious and bloody trek west is accompanied on film by thousands of violins and kettledrums." Harrison, during the *Detroit Free Press* interview, said, "Chief Seattle had a prophetic sense of the enduring presence of the Native people when he said, 'When you're walking in the evening and we are no longer there, we are still there,'" something Harrison must have felt walking home from the bar late at night in Lake Leelanau.

Hank says classes in the Ottawa language are now taught at the Grand Traverse Band of Ottawa and Chippewa Indians and at Northwestern Michigan College. He says the re-learning of the language is part of a Renaissance that's happening all across the country. In a country to which Europeans came, in part, for freedom of religion, it's a measure of the blind prejudice against aboriginal peoples that the Native religion was illegal until 1974, with the passing of the Indian Freedom of Religion Act. Hank says, "The idea of calling our way of life a religion is incorrect anyhow. The way we lived our life was a way of living in harmony within our universe. We understood we were not the best part of our environment. Just a part of the Circle of Life." Now, the Native people and culture, once on the brink of extinction, are experiencing a rebirth.

"Luck. Perseverance, my DNA," Hank says, is what has saved him from suicide and alcoholism. "I'm not sure who my spirit protector is, but I've got a beauty. I sailed on the freighters. It was late fall, 1975. We'd been up on Upper Lake Michigan. It was cold. Miserable. The decks were iced over. I just wanted to be back on shore." Hank's ship, the Joseph Young, was on its way down to Chicago, to go into dry dock for the winter. While they were waiting in the Chicago River, the bosun, in charge of the everyday running of the ship, went on a drinking binge and lost his mind, attacking imaginary beings with a fire ax, and setting off flares.

"I was on the steamship Joseph Young. The Edmund Fitzgerald was across the [Chicago] river. The flares were landing on their deck. Someone must have called the police or ambulance [to take the bosun]. We were all playing cards downstairs, when the bosun came to the top of the stairs. He was wearing boxers, these little slippers. His bathrobe was open. He had the fire ax. He was standing there in his," Hank pauses, "*outfit*. Nobody looked at anybody. He came down the stairs and started striking out at things no one could see. We thought we were gonna die." The ambulance came and took the bosun to the hospital. "He never lost his job," Hank says. "They must have covered it up for him some way."

The Edmund Fitzgerald's crew was preparing for another trip up the lakes. Heading for a western Lake Superior port. "I remember waving to three men on the deck of the Fitzgerald as they left the south side of Chicago port," Hank says. "The whole crew went down to the bottom of Lake Superior on the return trip. I could have been on the Edmund Fitzgerald instead of the Joseph Young." Twenty-nine men went down on the Edmund Fitzgerald, an event memorialized in the Gordon Lightfoot song. Hank says that while he was sailing on the Great Lakes, his marriage foundered. Married at 18 and a father at 19, with finally three children, the marriage breakup was "not a happy thing for my kids." He loves his children, and loves being a grandfather and great-grandfather, and is grateful now for having been restored to a good relationship with his children, but that rough early time in his life, after he got off the boats, "sent me into a spiral." He headed out west. For a few years he became a roustabout and a traveler.

Hank says he saw Mt. St. Helen's erupt in 1980 from a plane window. "If you ever think you're somethin', just look at a mountain blowin' up. There was thunder and lightning. It had its own weather in there." He chased the rodeos and fished in the Columbia River. He dated the granddaughter of Chief Joseph. He worked as a wildfire fighter in the mountains of Washington. It was dangerous work and he had a few close calls. He credits a childhood close to nature, and his Native ancestors, with his survival. He grew up in Benzie County, near Big Platte Lake. "We were poor, but we didn't think we were poor. We had the lake." He liked school, especially high school where he was a star athlete. He's proud of the fact that his father, Henry Bailey, for whom he's named, was a grandson of the great Ottawa leader, Cobmoosa, from the Grand Rapids area.

"Cobmoosa was a great orator. He was called the great walker. He could be on one side of the state at a meeting one day, and on the other side just a few days later. My cousin John [Bailey] calls him the Luke Skywalker of the Ottawa, because of his ability to get quickly from one side of the state to the other." Hank pauses. "Way back when, the people of this country called me a savage. Then I became known as an Indian. That was okay, we got used to it—so long as, you know, they said it with *respect*. Then somewhere along the way, I became a Native American. Now I look at the way people [in other countries] see this country. If I were to leave here, if I were to say that I'm a Native American, that's dangerous. Someone might want to shoot me because I'm an American." The word Indian, according to some, was coined by Columbus who thought he had reached India when he landed in Florida. Hank says the most respectful term is Native, as opposed to Indian, and even better is to use the specific tribal name.

Hank was one of nine children. "We were bringing game home all the time. We knew how to set snares [for rabbits]. I speared a 19-pound Northern Pike when I was 10. It was 43-

inches long and I was only 56-inches tall." He has a photo of the fish and his 10-year-old self. He was in a fish shanty on the ice at the east end of Platte Lake. His father had just left to run to nearby Honor to get lunch for them. "I could hear his footsteps walking away," Hank says, "when my spear struck [the fish]. He was so strong, he was swimming away with the spear."

Ultimately, Hank had to stick his arm in the water up to his arm pit to push the spear back into the fish before pulling it up and dragging it backward out of the fish shanty onto the ice. "A small battle ensued," Hank says, to get the pike out of the shanty, "with everything inside the shanty being knocked every which way." A Northern Pike is a predator with eyes situated on top of its head for sight. It's that fish with the underslung jaw. "My gal [Amy Russello], she's incredible. She knew the Northern Pike is my favorite fish. She commissioned a painting of a Northern Pike as a present. The pike is still my mother's favorite eating fish." Pike tastes like sole, but with firmer flesh. Because of the Y bones, a Northern Pike must be expertly filleted and eaten with care. Hank's mother, Betty Edwards, whose mother was Esther Jackson, was a woman Hank described as "quiet, resourceful," even in her 90s. In her later years, she lived near Omena, a mile south of where she was born near Northport. Hank's mother died in December 2017; he was very close to her and, based on the photo of Betty Edwards in the *Leelanau Enterprise*, he strongly resembled her, too. Hank said his mother's Ottawa name in English was All-Day-Woman, and true to her name, she had remarkable stamina and staying power all through her life.

Hank, now that he's retired, speaks to youth groups in churches and schools about the importance of taking care of the earth. He works with Jon Aylsworth at the Grand Traverse Band on a project called *The Edible Forest*. He's also part of a program at Dartmouth College called *Indigenous*

Confluence, with partners from the Grand Traverse Band, First Nations of Canada, and the Maori people of New Zealand, all working to restore the earth.

At a 2017 Northern Michigan Environmental Action Council (NMEAC) event, Hank Bailey received an award for his work to save the environment. Aaron Payment, the head of the tribe at the Soo and the keynote speaker at the NMEAC event, is also passionate about preventing environmental degradation. Both Bailey and Payment have been active in leading their respective tribes to protest the Canadian pipelines, liable to break due to age and poor engineering practices, undermining Michigan waters. The Canadian company, Enbridge Energy, with an outdated and increasingly controversial pipeline under the Straits of Mackinac, was responsible for the disastrous 2010 contamination of the Kalamazoo River. All of the company's pipelines are old; in many places, if they rupture, the rivers and lakes of Michigan will be irrevocably damaged. In Kalamazoo the company's carelessness sickened people and killed fish and wildlife for miles.

"This was all predicted in our prophecies," Hank says. "They said we would have everything taken from us: our children, our land, our language. But that then the eagles would come back, the bison would come back—and that *is* happening—and the white people would come to us and ask us how to save our mother."

Hank is a traditional dancer, a person steeped in his culture's beliefs. He says, "My spirituality stepped in [for me]. If I know in my heart that what I'm doing is a good thing, I'll push forward and let the Creator sort it out." After speaking about the importance of taking care of the earth at the NMEAC event, he used a sacred eagle-bone whistle to call to the four directions—north, south, east, and west—in a prayer with all of those attending, white and Native, standing in quiet reverence.

The Storm

Snow is falling softly. Snow is covering the scarred Alligator Hill where the rogue storm in August 2015 tore out a five-acre strip from the hide of the earth.

Glen Arbor Village is tiny. I went to sixth grade there. Out behind the school Gerry Barczak and Carl Oleson used to play baseball, honing their catching and throwing skills, determining whether or not the ball was in or out, if a foot was on or off a base, fine-tuning their sense of fairness.

In front of the redbrick school the girls sometimes had bird funerals, trailing around under the pines, trading on the poor bird's demise to try to understand the meaning of life; ramping up the emotions, and finally, after too many mawkish burials, tamping them down and joining the boys in baseball. If we couldn't catch, throw, or hit the ball with a bat, then one of the boys would take our last strike and let us just run the bases.

My family's home was a mile from the village on a high bluff above Sleeping Bear Bay. We lived in the Day Forest. Alligator Hill, where all the trees came down, was in that forest.

Alligator Hill was where Susy Schmidt and I liked to gallop our horses, on a road open under the pines, a road thickly covered in pine needles, a straight shot to the look-out. The panoramic views of the deep, blue-green lakes were extravagantly gorgeous but we didn't know this, having nothing with which to compare them.

That summer when "the big storm" came, I was in the Dennos Museum with American sculptor, Lori Park, visiting from London. She was looking at the aquatic-themed bamboo sculptures by Jinwon Chang, strange and interesting boats, or maybe fish, hanging from the ceiling, inspired by his three near-deaths from drowning.

I was in the wing with the Inuit carvings, thinking about the sense of humor in the face of the polar bear, when I heard a sound like a train in the air. The lights flickered; then went out.

Lori and I found each other again, along with a handful of other Sunday afternoon museum goers, all of us staring out the big plate glass windows at the storm.

"I think we should move away from the windows," I overheard someone say.

"They won't break," someone else responded, but everyone moved back.

"Maybe we need to get out of here," I said to Lori, under my breath.

"We might be in the safest place," she said quietly. She was watching the storm.

The air was fluorescent chartreuse, then fluorescent turquoise. Then rain drops the size of cats were falling from a black sky, trees whipping back and forth, with an occasional loud crack, like someone's leg being broken with a tire iron.

Finally, after what seemed like a long time but was probably not more than 30 minutes, we felt we could make it to the car. We crossed the flooded parking lot, checking for downed electrical wires, sprinting through the still falling rain and the sounds of breaking branches.

Along West Bay there were trees uprooted everywhere and sailboats thrown against the shore. When we drove back to the Leelanau Peninsula on Bugai Road we saw emergency crews. We learned that the storm had winds gusting up to 100 miles an hour. As far as anyone knew, there had been no deaths or even serious injuries.

For weeks one could hear the sound of chain saws. The village of Glen Arbor was closed for several days. This area seemed to have been particularly brutally struck and emotions were running high. Several people described themselves as having tears in their eyes when they described the way they felt seeing the downed trees. Glen Arbor businessman Bobby Sutherland, in a book he co-authored about the storm, *Storm Struck*, described his eyes as being "moist".

Trees are ancient and powerful entities in the human imagination. The "men as trees, walking" cited in the Bible, and "fear not, till Birnam Wood do come to Dunsinane" in Shakespeare's *Macbeth*, show the way images of trees strike deep in the human psyche. I've known expert woodcutters, manly and hearty and taciturn, who over time came to refuse to take down any trees but those that were dead or diseased. Do trees have spirits? Maybe, but their majesty is undeniable and the emotions they arouse in us are, too.

An article in the *Glen Arbor Sun* by Linda Alice Dewey, hiking up Alligator Hill after the storm with a friend, is about hers and her friend's deep childhood connections to this beloved summer place, how she and her friend associated the forest with picnics there in "an old '53 Plymouth" and how as a child her friend had found the ancient water tower "magical" and how it was "a bleak day" when she saw its rusted remains on the ground. They mourned together the loss of the storied childhood fairways of the latter-day Gilded Age golf course, abandoned during the Great Depression and, after a brief reprieve in the late 1930s when it functioned for a while as a golf course again, reforested with "little pines" and then no longer the same.

Patti Brandt Burgess, staff writer for the *Leelanau Enterprise* (she now writes for the *Traverse City Record-Eagle*), in an article entitled "Trail of Tears" wrote about people in Glen Arbor who bemoaned the changes the storm brought to the landscape. "I can't go to that one spot without crying," a

Glen Arbor woman was reported as saying. To see something one thought would last forever, gone, and to feel that loss acutely, is a universal emotional reaction.

Surely this is how Andrew Blackbird, the last chief of Harbor Springs, felt when he saw the virgin timber cut, the rivers polluted, the grayling and the passenger pigeons on their way to extinction, the children unable to get enough love or food, and his people put on reservations. "I thought my people were very happy in those [former] days," he wrote, "when they were all by themselves and possessed a wide spread of land, and no one to quarrel with them as to where they should make their gardens or take timber or make sugar. And fishes of all kinds were so plentiful in the Harbor."

My tiny grandmother, born in 1868 in White Cloud, walked north with her large husband, a lumberman, on the old Ottawa trail that ran from Newago to Northport. She said the stumps of the trees looked like yellow plates as far as the eye could see. She saw no Native people, most of whom were presumably dead, surviving incognito in marriages to whites, on reservations, or keeping a low profile somewhere out of sight of vigilantes.

Twenty-five miles from Glen Arbor, on a hill behind Tom's West Bay Shopping Plaza, someone has decided to sculpt a hill, right down to the sand, in order to put in a housing development on what had been a heavily wooded parcel roughly the size of the storm-damaged piece on Alligator Hill. The poor developer will have to wait 50 years for the trees he plants to be as big as the ones he's removed.

The entire M-72 corridor, starting in Traverse City, as it goes west toward Empire, is utterly changed from the road I knew as a child. Unplanned, random, industrial sprawl crowds the highway. The buildings could not be uglier even if they had tried to take a scenic landscape and make it as ugly as possible. A drive where the sweeping pastoral vistas once had the lulling, sweet rhythms of a waltz now has scenery as jarring as death metal.

If you take M-22 from Traverse City, going north out along West Bay, you can see mansions crowding the ridges, like people on a parade route trying to elbow each other out of the way so they can see. The shores of all the lakes, both Lake Michigan and the inland lakes, are cluttered with houses.

There were approximately two billion people on the planet when my parents were born at the turn of the century; soon there will be five times that many but the amount of land there is for that many more people is the same as it always was. You don't need to know a lot of math to see that the way things are going is bad. If we don't create—and enforce—wise and visionary zoning laws designed to prevent the way untrammeled development will ruin the landscape, then the Leelanau Peninsula will look like Paterson, New Jersey by the end of the century and in four centuries, the amount of time Europeans have been in America, we're probably going to look, and smell, like Calcutta.

Trees grow, but they don't grow through concrete.

Even the Sleeping Bear Dunes National Lakeshore, where they should have known better and cared more, installed an asphalt bike trail along the base of my mother's hill, killing the arbutus. It will never grow back.

I like the bike trail, I want to make clear. I think there should be gravel bike trails and hiking paths along all the roads, on both sides, wide enough that a person doesn't need to be afraid of being hit by a car. I also think more and better planning should go into all roads, trails and new construction generally.

Natural beauty is important. It inspires. It heals. It provides a moral baseline. It's how we understand the difference between life and death. It's our most ancient biofeedback system, one to which we are innately attuned and hard-wired to need. It has always been a birthright, but because we have an increasing number of people, and no effective zoning, it no longer is.

I grew up in a house on a hill and we had a cottage on the lake, too. But that way of life is not going to be sustainable if our great-grandchildren are going to be able to experience nature the way we did.

Residences and stores need to be clustered in cities, towns and villages—with green spaces and parks. Public transportation needs to replace cars. Solar and wind need to replace fossil fuels. We need to stop polluting our air and water. Trees should be replaced when they're cut. Industry needs to be where no one can see it. Farmland needs to be preserved. Parks and green spaces need to be everywhere and highways need to be landscaped. This is common sense.

It's normal to care about the tree that comes down in one's own backyard and normal to not care as much about the tree that comes down in someone else's. Novelist Karl Ove Knausgaard writing in *The New Yorker*, confessed that he didn't really think that much about the images on TV of the Syrian migrants crossing Europe until he saw "a dead toddler washed up on the gravel of a Turkish beach" and knew that could be his child.

We need to take the grief we feel about the loss of trees and the scarring of natural beauty in a landscape we know, and extrapolate, expand our empathy, and apply it to the loss of trees and scarring of natural beauty everywhere. If we sentimentalize our relationship to nature, without at the same time taking into account the need to preserve it for everyone and improve everyone's access, we cheapen our emotions. We risk becoming ridiculous, like grade school girls having way too many bird funerals.

We need to understand that natural beauty is important not just for a few sensitive souls like us, but for all; and, frankly, the least sensitive need it the most. A lot of poorly planned development is created by people never given a chance to appreciate natural beauty when they were young.

If we view trees coming down in the wind as a tragedy, a word used by several to describe the summer wind storm of

2015, we should nonetheless be careful to steer clear of associating it figuratively or otherwise with something like the Trail of Tears where thousands died.

Changing how we think about land will not be easy because we associate land ownership with freedom, with democracy. The men who wrote *The Declaration of Independence*, knowing that change is difficult for people, wrote, "mankind are (sic) more disposed to suffer, while evils are sufferable, than to right themselves by abolishing the forms to which they are accustomed. . ."

Ten thousand years ago, world-wide, people taught themselves to eat corn, rice and little grains of wheat, instead of meat on the hoof. The grain was less nutritious and probably less tasty, but it was steadily available. It meant people could stay in one place instead of chasing animals. This switch from hunting and gathering to agriculture created civilization as we know it.

As recently as 50 years ago we started to learn about the ill effects of smoking and began to educate ourselves not to do it. In an astonishingly short period of time, we've managed to reverse a trend that seemed insensible to change.

Now we need to teach ourselves to not destroy the land. This will feel strange at first because we're used to thinking that someday we would like a house on a hill or a cottage on the shore. But it's time. Unless we want our great-grandchildren to live in a world from which natural beauty has been obliterated, we need to change.

We need to navigate the distance between *this* land and *these* trees, to *that* land and *those* trees. It's about imagining the future. It's about seeing one's self as another. Access to natural beauty needs to be declared an inalienable right, not just for the few, but for all.

Vineyards and Hopfields

When someone wants to turn a place that was a church into a wine-tasting room, you know something's happening to the demographics. One warm June evening sometime in the early 2000s, Leland Township held a public hearing to consider a special use permit so the former Kingdom Hall of Jehovah's Witnesses at the corner of French and E. Duck Lake Roads could become a wine-tasting facility for CAB Vineyards. It was approved.

CAB Vineyards, 48 acres on French Road behind the Schaub dairy farm, is owned by William and Susan Braymer. William Braymer says he and his wife developed their interest in wine while living and working in California in the 80s. "We feel that between us, with my marketing flare," (Braymer works for Seimens Medical in Ann Arbor), "and her degree in enology from the University of California at Davis, we can make a good contribution." Braymer says advice from his neighbors, the Mathias family, vintners at Chateau Fontaine, is invaluable.

In the past 50 years the number of vineyards on the Leelanau Peninsula has grown from one, Boskydel Vineyards above Lake Leelanau, to more than two dozen; and most of those have emerged in the last 20 years, like the one Tony and Joan Ciccione, parents to the actress and singer Madonna, established on Hilltop Road.

There are also a growing number of artisanal breweries. Tandem Ciders on Setterbo Road north of Suttons Bay was one of the first but now there are more than a dozen. The highways are now lined, not only with vineyards, but hopfields. The hops, also a vine, like the grapes, are trained on ropes and wires that go up 30 feet in the air. The hopfields are distinguished by 50-foot poles leaning out to create tension on the ropes, creating a high, leaning-out fence around the hopfields, with a cat's cradle of wires over the top of the vines, criss-crossing. Hops look a bit like tight, new, green pinecones. Michigan is now the fourth largest hop-growing region in the United States, with 900 acres, still far behind Washington, Oregon, and Idaho where they have thousands of acres in hops, but the hop-growing ventures are increasing. Hops are a natural preservative in beer and the hops have long been known to have a calming or sleep-inducing effect.

The 30-mile-long Leelanau Peninsula offers nearly perfect vineyard conditions, according to several vintners. Many factors contribute: the Leelanau Peninsula is on the 45th parallel; it has a microclimate caused by the moderating waters of Lake Michigan; it has the 21-mile long Lake Leelanau up the center; the glacial till and sandy loam create good drainage; the mix of soils brought by glaciers offers variety; the peninsula has high hills allowing for "air drainage". Highly rated German Riesling wine, for example, is produced on slate in the Rhine Valley. Bel Lago Vineyards which has a vineyard with slate soil, won the 2010 Pacific Rim International Wine Competition for "Best of White" for semi-dry Riesling.

Gill's Pier Vineyards, now no longer operating, won a Michigan State Fair prize for a similar wine. "Riesling's a good wine for this climate," says veteran vintner Warren Raftshol of Raftshol Vineyards now owned by Nathaniel Rose, "because you can make a good wine out of the white grapes even if they don't ripen all the way."

Despite the Leelanau Peninsula's ideal wine-growing conditions, the *Oxford Companion to the Wines of North America* gives the Leelanau Peninsula only a brief mention and the *Wine Bible* and other similar books don't even do that. It's not on their maps; or it wasn't. However, when a wine tasting room goes in where a church used to be, maybe it's only a matter of time before the climate on the Leelanau Peninsula is no longer the world's best kept secret.

Bernie Rink, who would die in 2018 at the age of 92, was the original owner of Boskydel, the peninsula's first winery. He grew up on a truck farm in northern Ohio where his German father had vineyards so that even during the hard scrabble 1930s, he told me one day, "We lived like God in France." Rink wanted ordinary people to be able to afford wine on their supper table. "I consider myself a grape grower, not a winemaker," he said. "The more you do with the growing, the less you do," he gestured around his tasting room, "in here."

It was sleeting outside as he talked. Growing grapes, even in the optimal conditions afforded by the Leelanau Peninsula, is not without risks. "One year, Lake Michigan froze all the way to Frankfort. We lost all our grapes that year," Rink shook his head at the memory. "You can't plant the grapes too close together, they don't get enough sun. Grapes are like tourists. They like heat and sun. Some summers are too cool. One summer, a few years ago, I didn't even pick some of the grapes because they didn't ripen."

Rink was the wise old man of Leelanau vintners. Larry Mawby, a third-generation farmer, when asked what he wanted people to experience in a bottle of wine from his own vineyards, says, "The essence of Bernie-ness." Bernie Rink was viewed in most quarters as brilliant, fair, honest and curmudgeonly, a bit like Yoda in *Star Wars*, so if you can get that in a bottle, you've got something.

Boskydel was the first winery on the Leelanau Peninsula, but Rink wasn't the first person to plant a vineyard, or even the first German. In 1855 two brothers from Annweiler, about 30 miles from Heidelberg above the Rhine, immigrated to Lake Leelanau. Jacob and Simon Schaub brought their grape vines with them, according to Theresa F. Schaub. The Schaubs were devout Catholics and one might think the wine was needed for communion, but Theresa said, "It had nothing to do with the church," adding, "and they didn't think about it being the 45th parallel. They looked and thought, 'Ah, wine hills, like home'."

"Forty years ago, here, almost no one had wine with dinner," says Cris Telgard, one of the founders in 1985 of the Leland Wine and Food Festival, "I'm talking about people in their homes, with their families and friends, having supper together." Cris says he and his wife, Kathy, and a few friends, were sitting around one winter evening years ago in their little apartment above the Bluebird Restaurant, talking about how to get people interested in wine. At that time Cris and Kathy were still working in the family restaurant started by his grandparents in 1927. "People might have had a highball before dinner, a cocktail," Cris says. "Men drank beer in the bar, but no one had wine with dinner. Now you can buy wine at Sam's Club."

The Puritans were among the first immigrants to America and they set the tone. They valued going to work and going to church, not leisure time and fine dining. When Alexis De Tocqueville visited America in 1831, he found "very disagreeable" the lack of wine with meals. "It upsets all one's settled habits," he wrote, concluding, "The fine arts here are in their infancy." European customs, especially winemaking, hadn't crossed the ocean. Why? Time, maybe. It takes a lot of time and energy to grow grapes and make wine and it takes time to prepare and eat the kind of meal with which you'd like to have a bottle of wine.

Up through the mid-1800s, much of the continent west of Baltimore, with the exception of a few port cities such as New Orleans, Montreal, and St. Louis, was wilderness. Chicago was wilderness until 1833, and, even then, it was a frontier outpost of a few cabins. Abraham Lincoln born in 1809 in the wilds of Appalachia, whose grandfather, also Abraham Lincoln, was killed by a travelling Native war party of some unknown tribe while trying to cut trees on his Kentucky homestead, said if his family could sometimes afford to wear denim instead of leather, they thought they were doing well. Fighting random war parties and cutting trees came before everything else; basic survival took all of their time. Making cloth, it turns out, much less wine, takes time.

De Tocqueville, wanting to see real wilderness, was told to go to Michigan; when he got there, he wrote in his diary, "ceaseless trees." Michigan wouldn't be opened for settlement until the late 1850s. Henry Thoreau, already in the last stages of tuberculosis, strolled briefly along the shore in Leland one summer afternoon in 1861 while his steamer refueled. Leland then was primarily a wooding station. Thoreau's hasty scrawl in his naturalist's notebook was, "shepherdia leaves [bearberry], Indians, Carp Lake." Carp Lake was once the name for Lake Leelanau. Seventy years later when Cris Telgard's family was living in Leland, it was a sleepy fishing village where his grandfather, a boat builder, and his grandmother, Leone Carlson, a fisherman's daughter, started the Bluebird, a quaint dockside restaurant that in old photos looks like a moored fishing boat.

When vineyards first started appearing on the Leelanau Peninsula in the early 1980s, most people preferred red wines and sweet wines although the micro-climate here was better for white wine. According to winemaker Bryan Ulbrich, tastes have changed in the intervening 30 years and now the dryer white wines are preferred.

Deer season, late fall, is the time most people seem to want to visit the many wineries and breweries on the Leelanau Peninsula. Something about the cooler nights and the leaves coming off, makes them want to get together in groups and drink in a frenzy of socializing, often with total strangers, a kind of last gathering of the clan before winter sets in. The peninsula is also home to a distillery. Mark and Mandy Moseler who have the Distillery in Lake Leelanau say late fall and early winter is their busiest time.

"There's currently a nationwide awakening to what we're doing up here in Northern Michigan," Ulbrich says. "The kinds of wines we're making are the most popular in the country right now." At a time when regional foods and farm markets, with their underlying hopes of reigniting community connection and recreating an old-fashioned agriculture free from industrial pesticides, have captured the imagination of Americans, then the thought of those family-owned, microclimate vineyards and breweries on a remote Northern Michigan peninsula holds out a certain kind of tantalizing charm.

Where the Land Ends

The wind never seems to stops blowing at the tip of the Leelanau Peninsula. I've visited a few times and the wind is a constant. It's especially so in winter. This is where the land ends.

It's a sound you don't forget. It's the heavy breathing of the earth itself. I grew up with this sound. We lived above Lake Michigan, facing north. Every time I go out to the tip of the peninsula and hear the wind again, I feel nostalgic for something I'd known every day, but now know only on rare occasions.

There's just one road that goes to the very end of the peninsula and it's up the east side. The farthest you can go up the west side is to Peterson Park, more or less; there are some private roads but they don't connect one side of the peninsula to the other. My family often went to Peterson Park for picnics. We went there when it was called "The Wash-Out", the name derived from a deep fissure from the top of the bank, 500 feet to the shore. I still go there and the wash-out is still there but filled with trees now. I love the wind from the west and even on the hottest summer days, it is still pleasant. There are seldom any insects. There are grills to cook food. There's playground equipment for children. And you have the whole expanse of Lake Michigan out to the west, and the glorious sunsets.

You would think the road would cross over, and go up around the tip of the peninsula, connecting the west side to the east, but it doesn't. I know because I've tried. Up the east side you pass through Northport and go by the famous gathering spot, Barb's Bakery, on your way north out of town. This is where Barb makes donuts and sweet rolls all night and goes home to sleep at five. Someone else comes in to serve them. The joke in the bakery a few years ago was, "I guess GPS isn't all it's cracked up to be," after a tourist stopped and asked how far to Harbor Springs. Google and other maps offer 40 miles "as the crow flies" across the water. However, one cannot get to Harbor Springs across the water in one's car.

The day I find to drive to the tip of the peninsula is a winter morning. It's not even 10 a.m. yet, but it feels like late afternoon, like the sun already wants to go down. It's snowing. There's a winter advisory. The wind is blowing the snow across the road, sometimes in drifts. I drive slowly.

Driving to the end of a peninsula, approaching the end of anything, can probably be relied upon to set one ruminating on ultimate questions. Who are we? Where did we come from? Why are we doing what we're doing? And what is the meaning of life?

M-201, or Mill Street, curves out of the village, then straightens out, becoming County Road 629, or Lighthouse Point Road. At the bight, near the water, the northwesterly winds blow a cloud of milkweed fluffs across the highway toward the lakeshore—thousands of elliptical brown seeds, the diameter of a peppercorn, with their fuzzy parachutes, pirouetting across like miniature Russian ballet dancers, all dressed in white.

Earth is going to bed. Earth is in her nightshirt. The oak leaves are still on the trees. They'll be there 'til spring.

On the east side, or water side, there's the road going out to the famously gated Northport Point founded in 1899 when wealthy people came and built log cabin mansions, like those of the Rockefellers' in the Grand Tetons, complete with ballrooms and servants' quarters. Then on the west side of the road is the elfin cobblestone Woolsey Airport, unlike any airport in the world, named in honor of Clinton Woolsey, an early Northport aviator.

Then there's the strange, metal, tower-like thing, like a giant helmet on a Viking, a remnant of Vulcan Copper and Supply in Cincinnati, used for processing the highly toxic chromium-6, placed at a bizarrely inconvenient distance from the company's Ohio factory, necessitating dangerous transport between Cincinnati and the tip of the Leelanau Peninsula. I puzzle over this. Perhaps the thinking behind this was that there were a lot of people who could get hurt in Cincinnati, from a chemical spill, and only a few people who might die in faraway Northport. But it still doesn't make sense. Dead people in Northport don't matter as much as dead people in Cincinnati?

I think it's the kind of thinking, magical thinking, that our primitive ancestors used to address the world. For a long time, people had no idea where babies came from or how they got into the bodies of women. From the sky, maybe. Or, from eating round food, like apricots. They worshiped women because of the "big magic" they possessed. Then the men decided they'd had enough of that and determined that they were the source of babies. Then they all got religion and pretended they didn't know, at least not until it was either too late, and they had to put the baby in an orphanage, or they were legally married at the Justice of the Peace or in church. The toxic waste site was the illegitimate child of the Vulcan Copper Company. The toxic wastes were reportedly moved a mile inland by the federal government sometime in the 1970s or 80s and buried in sand, something that still smacks of out of sight, out of mind, not reassuring.

In somewhat of a reverse of Vulcan Copper burying their chromium-6 waste near Northport, Midland's Dow Chemical Company, through their department of charitable giving, has provided major grants to environmental nonprofits in Northern Michigan. Inland Seas, a Suttons Bay nonprofit devoted to protecting the waters of the Great Lakes, has received sizable grants from Dow. Dow people, both family members and employees, go to parties in the area; they're easy to meet. My friend Bill Meek was a chemist for Dow and his friend Dorothy Yates was my friend and one of my writing students; Dorothy's husband had been a patent attorney for Dow and they'd had a beautiful home overlooking Big Glen Lake. My sister Ann went to school with Mary "Lloyd" Dow at the Leelanau School in Glen Arbor. Mike Dow also attended the Leelanau School and has been instrumental in seeing that the Herbert H. and Grace A. Dow Foundation has given large grants to the Grand Traverse Regional Land Conservancy (GTRLC), most recently one of two million dollars from the Dow Foundation. Mike Dow, who sits on the Dow Foundation board, is quoted on the GTRLC website as saying, "We like to make long-term investments like this to keep Michigan a nice place for our grandchildren and beyond." Midland, a city in mid-Michigan, is home of Dow Chemical, and is one of the most toxic cities in the country, according to the *New York Times* in July 2018. The Tittabawassee River, which runs through Midland, is filled with poisons, including dioxins, a main ingredient in Agent Orange. You can't eat the fish you catch in the Tittabawassee River or eat the deer you hunt along the river. I'm glad the Dow Foundation is giving money to environmental groups in Northern Michigan, but I would feel more comfortable about this if they *also* cleaned up Midland; but perhaps it's too expensive to clean up Midland, or perhaps their grandchildren don't live there. It's hard to know what the thinking is.

Our thinking about toxic waste seems to be, evolutionarily, in the denial phase, a bit after magical thinking and somewhere before logic and reason: if we don't think about it, or see it, we don't know about it. It would be nice if we could advance rapidly to the reason and logic stage, but there will always be laggards, sometimes prominent laggards. Andrew Jackson, the U.S. president who didn't have much education and as a child often had to go without food, reportedly thought the world was flat. This was 2,200 years after Eratosthenes, a black-skinned man from North Africa, measured the circumference of the earth, with calculations so accurate he was within 100 miles of data from today's satellite photos. During the Inquisition, a thousand years ago, people wanted to put Galileo to death because he thought the earth revolved around the sun, notwithstanding the fact that several scientists had thought this for a long time. The Inquisition guys didn't kill Galileo, partly because he was willing to keep his views to himself, but they put him under house arrest for the remainder of his life. We will always have willfully ignorant people. Which is why we should keep public schools and make sure children have enough to eat, so they can grow up to be like Galileo and not like Andrew Jackson.

The road starts to curve and the sky opens up as the road begins to come to the end of the peninsula. I see a flock of crows, then a pair of ravens. That's how they usually come, crows in groups and ravens in pairs, no one knows why, and that's how I can usually tell them apart, at least at a glance, although ravens are generally bigger, maybe half again as big. They both walk in a waddling way, but ravens more so. Ravens thrust their heads forward, to give themselves momentum perhaps, the rest of the body following, with their bellies swaying like those of well-fed potentates. Crows, I think, are more aggressive than ravens. They work together, like wolves. Sometimes you'll see a flock of them feasting on road kill, some of them riding shotgun it seems while the others eat, and then they'll switch out. Crows care when one of their own dies. They will place "offerings" next to the body, a twig or a leaf.

Off to the south, there's a bald eagle in the field, just standing there, the size of a toddler. It must have found a rabbit or something. You think of eagles as flying, or perched high up in a tree, but see them standing on the ground sometime, they are not like a bird at all, but in some uncanny way like a person.

"Eight-hundred million years ago," according to retired geologist, Richard Cookman of Suttons Bay, "there was a major period of cold, probably world-wide. They call it Ice World, and they think all the continents were wrapped up in it, and of course the continents were in different places at that time." The whole mass of quivering geologic time lies in that downhome, tossed-off remark. One thinks about things like this when driving to the end of a peninsula that's spent a lot of its existence under water.

I get lost the first time I try to find the Leelanau Conservancy's Lighthouse West Natural Area at the end of the Leelanau Peninsula. This is partly because I'm driving in a snowstorm and partly because the entrance to it is south of the lighthouse. I arrive at a dead-end and turn around and go back the way I'd come, to the Grand Traverse Lighthouse. It was decommissioned in 1972, superseded first by marine radar and then by global positioning systems (GPS), however the historic lighthouse has been an integral part of the Lighthouse West Natural Area from the start, lending its name to the site, first and foremost, because it's the nearest and most visible landmark.

"The tip of the peninsula has a long, extended reef loaded with large boulders just under the water—very dangerous to vessels coming through the Manitou Passage and into Grand Traverse Bay," according to Dick and Sue Hanson writing for the Northport Area Historical Association, "and so the lighthouse was needed to prevent maritime disasters." The lighthouse remains—restored, but no longer in use—as a museum.

A gift shop on the east side of the lighthouse parking lot is oddly "open" in the quiet winter landscape. Asked if they get many visitors this time of year, a young woman named Amalia says, "Yesterday we had two." She adds that they will close in a week. I ask for directions to the Lighthouse West Natural Area and she says that I'm very close and tells me how to go back a little distance, to Cathead Bay Road, and turn where there's a bank of mailboxes.

Amalia wants to know how the roads are. She has a party to go to after work. I tell her the roads are okay, so far, but the storm doesn't show any signs of letting up.

Backtracking to the main road, I turn near the bank of mail boxes and head down a westward slope toward what must be Lake Michigan. There's a sign that says, "Private Property. No Trespassing."

I go back up the road and this time see the Lighthouse West Natural Area sign that I'd missed the first time, and a small parking lot. I'll meet Ed Ketterer, at that time the Director of the Leelanau Conservancy Board. Ketterer has been kind enough to agree to show me around. I'm early, as usual, and start reading the literature I'd been given at the Leelanau Conservancy office in Leland.

The natural area was created by the Leelanau Conservancy in 2004. It's on the migration path for birds flying between Mexico and Canada. It has over 125 different kinds of birds living here or passing through. Considering the small size of the natural area, only 42 acres, it has a diverse topography: rocky escarpment, dune ridge, cedar stand, an old field, and a remnant hardwood forest. Altogether, combined with the 1,700 acres of the Leelanau State Park and 600 acres of private conservation easements, it's a fairly large area of nothing but woods and fields. It feels like there's a quarter-mile or more in every direction with nobody around, especially at this time of year, no one but me and a few discreet wild animals.

In mid-December 2016, there's two feet of "lake effect" snow on the Conservancy land. The stalks of the dark brown great mulleins—their handsome, seven inches or more of abundant seeds at their head; a veritable feast for indigo buntings and American goldfinches—stand grandly upright above the snow. There's Queen Anne's lace in seed form, in the boll and in the little, light-brown, seed doily. If you break a stem of the Queen Anne's lace, it smells faintly of carrots, even in winter; it's a member of the carrot family. There's burnished, brass-colored chicory. There's amber-toned heal-all and evening primrose with an ebony sheen. These make elegant bouquets, beautifully subtle, when arranged to show the various shapes and soft earth-tone shades of the weeds.

On a blustery, winter day one wonders what it might have been like to live, out where the land ends and the wind never stops blowing, a hundred years or so ago. The first lighthouse, built in 1850, was put up when there were 50 Native families in Northport and two or three non-Native families. If geologic time on this promontory into the lake is so vast one can't take it in, colonial history is so recent, it's basically nothing.

In the early 2000s, one warm fall day, I had driven to the tip of the Leelanau Peninsula, taking an hour to myself to shift my perspective and clear my mind. Northport is about 13 miles up the peninsula from Lake Leelanau, where I lived then and lived for almost four decades. The Peninsula is an isosceles triangle with Lake Leelanau in the center, 20 miles on a slant from Traverse City on the eastern end of the bottom of the triangle and 20 miles on a slant from Empire on the western end of the bottom of the triangle. The finial, or tip of the peninsula, is about seven miles beyond Northport.

The Grand Traverse Lighthouse, on that beautiful September day, was open for tours. A tour isn't something I usually want, but this time it's different. There's a gnomic old man there, Douglass "Doug" McCormick, who had grown up in the lighthouse with his parents, who were the lighthouse keepers in the early 1900s, and his 11 brothers and sisters.

In the astonishing way life sometimes comes full circle, Doug, in his dotage, has become a live-in docent in the lighthouse he'd known as a child. I'm instantly interested in him. He's ancient, but the years seem to melt away as he talks, his eyes bright with memories of a different time. He says once as a boy he'd cut himself while scaling fish. His mother cleaned the wound with whiskey and sewed it up with fishing line.

Doug McCormick, before his family moved to the Grand Traverse Lighthouse, spent the first few years of his life living with the Ottawa at Cross Village, his family one of the only white families. He remembers learning to wrestle from the Ottawa boys, "They were good wrestlers." And he remembers the stories, too, of how his family, and all the families in Cross Village, had captured passenger pigeons.

People put smudge pots in the pines where they nested. The smoke from the fires asphyxiated the birds. Passenger pigeons are flightless when nesting and so they couldn't escape the smoke. There were so many. They darkened the sky when they came in the spring. People salted them and shipped them in barrels to Chicago. They were delicious. People could make money. No one knew that the passenger pigeons would become extinct from such wholesale harvesting. "We didn't know any better," McCormick says, shaking his head. "I'm sorry for it now."

We walk around the grounds. He shows me a birdbath made of pebbles, pink quartz. "My father," he says. "he liked to do it for my mother. She liked the pink stones." He pauses, reflecting. "I think we were all quite happy then." McCormick would die in 2012 at the age of 97. I was struck, as I listened to him reminisce, by how recently anyone white was in Michigan.

If McCormick, who wrestled Native boys when there were more Native people than white settlers, and who could recall the stories of the passenger pigeons, is a man I talked to, both of us sitting on a stone bench, looking at a bird bath his father had made for his mother with all-pink pebbles, that's what's called "living memory," talking to someone who remembers. White people, my tribe, have inhabited the Leelanau Peninsula for fewer than 17 decades, and have been colonizing the continent of North America for a mere 40 decades, about as much time as the Romans were the colonial rulers in England. History, like lighthouses, helps position us so we can understand where we are, relative to where we were, and relative to where we might be heading. Metaphorically, history helps us around the shoals under the water, something unseen; if we know history, we can extrapolate, hypothesize, and plan for what might be up ahead.

Later I learn from other people that McCormick had been such a skilled Coastguardsman that he had been chosen to train members of the U.S. Marine Corps in New Zealand in the amphibious landings used on the beach at Normandy during the Second World War. Then he was at Gaudalcanal, Africa, Europe, returning to the Coast Guard on Lake Michigan after the war. He was made Group Commander in 1955, in charge of 18 lighthouses, and later served at the Coast Guard Officer Candidate School in Yorktown, Virginia. He captained a ferryboat on Lake Champlain for a decade, before finally coming home to Northport. He was an honorary member of the Sault St. Marie Band of Chippewa Indians, perhaps because he had wrestled them as a boy and earned their respect: a brave and fair fighter, a good friend.

I had visited the tip of the peninsula another time, in 1979, camping overnight. That's when I learned that in the spring huge carp come in to spawn in the rocky shoals that surround the spear-end of the land. This is the common carp, *Cyrinus carpio*, and they are a reddish gold or brown, and large. That June, as the brilliant morning sun rose and covered the rocks in the shallow water near the shore with crimson light, these common carp, hundreds of them, shining like gold in the sunlight, gamboled in the waves. It was a display of primordial fertility, like a scene from a dream of peace and plenty. A few people, myself included, enticed by what appeared to be easy pickings, went out and tried to catch the carp with our bare hands. But there were stones under the water—that's why the carp were coming in to spawn there, because of the stones—and the stones were slippery. It's not easy to catch a carp, even when you aren't standing on slippery stones. Carp are big and strong, much bigger and stronger than they look. Their scales are sharp and hard and they can jump out of your arms in two seconds.

Matt Heiman, a veteran staff member at the Leelanau Conservancy, says the Lake Michigan carp are a species introduced from Europe. These are not the Asian carp now threatening to invade the Great Lakes but an earlier foreign carp, deliberately brought over in the 1800s from the Caspian Sea as a potential food fish, but they never really caught on in America. Now they're mainly used in cat food. "They're a bottom feeder," Heiman says. "They have a muddy taste." Heiman studied ichthyology in college, among other subjects, and spent his childhood in Midland. Heiman learned to fish in Midland's Tittabawassee River. Heiman wouldn't have been able to keep the fish he caught or eat them. Heiman's family also had a summer cottage on Platte Lake, and he had fished there, too, and had been able to keep and eat the fish.

Fishing is something the late Michigan writer Jim Harrison loved, "Fishing makes us less the hostages to the horrors of making a living," he wrote once. Fishing, if you think about it, was a way to *make* a living not too long ago, or at least to supplement it. My father regularly supplied our table with fresh and delicious fish, as well as grouse, partridge, teal, venison, food he prepared, too. My urban mother was understandably reluctant to cook foods so totally unfamiliar to her. Those meals are now a distant memory.

An avid fisherman, Heiman says he prefers to fish in the Upper Peninsula because the fishery is healthy there and he can keep what he catches. He's fished in Utah, Florida, Mexico, Traverse City. In the Lower Peninsula he often returns fish in order not to deplete the supply, or in some cases, because the waters are polluted and the fish are not safe to eat. Heiman is a land protection person for the Leelanau Conservancy, specializing in stream restoration. "Whenever you can make permanent impact by protecting large swaths of natural land," he writes on the Conservancy website, "you can help guarantee someone's legacy for the land."

Jim Harrison grew up in Michigan near Grayling, the son of a county agriculture agent, and lived on the Leelanau Peninsula for more than 40 years, before he and his wife, Linda, moved to Montana to be near their two daughters and their grandchildren. Jim wrote authentically and uninhibitedly about his love for the land. "You can be in terrible shape," he wrote, "and if you take a three-hour walk through the woods and along the river, you're simply not the same as when you started out." Jim loved to cook and wrote a whole book about food, and what foods he loved to eat, and how to cook them all. I've known a few writers who love to cook.

Matt Heiman, too, loves to cook, as well as fish. He says he prepares fish many different ways: on the grill, baked with vegetables, and of course pan-fried when it's very fresh. Fishing, for Heiman and Harrison, and countless others, was "a way in" to their interface with nature and their understanding of the importance of nature, not only to the sustenance of the individual, but to the sustenance of human existence generally, and for the need for all people everywhere to love and respect the natural world.

The carp, a feature of myth and legend in Europe and Asia, is, for some, a comfort food, associated with special occasions, fish cakes poached in a salty broth seasoned with celery and onion. There's a children's story about this fish, *The Carp in the Bathtub*, about a mother who kept the carp alive there for days, until she was ready to prepare it for Passover.

Chanie Apfelbaum, quoted in the *Wall Street Journal*, said, "I ate gefilte fish [carp] straight from the jar as a child, and I still have nightmares." Any fish that can stay alive in your bathtub might well qualify as the fish of the future. If the water quality in Michigan's lakes and rivers goes the way of some of the lakes and rivers in Asia and Europe, or even Illinois, Ohio and southern Michigan, as it well could since things have changed so dramatically here in the last several years, we might all need to learn to eat carp.

My father was a contemporary of Doug McCormick. My father's father, Walter Stocking, a teamster in the timber industry, was born in 1862 near Newago. Walter's father, Erastus Post Stocking, was born in New York State in 1825. All the Stockings can trace their ancestry back to George Stocking, who came from England to America in 1633, a Dissenter from the King, and helped found Hartford, Connecticut in 1635.

In my lifetime, but also through the memories and stories shared by my parents and grandparents, I knew this land when it was new, or at least when it was "newer." The wonderfully fragrant ground cover, arbutus, grew in many places when I was growing up. I haven't seen it for years. The sound of whippoorwills filled the woods behind our house in the spring when I was a child. I haven't heard them since. Urbanization, large-scale farming, and carbon emissions from cars and factories, caused, and continues to cause, air pollution, water pollution and climate change, which in turn have altered or destroyed the habitat for the native plants and animals.

Out at the Lighthouse West Natural Area, waiting for Ketterer, I think about the 2013 poisoning of the water consumed by the children in Flint, all the while the state government was telling them the water was safe to drink. In 2010 an Enbridge pipe broke in the Kalamazoo River; the company said it was a one-off, an unfortunate mishap that would never happen again. There was the Deepwater Horizon oil spill about the same time, which killed 11 people, sickened others, and ruined the shrimp, something British Petroleum could have easily prevented, as—with a little more thought and care—the Flint water crisis and pipeline break in the Kalamazoo River could have been avoided. And the list goes on and on. We don't want to know about these things, but of course we do know about these things.

According to *The New York Review of Books* in December 2016, a group of retired American generals and admirals who studied the national security implications of climate change, concluded in 2007 that "economic and environmental conditions in already fragile areas will further erode as food production declines, diseases increase, clean water becomes increasingly scarce, and large populations move in search of resources." All of which will increase the vulnerability of populations and governments—a case in point being all those people drowning in the Mediterranean trying to escape war and drought—and all of which has occurred within living memory. No wonder people want to live in gated communities on Michigan's remote Leelanau Peninsula, as far from Thomas Hardy's "madding crowd" as possible.

William Catton, son of the Pulitzer-winning Bruce Catton, in a 1987 preface to his father's memoir, *Waiting for the Morning Train*, wrote about his dad, "He saw only three possible endings: eventual destruction of the planet and everything on it; the dying out of the human race; or just maybe, a turning away from our present course in time to permit humanity and its habitat to survive." History is our moral compass, or one of them, and whether embodied in an individual like Doug McCormick or in books, it's what tells us who we are. Bruce Catton and his son knew it.

Bruce Catton was born on the Michigan frontier in 1899 and grew up in Benzonia. His parents, along with others from Oberlin, Ohio, established the Benzonia Academy. Catton saw the wilderness in its primordial natural beauty, and saw it likewise being horribly, thoughtlessly ravaged. And each time, the damage would become normalized, people would get used to it and, with time and the next generation, not knowing anything else, would think it was the way things had always been. He saw the destructive environmental changes coming. And, since then, the changes have been coming faster and faster.

Ed Ketterer, the Chair of the Board of Directors of the Leelanau Conservancy at the time we met, lives near the Lighthouse West Natural Area. He arrives in his little gray car. He gets out. I can see just by his walk that he's a bouncy guy, geared-up and enthusiastic, ready for anything. This day he's all ready for a hike, dressed in warm, light-weight, modern hiking clothes, his pantlegs tucked into his boots to keep out the snow.

He points out the tracks in the snow. "A deer," he says, "see how they drag their feet?" Other small tracks he thinks might belong to a fox. "We have a lot of fox here," he says. "We have bobcat. Sometimes bear." He moves through a clearing and points out the old apple orchard, and pointing again, a cedar hedge that used to be part of the surroundings of the farmhouse that burned down some time ago. "Wild blackberries," he says, "in the summer."

These blackberry bushes look strange. Their brambles seem too long. They arch over each other, every which way, weaving together an impenetrable tangle. In December there are still leaves on the brambles, and even berries. The animals don't seem to have eaten them; by this time of year one would expect they'd all be gone. Walking around before Ketterer arrived, I'd tried one. The berries are large and look like they would be delicious, but they are hard and slightly bitter, as though maybe they never ripened. But why wouldn't they have ripened? And wouldn't the cold weather have made them sweeter?

I mention the wind and Ketterer says that Brian Price, the now-retired first director of the Conservancy, described the place as a "high energy" area. Once I was teaching in a special program for at-risk kids, trying to get them to describe things, lots of things, anything at all, trying to get them to connect to something outside themselves. I played a Rachmaninoff C-minor piece. One of my students, a girl in foster care who'd had one of the hardest lives of anyone I'd ever met, and who had, up to this point, not responded to anything in the class, spoke, surprising me by describing the Rachmaninoff piece as "agitated." And it was the perfect word. And it's that way out at the tip of the peninsula. It's the wind, but it's not just the wind. Even in summer, there's something where the land ends that I can't quite put my finger on, but "agitated" comes close.

Sheltered by the cedars surrounding the parking lot, it's quieter than in the open, but there's still the ever-present wind. The wind makes a faint music as it passes through the trees and over the water. The Aeolian sounds, the strong winds flowing past the tree branches, produce an almost musical tune and at first you think you've imagined it and then you realize that it is, in fact, the wind, and that the day is so quiet, you can hear it make its music. The wind is the proud natural element here at the tip of the peninsula.

The woods to the south, on the other side of Cathead Road, are also protected as part of the Lighthouse West Natural Area. The trees look like the black, enharmonic keys on a piano, black against the white snow. This is the kind of day, and this is the kind of place, where one can imagine seeing a bobcat. But, one reminds oneself, bobcats are nocturnal and in winter are likely to be somewhere out of the wind, in a tag alder and cedar swamp, preferably one with rabbits.

A bobcat looks like a large house cat, but it's not a house-cat. It has daggers for teeth and razors for claws. It is very strong—all muscle under that fluffy fur. It can bring down a small deer. They are good hunters. One imagines trying to make friends with such an animal. *You and me, bobcat, we're the same. We're all bobcats here. Come sit down, right here by me. Oh, please, yes, do, I would love it. Do you mind if I call you Bobby?* But looks can be deceiving. You can't make a bob-cat into a housecat. Bobcats are wild.

I had experienced the little area as desolate, before Ket-terer got there. The old foundation of a farmhouse. Lilacs. Second growth saplings, tangled underbrush covering the barren ground. The strange-looking blackberry briars with some of the berries still on. The wind. The storm. I tell Ket-terer I would love to hike, but I'm going to a Christmas party after this and I'm dressed more for the Christmas party than the storm. I can sense that he's disappointed, but we decide not to walk to the shore.

Sitting in his car, Ketterer shows aerial photographs of the land. "In 1938, this was an open field. You can see in the photo, how it was still a field in 1963, but you can see how it's been reforesting itself from the northwest, the direction of the prevailing winds. The field is reforesting itself with the pio-neers: staghorn sumac, juniper, poplar, cedar, birch. Now we have cedars thirty feet high." He's clearly pleased with the positive direction the woods are taking.

Ketterer grew up in Lorain, Ohio. I know Lorain is near the industrial port of Cleveland, not far from where the Cuya-hoga River caught on fire in 1969. I don't mention this. In-stead I ask him what it was like to grow up in Lorain.

Lorain, according to Ketterer, was semirural, adjacent to areas that had trees and a stream which Ketterer and his friends explored. Ketterer says his parents' home was half-a-mile from Lake Erie and he always loved the beach there. "But this area is different," he says. He and his wife retired to Northport and he began to volunteer at the Leelanau Conservancy. He has formal training and degrees in engineering and law, self-training in the natural sciences, and a passion to restore damaged lands to their former health.

On the Leelanau Conservancy website he has written, "Early on I developed an affinity for the north, with its clear air, sparkling waters and abundant wildlife. Leelanau is true north country. It's a different environment than we have down state, and it provides a different sense of place for those who "tune in." That's the essence of what we seek to accomplish with guided walks on the Conservancy properties—[to] help [people] develop a sense of place."

It's November 2017. I drive through Suttons Bay, coming from Traverse City, going up once more to the tip of the peninsula to meet Ketterer. I've been up there several times since Ketterer and I first met in 2016 in a storm. Sometimes I would ask other people, people I thought might be able to help me understand the place, to go with me, and sometimes I would go alone. This day I've been up since 4 a.m. I'm hungry.

I stop at Boone's Prime Time Pub on the southern edge of Suttons Bay. I order a hamburger to go, extra pickle. I know the people who work here, some by name and others by their face. Wendy Herman is the manager. She started here as a kid. It's her meatloaf recipe, the best meatloaf in the county. Sheila Snyder, Marianne Spriet and Melissa Zelinski are waitresses. Lori Pease and Maria Rivera work maintenance. Young Bob Neddo is a cook. I thought he didn't know how to smile, until one day I saw him when his kids came in, and witnessed a miraculous transformation, from shy guy to happy man. "When Bob sees his kids," Wendy concurs, "he lights up like a Christmas tree."

In November 2017 the nation is in the throes of the Harvey Weinstein scandal. In *The New Yorker* Ronan Farrow, one of the first journalists to break the story, interviews Zelda Perkins, a former assistant to Weinstein. Perkins says, "What I want to talk about at this point is not what Harvey did." She goes on, "Money and power enabled. And the legal system has enabled. As a culture, that's our fault." And the same could be said about the degradation of the environment: we, as a culture, including the legal system, which is only a reflection of our culture, have colluded and enabled by our silence and apathy.

Destruction comes in stages, but restoration does, too. There's been a proliferation in the last 40 years of nonprofits working to protect and restore the environment. Like the Leelanau Conservancy, they work to protect the land with conservation easements, bequests and donations. More people all the time have life-threatening illnesses, everything from stage IV cancer to severe asthma, diseases caused by and exacerbated by the pollution in air, water, soil and food. Trees and grass help fight pollution by cleaning the air and making cities cooler. In Paris, according to an August 2018 article in *The Guardian*, people are planting trees in schoolyards to mitigate the hot weather and the pollution. City parking lots across America are being turned into green spaces as people become aware of the need to restore the earth. And people can do amazing things when they work together to make things better.

In November 2017, almost a year after we'd first met in a storm, Ed Ketterer has graciously agreed to meet me again. Since I first met him at the tip of the peninsula, I've learned that the blackberries looked strange to me because they're Himalayan blackberries, not the ones I'd grown up with. I won't mention this to Ketterer, but I feel better knowing it; it means my eyes weren't deceiving me.

I've asked Ketterer to meet me again, so we can walk to the ledge near the shore, as we'd planned to do the year before, so he can tell me about it. He arrives early, saying he thought I would be early, which elicits, as I think he'd anticipated, a smile from me.

The second time at the Lighthouse West Natural Area with Ketterer, we do walk to the edge of the escarpment, the old shore of a glacial lake, a steep ledge above the boulder terrace. There's no snow this time. We see rabbit scat, right on the trail, not off to the side of the trail, and then, also on the trail, something that might be from a gopher or skunk, and then, also on the trail, something that might be coyote scat with what looks like deer fur in it. "Animals use the trail," Ketterer says. He smiles. We know that animals use human and other trails. It's easier. And they mark the trails in the only way they can. It's oddly comforting to know that this is their place, before it's ours. They're at-home in it. We're tourists.

In the spring the birds will come back. This is part of the flyway for birds coming south from Mexico and going north to Canada. Birds seem to have their own internal, built-in GPS, but they also are thought to fly by sight and the shore of Lake Michigan is easy to see. The Conservancy lands, plus state land and conservation easements, have created a haven for birds and wildlife, here where the land ends.

The brown thrush will be here in the spring. This bird likes the deep woods and often sings at dawn and at dusk. It has a double voice box and can harmonize with itself. Something about the tone of the notes, especially when they sing in the woods, pierces through where words can't reach. Poet Gerard Manley Hopkins describes the sound of the thrush, "through the echoing timbers" where the sweet notes, "do rinse and wring the ear" and "it strikes like lightnings to hear him sing." Shakespeare, Milton, Keats, Melville, Dickinson, Whitman, Twain, Thoreau, Harrison, all the great writers of the past, knew the thrush and were amazed by the sound it could make, a sound that could reach into the soul where words could not. How many writers living today know the sound of a thrush? And in another 400 years, how many will?

On a mellow Michigan winter day, when the sky is a faint yellow and gray-white, I go out again to the tip of the peninsula. This time I'm not meeting anyone. The fields of the Light House West Natural Area are an expanse of faintly blue, soundless snow. The sun rose this morning out over the water to the east and tried valiantly all day to break through the heavy cloud cover, but the vulcanized skies were too much for it. Now, at two in the afternoon at Cathead Point, as the sun is sinking in the west, it feels as if the sun is exhausted. The sun is a fluorescent-white swirl in the dense gray sky. One can understand the impulse behind the ancient solstice custom in Sweden, where beautiful young girls put on helmets of candles to invoke the light, seemingly by flirting with it.

I know now why I've made so many trips to the tip of the peninsula. I'm trying to understand what has to happen to the way people think about themselves in relationship to the land, so they can stop destroying it. It has taken so many successive trips, not because it's hard to understand what to do, but because it's hard to see how people will be able to go from dumping toxins everywhere, and denying it, which is easy, to not doing it, and not denying it, which is hard.

It will happen, collectively, with awareness, is what I'm coming to, just the way agriculture happened 10,000 years ago, world-wide, and hieroglyphic picture writing—with a sharp stick in wet clay or a sharp arrowhead on birchbark— happened 5,000 years ago, sometimes a little here, sometimes a little there, because people, individually and in groups, will realize it's better for them. The awareness will grow. It will reach critical mass. And then everyone will know.

Overall, my sense is that there's hope for humanity. One of the most interesting things about us, as a species, is how we all tend to start doing the same thing about the same time, even when we're on opposite sides of the globe and don't know that others are doing the same thing. In Mexico, according to a 2016 *National Geographic* article, corn began to be cultivated about 10,000 years ago, and a continent away, the same was being done with wheat in Syria and rice in China. Weaving occurred all around the world about 12,000 years ago, give or take, and evidence of it has been found in the mountains of Peru (where it's cold and dry and fragments could survive) and in the caves of Albania (where it's also cold and dry and fragments could survive). An article in *The New York Times* on November 7, 2018 reported that cave paintings of figures had just been discovered in Borneo, that big island in the Pacific Ocean in between Malaysia and the Philippines, paintings that date to 40,000 years ago, which was about the same time some people in caves in Spain and France started making figurative paintings. The author of the article, Carl Zimmer, notes, "The finding demonstrates that ancient humans made the creative transition at roughly the same time, in places thousands of miles apart." Why? How could this be? It's a mystery, but one with implications, albeit possibly metaphysical ones. On October 22, 2018, Alice Walker, the famous author of *The Color Purple*, who has written many books, with sales of 15 million world-wide, translated into just about every language, was in Traverse City, speaking at the City Opera House, a block from my apartment, a short walk down the ally in the rainy night, and Walker said, "Human consciousness and universal consciousness are one." Seems true to me.

The difference between learning how to farm, or learning how to write, however, and learning how not to take down the planet that we're living on, is that now we have to learn about five-thousand times faster. Then we had lots of time, now we barely have any. But, because of the Internet, we communicate faster, too, so we can do it. We are barreling toward a world-wide culture, at breakneck speed, and our growing awareness of the need to protect the natural world, on which we all depend in order to stay alive, is part of our becoming a more enlightened and a more coalesced global civilization. I believe in the overall goodness of people, in the transcendent and increasing intelligence of people. I believe in our will to survive and our ability to think of new ways to help us all survive. I've been watching, I've been reading. I've been adding it all up. I think we can do it.

Standing on the tip of this wind-buffeted peninsula, this small cape of boulder-strewn land stretching out into the iron-gray waters of the lake, one is aware of one's short-lived, human littleness, especially in comparison to the vast ice ages, the millions of years going back to when the continents were in different places. Relatively speaking, we are breath on a mirror.

I think of ancient paintings that have had other paintings made on top of them, a pentimento. I think of ancient manuscripts, when vellum and paper were scarce, that had other writings over them, a palimpsest. And I think that's where we are now, with what came before, hidden under what is now, and what is to be, in the unseen future, hidden in the implications. I'm awed by being on this peninsula, this palimpsest, this pentimento, this place of succession forests and fields and dunes, by being part of something that was here before, something that will underlie something that is yet to come.

Standing in the waning light of a winter afternoon, with the soft soughing wind, the bluish snow beneath the lowering sky, the trailing, tattered, still-green leaves on the grapevines, valiantly fluttering in the breeze, is wonderfully, exhilaratingly, humbling. Be here with me for a minute in the gently falling snow. Think about the snowflakes, big as cookies, melting into the dark waters of Lake Michigan. Catch one on your tongue. Think about becoming friends with a bobcat. Think about the Ice World of 800 million years ago. Let the universe shoot through you.